Happy Anniversary
Feb. 14th 1992.

SO FAR
SO GOOD ...

ALSO BY MATTHEW PARRIS

Inca-Kola: A Traveller's Tale of Peru

SO FAR
SO GOOD ...

SELECTED PIECES

*Matthew
Parris*

Weidenfeld and Nicolson
London

First published in 1991 by
George Weidenfeld & Nicolson Ltd
91 Clapham High Street, London SW4 7TA

All the pieces in this book previously appeared in
The Times, with the exception of those on pp. 92–
3 (*The House Magazine*), 125–6 (*Investors'
Chronicle*), 231–6 (*Sunday Telegraph Magazine*),
244–6 (*London Evening Standard*), 263–5 (*Sunday
Telegraph*), 267–9 (*London Evening Standard*) and
286–8 (*Sunday Telegraph*).

British Library Cataloguing in Publication Data
applied for

ISBN 0 297 81215 7

Printed in Great Britain by
Butler & Tanner Ltd, Frome and London

Contents

Acknowledgements

My best ideas usually come from other people, or from at first mistaking or misunderstanding what I hear.

The Times' room at the House of Commons has been a source of inspiration, accurate quotes, cheerful encouragement and judicious restraint. To Ivan Barnes, then Roger Wood, and to Bob Morgan, John Winder, Peter Mulligan, Derek Barnett, Carolyn Oakley and Sally Dealler (in the Commons), and Sheila Gunn (in the Lords), I owe good advice, true facts and some excellent jokes.

Xandra Hardie and Allegra Huston have helped me sort through a thousand articles, tirelessly filed by my secretary, Eileen Wright, who has ever urged me to accept that some of them were better than others.

To Lawrence Newcombe

1
Animals

Panda points to ponder

THOSE REQUIRING proof of the socialist bias of the BBC need go no further than its coverage of the Worldwide Fund for Nature controversy. Everyone is blaming the Fund. Why is nobody blaming the panda?

Responsibility for the imminent demise of this ludicrous species should be placed squarely where it belongs: on the panda. By their own indolence and fussiness they have got themselves into this; and now they won't lift a paw to get themselves out. As Confucius put it: 'Buck stop at desk of panda.'

So they are on their way out. Well, who isn't? In the long term, as Keynes said, we are all extinct. Let us have an end to the wildlife dependency culture. Let the message go out loud and clear to the rest of the furry flotsam and feathered jetsam, scrounging flora and couch-potatoes of the animal kingdom: the party's over.

In the space allotted, I can only scratch the surface of the great shambling fluffy heap of inadequacy which is the giant panda. Gaw' bless you Prince Philip, but you are out of your depth on this one. Let me put you straight, Your Royal Highness: *Ten Things You Didn't Know About Pandas* ...

● They are not cuddly at all. Their adorable 'sunglasses' are a trick. They have foul, grumpy natures. They smell.

● They are the world's ultimate fusspots about food. They refuse to eat leftovers. They are actually carnivores but are too idle to catch anything, and have opted instead for bamboo.

● But their digestions are not designed for bamboo. So a panda has to eat about 40 pounds of it a day to keep going. Bamboo dies after flowering. The pandas do not appear to have thought of this, and expect Western charities to organize relief supplies.

● Pandas have no sense of fun and none of community. Disliking the company even of other pandas, they have no family life. Pandas cannot return affection.

● They will do nothing to help themselves. They refuse to try new diets, adapt to new habitats, or learn circus tricks or television acts.

● Among expensive requests to the Worldwide Fund for Nature, these lovable welfare junkies are now demanding 'bamboo corridors' between the patches of their habitat. Otherwise they refuse to travel.

● Their fur is host to a multitude of small vermin.

● They are horribly prim about sex. They reject perfectly acceptable mates, or sulk just when the other is ready for romance. This is disastrous for panda procreation, as the female is on heat for only one or two days in the year.

● In the unlikely event that they do mate, the period of gestation is interminable, the result a single, bald, half-formed mouse of a thing, which the mother then rolls on and squashes. The father doesn't want to know. Pandas make useless parents.

● Never once has a panda been known to express gratitude for Western efforts to save it. They take our bamboo leaves then spit in our faces.

Frankly, this shower are going nowhere. Pandas are not pulling their weight. I did not vote for Mrs Thatcher to featherbed a load of fluff-balls who think the world owes them a living. As Alan Walters says, 'There's no such thing as a free bamboo shoot.' We don't subsidize uneconomic coal mines, so why should we subsidize uneconomic pandas?

These johnny-come-lately species don't know they are born. We humans were a young species once. And there were no charitable trusts to mollycoddle *us* when we were clobbered with ice ages, showered by molten lava and chased by mammoths. No sir! We got on our bikes and evolved.

So my advice to the BBC and the Worldwide Fund for Nature is to ditch pandas and get into rats. Rats are smart. Rats are survivors. More about rats soon.

4.8.90

Rats

AS ALL who use buses will know, there are lucky and unlucky bus stops, even on the same route. Wait at one and a bus will come. Wait at another, perhaps only a few hundred yards away, and you will be there forever.

There are London Underground stations like that, too, and White-chapel is one of them. At Whitechapel the universe goes into a small but intense time-warp.

I was stuck there the other morning. It was eleven – too early for the homeless. I was on the New Cross line, in no hurry, and alone.

Or so I thought. Sitting on the empty platform, staring across the empty tracks with vision unfocused, a blurred grey movement – very sudden – broke the stillness. I focused. Something was stirring down by the electrified third rail. It was a rat.

The instinctive reaction might be to shudder or draw back. Yet I felt relaxed. After all, this was not my territory, and my temporary accommodation, the platform, was safe. The rat was in his domain, down by the live rails where I had no reason to go. He was in his own world and I in mine. I felt at peace.

He was relaxed, too, going about his business without regard to me. In some part of himself he knew with an absolute certainty that passengers do not come down to the tracks. So he ignored me while I watched him for the better part of ten minutes, very intently.

This was an adolescent rat, only three-quarters grown, and in peak condition. It was difficult to imagine a finer example of the species. His fur was battleship grey, soft, clean and shiny. Beneath it – for there was no fat on him – you could see his muscles working: strong, sleek sinews. They rippled the surface of his grey pelt.

He was searching for food. He had finished some crumbs from a crisp packet and was investigating a sliver of rotten fruit. His tiny feet worked fast and nimbly: each claw as strong as it was feathery, like steel wire. He had learned which rail was live and how to avoid it. He had no fear of trains for he knew their certain path.

The rat's eyes had all the brightness of youth. He could see *everything*. The slightest movement riveted his whole attention at the instant. He was alert to his whisker tips. Every part of this lean creature, every inch, was on the qui vive. All was muscle, speed, reflex, aggression, defence, survival. He was in his element yet ready for anything. To this rat the unexpected was his whole life. He was a destroyer. He relished danger. He was beautiful.

And out of such dirt and decay was brought forth such a creature! So clean and strong: like a bright flame, burning above the rubbish it consumes. Pollution was his meat and drink. Here was nature really working: adapting, discarding, killing, testing and multiplying.

We talk of our reverence for the natural world, but this rat was the glory of the natural world and had reverence for nothing. He was an evolutionary triumph. He was not threatened.

Yet are the survivors not the most beautiful of all? I saw a starling, sitting on a tree, his feathers shiny, breast puffed out, singing for all he was worth. Crows – the rats of the air, wonderful birds – flies, ants, bindweed ... each of them the rats of their element. And humans? The rats of our own domain, endlessly resourceful.

Perhaps that is why we hate rats: rivals, too close to home. Instead, wringing our hands, we grasp dying species to our breasts, misty-eyed, and call that 'nature'.

But that is not nature. Nature is extinction. Nature is survival. Nature is rats, our brothers; and we are nature.

6.8.90

Melancholy mouse memories

I WAS one of those little boys who kept mice. The first breeding pair came from a petshop and cost a shilling each. Later immigrants to my cage came from friends and, once, a wild mouse came to stay, though she did not get on with the others and had to leave.

The mouse population soon grew, as nests of chewed newspaper filled with litters of tiny pink babies: blind, delicate, almost translucent -- like underdone cocktail sausages. Those were exciting times and I would cycle back fast from school, to be present at the birth whenever possible – decades ahead of the fashionable men of today. Once, when a newborn litter's parents fell victim to the cat, I raised the babies by letting them suck pieces of string dipped in milk.

Mice are beautiful creatures if you look at them quietly. Mine were mostly white, with little cherry-coloured eyes; but there were a couple of black ones (two shillings), while a prized possession was a honey-coloured mouse, unusually tame. Sadly, the cat got her. I always hoped that the mating of black and white mice might produce a piebald issue, but it never did. The chapter on genetics in my encyclopaedia explained that the chances were slim.

I built the cage myself. It was based on instructions in a *Pets Annual*, but it was more ambitious. In addition to a home-made exercise wheel (which they never used) I constructed jumps, ladders, ramps and a series of mezzanine galleries on different levels. It looked like a stage-set for an avant-garde opera.

I felt sorry for the mice being shut in, but experiments with free-range in my bedroom had alarmed my mother and ended in tragedy with the cat: so the aim was to make their prison as big and as interesting as possible. They even had separate sleeping quarters, though they never used them. They had minds of their own.

Each mouse has a distinct personality. They are not alike at all, once you get to know them. Some are forgiving, some placid, others wary. Some are lazy, some greedy, others pull their weight in the mouse community. Some can return affection, some not. Some are mentally ill, some imagine they are physically ill when they are not.

Mice suffer, in fact, from most of the same complaints as us. Luckily I found a vet who took my pets seriously: Dr Sugden (but I called her 'Mrs'). I would cycle to her surgery with my small patients in shoebox ambulances. Once, after a disastrous raid by the cat I took a mouse whose hind leg had been all but severed, and Dr Sugden saved him, though he always limped.

Each had a name: not silly names like Ophelia or Stilton, but real names like George and Claire. All too often we had to resort to 'George Jnr' or 'Claire No. 2' after incidents involving the cat; but generally the population held up well and later multiplied. We racked our brains for new names.

But it is not true that I called one of my mice 'Twinkletoes'. My mother – who wrote and read children's stories for the radio – made that up. My reception the following morning in the school playground taught me an early lesson about irresponsible journalism ...

And now it is the beginning of winter in Derbyshire, when the mice start to come in for refuge. Look at it all ways – and I really have – there is only one answer. I did try letting the first immigrants stay: am I so mean, I thought, that (living alone) I cannot share a big house with a couple of mice? But they were a married couple: and soon there was the patter of *very* tiny feet, and mouse droppings on my pillow. So I had to ... must I spell it out? You will know what I had to do.

I arrived from London last night. One trap had killed the father cleanly. But the mother was still struggling in the other trap. It had almost severed her leg.

Mrs Dr Sugden could have mended it, but she is gone. And the string dipped in milk for feeding the orphaned babies is gone too. And a lot else, besides.

16.12.89

Sunbathing among worker ants

VARIOUSLY COMPARED with volcanoes, eagles, snakes and hurricanes, politicians inspire comparisons with the best – and worst – of the natural world. But to watch the ministerial bench during Health Questions yesterday, was to be struck with a humbler comparison: the comparison with the workaday world of insects.

Kenneth Clarke, Secretary of State, basked on the green bench, beaming gently, his wings opening and closing gently in the sunlight of his Mistress's favour.

'... A system which encourages good performance ... improved service to the patient ...' Mr Clarke spread his wings further: 'I'm meeting hundreds – *thousands* – of doctors ... *wide* range of views ...'

There may be some to whom Mr Clarke is not an obvious butterfly. Butterflies are lightweight – a word neither of whose meanings fits him. Yet something about Clarke smacks of the political sunbather. Minister for almost everything at one time or another, it is hard to remember quite what or when.

One suspects that he finds it hard to remember, too – confident, well-briefed and skilful though he conspicuously is at any brief at any particular time. Mr Clarke perches lightly upon his portfolio, always ready to wing his way off after the next reshuffle to one more blossom, one more Department of State.

'But Snapethorpe Hospital hasn't had a patient since 1984,' sneered junior minister David Mellor at a Labour backbencher, David Hinchliffe (Wakefield), who had asked about a hospital closure. Laughter followed, at Hinchliffe's expense. Only later did one reflect that Health Authorities do actually empty hospitals before closing them. Mellor was offside.

But then Mr Mellor is a warrior ant of a minister: the kind that bites, stings and enrages. Every morning Mr Mellor resolves that today he will be just a worker ant. Every afternoon he bites someone.

'And tell the BMA to stop their campaign of doctors scaring old ladies,' snapped Robert Jones (C, Herts W). The hunched figure of Windsor's Dr Alan Glyn stirred uneasily in a dark corner bench. One smiled at the thought of Dr Glyn jumping out at old ladies from behind bushes and howling 'hawoooo!'

'No mental hospital should or will close unless there are adequate facilities in the community ...' intoned Parliamentary Under-Secretary Roger Freeman, gently, to an incandescent Nicholas Winterton (C,

Macclesfield): '... "*Care in the Community*" in place for 30 years ...
Government issuing guidelines ...'

You knew Winterton was right, of course, but only a Winterton could
withstand the chloroform. For Mr Freeman is a drone among ministers:
an exceptionally well-combed, soft-toned and nicely-tailored drone, but
a drone: one of a swarm of reliable, pinstriped buzzers. 'Resign! Resign!'
shouted Labour. On zizzed Mr Freeman: community-this, community-
that, 'adequate care by 1991 ...'

And in hummed the Queen Bee, in pink and grey. If there was any
seemly way in which she could be borne in on the shoulders of besuited
drones and lowered, gently to her seat, then the whips – sentinel ants –
would have organized it.

26.4.89

Saving Badger

'*A BILL to make provision for the protection of badger setts; and for
connected purposes.*' The story so far ...

Nice Mr Badger (Lab, Newham NE) has been trying to persuade the
other animals in Parliament to pass a law preventing evil badger-baiters
from blocking up the entrances to his house.

But wily Sir Nicholas Tally-Ho (C, Upminster), his corpulent friend,
Yaroo Soames (C, Crawley), and Jorrocks Colvin (C, Romsey & Water-
side) have thwarted him. They are Tory fox-hunters, an unspeakable
gang who like nothing better than to block up Mr Badger's doorways –
just in case cunning Mr Fox should try to hide here. They have nothing
against Mr Badger, they say, but why should they let him harbour a
Wanted Fox?

Poor Badger! He only wants to stop people baiting Mrs B and the
cubs. If the truth be known, he does detest fox-hunting and wouldn't
be sorry if Parliament did make it harder for people like Yaroo. But
that wasn't his motive, honestly; and now the hunters are wrecking his
Bill.

In Committee, feelings have been running high. Badger has called
Yaroo 'the Crawley food mountain'. Badger's friend, Jeremy Corbyn
(Lab, Islington N), has accused Yaroo's grandpa of running a badger
over in his car, while another has called Tally-Ho a 'smelly old farmer'.

9

Retaliating, Yaroo has regretted that he can't hear this because he is 'deaf, from shooting'.

The story moves: to Committee Room 10, 10.30 am yesterday. Tony 'Badger' Banks is speaking ...

'Some people want a lot more holes stopped up, including one in Mr Soames's face which is large enough for not just a badger but a whole pack of hounds to go down.'

John Bowis (C, Battersea) has protested that 'the debate has taken on a rather unreal air, with old ladies disappearing down holes in the ground, taking chihuahuas and Rottweilers with them'; while Banks has ruled that to injure a badger deserves punishment so severe that 'almost nothing is suitable'. His colleague, Peter Hardy (Lab, Wentworth) has proposed offering such people 'NHS surgery, without the anaesthetic'; and the hapless Home Office minister, Peter Lloyd, is poised to resist an amendment designed to swell the prison population with innumerable badger-baiters – to face the lynch mob, no doubt, along with sexual offenders, in the next prison riot.

On all sides, MPs are proposing special policemen for each constabulary, trained to handle badger-related issues. Simon Hughes, a Liberal from badger-rich Southwark, has an amendment about filling paper bags with straw and stuffing them down badger holes; and Soames is poised to move an amendment protecting owners of badger-hair sporrans and shaving brushes from prosecution ...

In short, the thing has got completely out of hand. The owlish chairman, Patrick Cormack, is near despair. Mr Corbyn shouts, 'On their heads will be the public anger!' And, from the direction of Mr Soames, something like 'tally ho!' seems to drift.

Your sketchwriter tiptoes out ... and in, later, to the Grand Committee room. Here, Agriculture minister John Gummer awaits interrogation by the Select Committee on Mad Cow Disease.

24.5.90

Dead bats

IF SCIENTISTS wish to investigate the human body's defences against stomach upset, I offer my own findings for their research. These days, I never, simply never, get an upset stomach. For the last year my alimentary canal has been proof against the most appalling assaults. More than a month in Peru and Bolivia, followed by a week in Albania, followed by the ultimate test, the Labour party conference in Blackpool, saw me sail confidently through digestive storms that reduced comrades to hunched, quivering wrecks.

What is my secret?

Well, now I think I know.

Let us start at the beginning. The water supply at my house in Derbyshire comes from a spring in the hillside. It pours into a stone trough and is then pumped up to a small storage tank in my loft.

The water is uncommonly pure and I do not treat it. I just drink it.

But for the last year or so, I have noticed a slight – very slight – 'taste' to the water. Nothing to complain of, but you can tell: it makes the tea taste different. I thought little of it, though, until last weekend.

Now the taste was unmistakable – that same taste, but stronger. It was *almost* unpleasant. There was a very faint smell to the water.

Still, I was too busy to do anything about it. I drank the water as usual, and washed a couple of machine-loads of sheets, which should see me through to 1992. By Sunday I must have drunk a few gallons of the stuff, and felt fine. But that taste really wasn't right.

So I decided to check, starting with the stone trough. Frogs sometimes get into this trough, but I take the view that if they are still swimming, that is a good sign. I unlocked the cover. No, no frogs, dead or alive; no slugs either.

I tried a glass, removing a lively waterboatman. Tasted fine. Bother. That meant the loft, and the ladder with missing rungs, and the torch with the flat battery. Up I went.

As my eyes adjusted to the dark, I realized that the cover was off the little storage tank, and remembered taking it off last year and never replacing it. Hm. I shone the feeble beam into the murky depths, and looked. Something horrible looked back at me.

It was a bat. A very big bat. A very big dead bat. A very big *long*-dead bat. Oh yes, my friends, this (as Mrs Thatcher would say) was an ex-bat; a late bat; a previous bat. This bat had gone to meet its maker. So long ago, in fact, had this bat gone to meet its maker that it was only just recognizable as a bat. You could have mistaken it for a bad case of mushroom soup. Except, that is, for the little, sodden, furry face, which now stared eyeless up at me in unspoken reproach.

And I had been *drinking* that, probably all year. I fished out the bat bits and descended, queasily, to begin flushing the tank.

But have I not found the answer to stomach problems? Is not putrefied bat the way to immunize yourself against internal upset? Was it not the homeopathic drip-drip of ever more concentrated decaying bat that had, over the months, fortified my stomach against Peruvian bacteria and Blackpool toxin?

This, surely, is the way to guarantee the health of the water-drinking masses: pollute the water! Forget your chlorine and your fluoride; a dead bat in every loft tank in every home throughout the kingdom should be our environmental health officers' goal.

There is now a flat taste to the Derbyshire water. Water-with-a-hint-of-bat was what I had become used to. I miss it. And I shall not bother to wash those sheets again. On a warm night, if I bury my face in them, they remind me.

20.10.90

Okapis and dachshunds

A FRIEND was amusing us at lunch recently with his account of a Save the Rhinos Ball. 'Why?' asked a little girl at the table. Solemnity fell upon the grown-ups. We had been shamed in our giggling. 'Because rhinoceroses are an endangered species,' said one of us, in a *Listen with Mother* voice. 'There are only a few left, and hunters keep killing them, and soon they'll be extinct. We don't want them to disappear.'

'Why?'

'What do you mean, "why?"?'

'Why don't we want them to disappear?'

'Well, it would be sad, dear, if there weren't any. Wouldn't you be sad if rhinos didn't exist?'

'No. They're horrid.'

'Well maybe you don't *like* them, darling, but that's no reason for wanting them all to die.'

'Why not? We've got a magpie trap. We don't like them either ...'

'Oh no, that's different. You see, there are lots and *lots* of magpies, so it's all right to kill some because ... well, there are lots left.'

The adult was plainly faltering in the face of relentless infant scepticism. Happily the child desisted. She had won, articulating doubts half-formed in more minds that her own. *Why* should we put clapped-out species on life-support machines?

I once saw some okapis in a zoo in Antwerp. These creatures, from the Congo I think, are a sort of cross between a giraffe and a zebra. They looked absolutely miserable, as you would if you were a moth-eaten traveller down a dead-end evolutionary track.

The okapis realized that it was all over bar the shouting, and stared bleakly into the Belgian drizzle, as little Walloons offered them chips with mayonnaise. I felt for them. Imagine the shame of knowing that your long neck and long tongue were not needed for chips or mayonnaise, that your stripes had given you away to every passing pygmy, and that you now faced the indignity of seeking sanctuary in a Belgian zoo. I would want to end it all on the spot. You could tell the okapis did.

Man, we are told, has evolved from the ape, passing through a number of disagreeable interim stages. Is it a matter for regret that these beasts have disappeared, yielding to the improved model? Would conservationists wish to freeze species that are still evolving, as well as those that are disappearing? Think how many 'endangered species' fell beneath the glaciers of the advancing Ice Age! I suppose the Nature Conservancy Council would have wanted more money to melt the glaciers.

Or are we concerned because it is at our hands that some species are dying? Species have been dying at the hands of others since the world began. Our attempt to take control of the destiny of species, presented as humility before the altar of Nature, is the grossest arrogance. It will take us back to Noah's Ark, with a sample of every species but our own retained in glass boxes and allowed to breed for posterity. And we call that reverence for nature!

Survival, with ignominy – or death with dignity? Okapis! Dachshunds! Fight for the right to extinction!

23.6.90

Guinea-pig and chips

HERE IN Ecuador, some things are familiar, others strange. Fast-food joints such as Mr Chicken blend, a merry confusion, into a landscape of brightly coloured shanties and towering volcanoes. There is even a McDonald's and, queuing within, Indians in ponchos each sporting a single pigtail – its length an indication of virility.

Or so Mary Magdalene told us. Mary is our guide. As we drove along the Pan-American Highway, she explained some of the Indian customs and language.

'Many Indian words have been incorporated into our Spanish,' she said. 'Cuy, for instance, means guinea-pig in the Indian language. It mimics the – how do you say? squeak – of the animal.' *Cwee, cwee, cwee*, she squeaked.

'Do you eat guinea-pig in Ecuador?'

'Absolutely!'

It was my childhood friend in Africa, Jill Bleakley, who introduced me to these deeply unsatisfactory pets. I helped Jill to tend her half-dozen piebald bundles of mindless fluff, and wondered, even then, if their flesh could be as bland as their personalities. Jill's brood came to a sad end one evening, when she gave them oleander leaves to eat.

One hundred per cent mortality in the cage! Six former guinea-pigs, twenty-four little feet pointing skywards. I comforted the weeping Jill, but secretly I thought her grief disproportionate. Guinea-pigs, like humans, are unable to return affection and, like humans, make hopeless pets. For years I have longed to eat one.

Could Ecuador, and 1991, be my opportunity? Our van rounded a corner, scattering a family of polka-dotted pigs. And there, by the roadside, was the sign, 'Mr Cuy'. It was January 1. What a way to start the year! Beneath the sign was a shack, a charcoal fire, and what looked like a spit, turning. Wow!

'Mary Magdalene, can we stop?'

'But you've just had lunch.'

'Mary, a chance like this may not come again.' Our driver, Santiago, stopped the van. I jumped out.

As an old Indian woman in petticoats and a trilby hat turned the handle, six skinned guinea-pigs rotated on a grisly carousel. Each was, well, *shafted*, if I may express an undignified position delicately. Six little faces, six little jaws of tiny teeth, open, frozen in expressions of guinea-pig rage, spinning gently through the air as the charcoal spat and the woman sang a sentimental song.

She paused. 'Which?'

'That one's done nicely,' said Mary Magdalene.

'Sit down,' said the woman. 'I'll bring it.'

Five minutes later it arrived, with chips. 'That will be 2,000 sucres,' she said (about £1.20) – roughly what you would pay in an English pet shop, and that would be without chips.

No knife and fork was supplied. Mary Magdalene and Santiago were watching. I felt my virility was on test. I took one final glance down at the head, which seemed to be taking one final glance back up at me. I noticed the two long, curved bottom teeth and remembered Jill's fatalities after the oleander leaves. A sudden queasiness gripped me.

But there was nothing for it. I picked up the guinea-pig. I bit. Paws flailed from my mouth and minature ribs fell like needles. It was good. Not at all bland, but rich, sweet, strong and gamy.

In the old city of Cuzco, in Peru, one of the churches has a Last Supper (seventeenth-century) painted by an unknown Indian artist, after the European style. It follows the customary forms, except that Christ is eating a guinea-pig.

'Coca-Cola?' asked Mary Magdalene.

7.1.91

Eat your own pet

'PLEASE HELP the RSPCA to fight the needless transport of live animals.' I sat staring at the advertisement in the Underground as Waterloo flashed by. The poster was advising us to eat our own pets.

At first I found that hard to live with. Turning the RSPCA's recommondation over in my mind, I looked for objections, trying to reason them through. None could be sustained. After all, what was I saying – that, rather than eat your own pet, it is better to eat somebody else's? Do we maintain that farm-raised animals are nobody's pets, inferring that an animal which nobody loves has less right to live than one which a human has chosen to cherish? No. We are not gods. Our affections cannot be the criteria. At Clapham North I concluded that the RSPCA was right and we ought to eat our pets. I alighted at Clapham Common to consider the practicalities over lunch.

The theory is challenging, but the application surprisingly straightforward. Dogs are apparently delicious. Paul Levy, an *Observer* food critic, tried dog in China and has described the experience approvingly in his book *Out to Lunch*. Eating dogs would lead to heightened interest in the breeds which yield the best cuts – 'table dogs' – and whippets would decline. The criterion of edibility is at least as fair as whether their ears stand up. Crufts could add a 'culinary' category, though if your dog lost, there would be no going back.

Rabbits we already eat. A brace of hamsters is an idea as mouthwatering as half a dozen fresh gerbils with a twist of lemon. I know someone who once had Kentucky Fried Mouse, by mistake, while 'edible dormice' (which you need an Agriculture Ministry licence to trap) have been the subject of questions in Parliament. The Italians already eat songbirds. Tropical fish come into this category, too, and what about a bowl of goldfish lightly tossed in sesame oil over a hot griddle?

Cats present a problem. I understand that they are best curried, and often are. Or they can be presented in a sage and garlic sauce, on a bed of fluffy white rice. The whiskers should always be removed ...

But back to the RSPCA. One of their immediate concerns is the transport of British horses to France, to be eaten. Sadly, it is a truth of economics, that if there is a hungry Frenchman in one place and a redundant horse in another, no law on earth will prevent their converging. So can we not go with the grain of the market? Can we not eat our own horses, and invite the foreigners here? 'The transport of live Frenchmen.' Now who could object to that?

9.3.91

2

Parliamentarians –
Their Habits and Habitat

Joe's prophecy

'*IT IS a very curious thing,*' said Joseph Chamberlain in an after-dinner speech reported in *The Times* on 21 March 1892, '*the types of the House of Commons are constant, although the men change.*'

Let us examine Foreign Office Questions yesterday, to see whether the intervening years have altered its truth.

'*I have never known the House of Commons without a funny man. (Laughter) ... When he dies ... there is another immediately to take his place. He is a man with a natural taste for buffoonery ...*'

Mr Andrew Faulds (Lab, Warley E) is an ex-Shakespearean actor, resting at Westminster. 'Mr Speaker, as to Romania, a country I have not visited recently ...' (Prolonged laughter. Mr Speaker rose ...)

'... Oh Mr Speaker! I thought you were going to arrange it for me!' (Shouts of 'we will, we will!' from all sides, more laughter.)

'*Then there is the House of Commons bore – of course there is more than one (laughter) ... He is generally a man who is very clever, a man of encyclopaedic information ...*'

Yesterday, Mr Nigel Spearing (Lab, Newham S) rose. 'Will not the minister reconsider his use of the phrase "the principle of subsidiarity"? Has he seen the report of the Select Committee on Foreign Affairs about the operation of the Single European Act, HC 82, when I was a witness ...?'

'*Then you have the weighty man and, gentleman, the gravity of the weighty man of the House of Commons is a thing to which there is no parallel in the world.*'

Yesterday, Mr Patrick Cormack (Con, Staffs S) caught the Speaker's eye. 'Is my Rt Hon Friend aware that in Romania, which I had the chance of visiting recently ...' Mr Cormack has been there, you see.

Do you have a question about Da Vinci? Mr Cormack knew him well. Does your inquiry concern King Zog of Albania? He was one of Mr Cormack's oldest friends.

'*You have the foolish man ...*'

Yesterday Mr William McKelvey (Lab, Kilmarnock & Loudon) sprang to the defence of Fidel Castro. Was it not 'bullying' for the United States to broadcast to Cuba?

'*The man with one idea ...*'

John Carlisle (C, Luton N), the last man still defending what even Pretoria has abandoned, urged Mrs Thatcher not to tread where Mr de Klerk himself has trodden: 'it would be irresponsible to see Nelson Mandela' until he has renounced violence.

'You have the independent man ...'

Mr Nicholas Budgen (C, Wolverhampton SW) bobbed up and down, hoping, as ever, to catch the Speaker's eye to explain where he thinks his own party are going wrong over the EC. Budgen was once a junior whip but resigned because he disagreed with the Northern Ireland Assembly: a resignation which saved him having to resign because he disagrees with European integration: which resignation would in its turn have saved him from resignation over the looseness of the Chancellor's monetary grip. He was not called yesterday, but left the Chamber with a jaunty step, as ever.

'All these men are there today, were there fifty years ago, will be there fifty years hence.'

Nay, Joe, ninety-eight years hence.

5.4.90

England eyes Welsh organs

NOW THAT the whales have been freed and swum off to be harpooned by the Japanese, there is a huge reservoir of public goodwill for endangered species waiting to be tapped. So it is natural that concern in the House focuses on Mr Peter Walker.

The Government benches were unusually full (about 11 Members) for the commencement of Questions about Wales on Monday. Some of this interest may have arisen because a few of the simpler souls, having heard about whales on their wirelesses and seen the Prince of Wales on their televisions, probably thought one of the PM's new 'green' ideas was to have a special session on this endangered species. But most knew otherwise: that Mrs Thatcher dreams not of preserving that largest of mammals, but of driving into extinction that comparatively small, birdlike creature, the very smoothest, crispest, sleekest of mammals, the Secretary of State for Wales, wet as a Welsh weekend.

It was said when she offered Mr Walker the job, that, tied to a humdrum department and starved of the oxygen of publicity, he would fade away. Holes have been punched through to Wales in the nick of time. So, though he may be only a bird in a gilded cage, I can report that Peter Walker is hopping up and down on his perch, pecking enthusiastically at his little mirror.

Heaven knows it can't be easy. Never the most trusting of races, the

Welsh are convinced that the latest English plot is to sell 'their' water to foreigners. While control of Welsh Water rested in the Government, the complaint was that the English had stolen it. Now it is to be privatized, the complaint is that foreigners will.

Gwilym Jones did us all a service with his question on donor organs. Question and answer implied what few had realized: that Welsh organs are handled by a different authority from English ones. It cannot be long before it to occurs to someone in Wales that the English are planning to steal their internal organs.

Suddenly (it being 3.10) we switched from Welsh organs to questions to the Church Commissioners.

I often like to imagine, as He trudged through those deserts in Palestine, or lay upon stones, staring at the night sky, whether Jesus would have looked into the future. Did He wonder where it was all going to lead? Did He know? Did He see a grey-suited Sydney Chapman ask a grey-suited Mr Alison whether wise investments by the Church Commissioners gave the Church an excellent 'stake in capitalism'? Did He hear Mr Alison reply?

It took me back to the first Commons debate I attended on Church matters. As I remember, it addressed the question whether the Church of England should call itself 'in' Gibraltar or 'at' Gibraltar; it was argued at length and with passion. It is interesting to speculate upon what part Jesus Himself would have wished to take in these occasions. I seem to remember something about driving the whole lot of them out with a whip. But no doubt that was another issue, another Temple.

1.11.88

Bird's-eye view of egg crisis

THE VIEW we sketchwriters enjoy, down on to Members' heads, offers rare insights.

At Health Questions yesterday, during an important exchange on cervical cancer, one's attention wandered momentarily to the roof of the little four-poster canopy erected above the Speaker's Chair. It takes the form of a sort of neo-Gothic, oaken bus shelter. Now, have you ever looked down on real bus shelters from the top of a double-decker? Yes? You noticed, then, the leftover fish and chips, empty beer cans and other unmentionables slung out of the street-cleaner's view? Well, the

Commons cleaners cannot reach the top of the Speaker's canopy, either; and MPs cannot see it. It is thick with dust, and snaked across with a bit of discarded wire. One awaits the first beer can and crisp packet, cunningly placed where Mrs Currie will never see.

There is no denying that she is under pressure. Tuesday saw a number of Members taking a swing at our heroine – not just on eggs, but on the woolly-hats-for-pensioners issue as well. But she was not without allies. Was Mr Speaker aware, asked Sir Michael McNair Wilson, that up to 20 per cent of body heat is lost through the top of the head?

MPs, who already face massive heat loss from the aperture in the front of their heads, gasped. But your sketchwriter, from his eagle's nest, immediately understood the shiny-pated Sir Michael's problem.

To listen to backbenchers baying for Mrs Currie's blood, you would think nobody in this country actually *ate* eggs, the citizenry being composed entirely of people who produce them. A passionate Paul Marland (Conservative, Gloucester W) implored the Prime Minister to take pity on an egg industry facing a bleak Christmas. We were even asked to spare a thought for all those egg-laying birds who would not see the New Year. When would she sack Mrs Currie? 'Hear, hear!' howled the mob.

It made one wonder how the House would have reacted to the discovery that blue asbestos can cause cancer. Would the Chief Medical Officer have been called to account and blamed for redundancies in the construction industry? The answer is almost certainly yes. He probably was, at the time.

Wiser heads at Westminster (well below the parapet) suspect that if Mrs Currie has farmers, food manufacturers and the Ministry of Agriculture all united in protesting that there is no cause for concern, then she is almost certainly on to something. Your sketchwriter suggests that she ignore the pinstriped rabble, and write a special notelet to Father Christmas: 'Dear Santa, would you send me a couple of well-publicized salmonella deaths? Quickly, please. Christmas may be too late. Thank you. Love, Edwina.'

Very much in the festive spirit was Hereford's Colin Shepherd. Were ministers aware, he enquired pleasantly, that in judging the health of the elderly, 'Morbidity is a better measure than mortality'? To be perfectly frank, one had not realized that *either* was an especially encouraging sign. But there may be aspects of Government policy for the elderly that one had overlooked.

14.12.88

One day I'll show them

WHY ARE all those MPs – those, that is, who are not called Norman – called Reggie, Ronnie or Stan; Cyril, Cecil or Archie? Why are people with ludicrous names driven by some unseen force to stand for election?

As with so many great discoveries the answer came to me by chance, while pondering another great question of our time. Why can so few politicians pronounce their r's?

In a flash it was all clear. Both questions have the same answer. *MPs were desperately unpopular at school.*

They were the boys and girls who got teased in the playground. Some had funny names. Some had speech defects. Some had squidgey little faces, awful freckles, or problems with girls. And the whole of their life since has been a desperate attempt to compensate. Plump little Kenneth hid in the loo from the other boys, sobbing silently: '*I'll* show them. One day, I'll be Secretary of State for Education. I'll wear flashy ties and be popular with all my mates.' Correct Miss Margaret-Hilda flinched at classmates' taunts: 'Snobby-Roberts!' Inwardly she vowed to work even harder, to be even *more* superior, and – one day – to be the first woman Prime Minister in the Western world, *and* end up a Duchess.

Thin, shy, studious young Michael Meacher ('Meacher, Meacher, suck-up to the teacher') knew he'd grow up to be a working-class hero. Oh yes! They'd be sorry they'd bullied the bloke they now needed to protect *them*! He'd stand at the Opposition dispatch box championing the unemployed.

So he did yesterday, at Employment Questions. Opposite him was the Secretary of State. Who is called Norman. And cannot pronounce his r's. When he was Minister of Transport his Labour opposite number was called Albert (really!) and couldn't pronounce r's either. The repartee on 'redundant British Rail rolling-stock' was richly rewarding.

Someone called Conal from York wanted to know why some tourist information centres were closed in winter. Then Cyril from Rochdale spoke. But soon Cecil from Barrow-in-Furness was on his feet, worried lest Norman's relaxing of the rules about employing teenagers might usher back chimney-sweeps.

Norman from Chingford looked in. Dale, Derek and Kenneth (Workington, Leeds and Blackley) intervened.

Then on to a Mr Rooker's question ('Rooker! Rooker! You're a silly ...') where Bernard from Castle Point came to Norman's aid. Alistair's exchange proved interesting to Dafyd, so there was hardly time to hear

Irvine. And none for Dudley, Archy or Spencer. As for Hugo and Trevor, there was no chance at all of questions 79 and 80 being reached.

For it was time for Prime Minister's Questions with Hilda. The first was from Keith of Manchester; the second from a Ms Walley. Hugh from Hornsey was away, but a freckled person called Neil seemed especially agitated, while a chap called Robin Maxwell-Hyslop was furious about a girl called Edwina.

With Hilda sat Tristan (a whip, or class monitor). In garish tie was Kenneth who (since our story started) has become Education Secretary. Still waiting at the back was Sydney from Barnet. Standing at the Bar of the House, yet another Kenneth, next to a Miss Fookes and a Mr Brandon-Bravo.

We never reached Humphrey's question.

7.12.88

What do they care?

THE HOUSE met (Sir Philip Goodhart reminded us) under a shadow. He meant the air crash at Lockerbie, on which a statement from the Transport Secretary was promised for 11 am. First, though, on this last parliamentary morning before Christmas, Sir Philip had called a debate on the plight of Vietnamese refugees.

Why did that seem a trivial distraction from Lockerbie? By the end of his speech, Sir Philip made one ashamed to have felt so.

He stared unhappily around him at an almost entirely empty chamber. Even the journalists looked inattentive.

Sir Philip did not minimize the horror of Lockerbie. Gently, though, he pointed out that perhaps 300 have been killed there; while more than 30,000 had been killed, or drowned, trying to flee Vietnam. Sad, he reflected, that slow tragedies never attracted the interest of sudden ones.

It was strictly according to custom that Mr Speaker left, here, for a deputy to take over. But it was an unlucky coincidence.

Sir Philip described conditions in camps in Hong Kong for those who escaped alive.

His halting manner seemed unmatched to the force of his argument. One of the two backbenchers who had wandered in, wandered out.

Britain accepted twenty refugees a month, Sir Philip concluded. Could we not take a handful more?

And would the minister promise we would not forcibly repatriate refugees to who knows what murderous reception from the country they had fled?

The Principal Doorkeeper, all in black and tailcoated like a slender beetle, buzzed in muffled conversation at the Bar of the House with the bestockinged Assistant Serjeant at Arms. Perhaps it was about the plight of the refugees.

Roger Sims spoke in support. Then came Mr Eggar's reply. It was polished: designed (like all Foreign Office drafts) to explain that everything is more difficult than it seems.

Besides, in this 'difficult and sensitive issue', 'screening' was 'in accordance with established international criteria'. *Economic* refugees are 'screened out': 10 per cent who are *genuine* refugees are 'screened in' and a few extra-useful ones can come here.

The screened-out 90 per cent are now 'temporarily' in Hong Kong till arrangements can be made for their 'future'. They were very much 'a residual problem'.

The thought occurred that, if he meant repatriation, the future of this residual problem would be to be screened out in the Vietcong sense. But there was no need to worry. 'Assurances' had been given and would be 'monitored'.

So, no, he could not pledge that there would be no compulsion, or – in his words – 'We're certainly not talking about compulsion at this stage.'

Next came Paul Channon's statement on Lockerbie. The unhappy ritual was sensitively handled, but, as an undoubtedly sincere voice intoned, 'Our thoughts at this time are also with . . .', one's own thoughts had left the mock-Gothic carving, green leather and muted microphones.

What could it matter to those hundreds of people in Scotland; and to those tens of thousands of refugees, murdered, drowned or 'screened out' as the Foreign Office might put it; and to those still alive? Sorry: 'the residual problem'.

23.12.88

A fatal pause

MR DAVID ASHBY (C, Leicestershire North West) is not a fat man. Far from it. But there is about him a certain plump sufficiency. And, like so many barristers, he has a chubby aura. Call it self-assurance, call it good-humour, but lawyer MPs speak always with their metaphorical thumbs thrust into their metaphorical braces, rocking gently on their metaphorical heels, their metaphorical tummies swelling confidently as the clichés roll.

'Is my honourable friend aware,' said Mr Ashby yesterday, savouring each syllable, 'that St Clare's school is an *excellent* school?' He paused, for effect. 'But it is *bursting* at the *seams*.' He paused again, fatally.

'Like you!' came a shout from the Labour benches. Poor Mr Ashby's question was swamped in general mirth. To the end, he could be seen bailing manfully.

It was Leicestershire's day at Education Questions. Mr Keith Vaz (Lab, Leicester East) asked a most complicated question about resources, defects and repairs in schools that had been waiting '175 years' for improvement. That remarkable figure came from adding together all the waiting times of all the schools. The method holds possibilities. Looking down on the Tory benches we saw a Prime Minister flanked by senior colleagues who have been waiting seventy-three years for her to go.

Behind her were the massed ranks of backbenchers who have waited 4,684 years just to be PPS to someone like a parliamentary under-secretary. Surprising, really, that accumulated frustration has not blown the lid clean off Westminster.

Mr Vaz was on his feet again at PM's Questions. 'In the course of a busy day,' he asked, 'will the Prime Minister find time to look at her shoes, and . . .' But he was engulfed by howls of general puzzlement.

'Her *shoes*,' he repeated, 'her *shoes*.' His question, about the footwear industry, included a challenge to the Prime Minister to name the origin of her own shoes.

It does not come easily to Mrs Thatcher to look at her feet. Modest lowerings of the eyes have not been her style for at least the last half-century. But she managed it. 'Marks and Spencer's!' she declared.

Mr Andrew Bennett (Lab, Denton & Reddish) was fielded easily enough; but then it is always hard to take seriously a small man with a large beard and a falsetto voice: never can such a squeaky noise have emanated from amidst so much hair. But Dr Owen proved harder going.

In his gravedigger's tone, he told us the NHS was not safe in Mrs Thatcher's hands because it had no place in her heart. The Prime Minister adopted her really-*very*-surprised voice, as though Dr Owen had just goosed her.

Then Neil Kinnock scored a bull's-eye. He pricked her outrage at the leaking of the NHS report with the remark that the last big leaker (over Westland) had just been knighted and made a European Commissioner. He meant Sir Leon Brittan.

Only Mr Donald Thompson (the junior agriculture minister) smiled. But then the ample Mr Thompson smiles continuously: a gentle, internally radiant beam whose occurrence does not reflect any changes in the external stimuli to which Mr Thompson may be subject. Mr Thompson is *not* in fact subject to external stimuli.

1.2.89

Green men and blue leaders

A MARTIAN peering in for the first time at Prime Minister's Questions yesterday would have sent a most bewildered report back to his home planet.

A strange Earthling (he would have to explain) dressed all in electric blue, who appeared to be the Leader, stormed into the Chamber with what looked like two enormous silver eggs pinned above her left breast in flying-duck formation.

The blue Leader rose and delivered a fifteen-minute lecture, punctuated by what another Earthling (in black tights and a white wig, who had arrived earlier pursuing a golden wand) called 'Questions'. These bore no relation at all to her lecture, which was divided into three parts.

The first part was about Israel. The Earthling's status in this matter seemed to be high, for she offered advice (and her own good offices) to every other nation in what sounded like a major territorial dispute. From time to time, craven-looking creatures behind her (obviously vassal Earthlings) rose, wringing their feelers, and told her how wonderful she was.

Then rose an Earthling who led the creatures opposite. He had much less fur on his head than the blue Leader: ginger fur, and he looked a bit downtrodden. But when he put his question she became very angry.

He asked her what she had had for lunch.

It seemed to touch a nerve. 'Cheshire cheese and very good it was,' she shouted: and this began the second part of her lecture, which was not about wars or nations at all. It seemed to be a detailed set of instructions to other Earthlings on how to cook their food. 'The Government's Chief Medical Officer' was constantly referred to – reminding the Martian of another absent personage called 'The Marquis of Carabas' in *Puss in Boots*, a less bizarre pantomime.

The cookery part of her lecture went on for a very long time indeed and only ended when everyone began shouting wildly. Even the thing in tights and white wig began to get impatient.

Then came the third part, equally strange. A creature with no fur at all, very tall and anxious, referred to as 'Sir Anthony Buck', asked the Leader to say something nice about the departing American Ambassador, Mr Charles Price. Why? Nobody had said anything *nasty* about Mr Price. But, immediately, all the vassals on the blue Leader's side started to make a weird growling sound – '*Yer-yer-yer-yer*' – and the Leader said Mr Price was wonderful and added her appreciation of '*Mrs* Price, who has been *absolutely marvellous*'.

Then she departed, as suddenly as she had arrived.

The moment she was gone, the remaining creatures stopped talking about how to cook chicken, and how marvellous Mrs Price was; and started to talk about a great storm which appeared to have devastated large parts of a distant place called Scotland.

But, strangest of all, a few seconds after the blue Leader left, almost all the Earthlings on her side left too. After ten minutes, even the thing with the ginger fur departed. Soon the Chamber was nearly empty.

What should the Martian do now? Should he seek out the thing in blue ribbons? Was it 'Take me to your Leader' or 'Take me to your Cook'? Or Nanny? Or Hostess?

But here our Martian laid down his pen, in utter disbelief. For into the Chamber walked another Martian, speaking impeccable English and talking about local government. The Earthlings called it 'Nicholas Ridley'.

15.2.89

Here comes the sun

FROM THE high windows which light the Chamber, sudden flashes of winter sunshine illuminated Social Security Questions yesterday: brilliant, acid and brief. The argument, likewise, dissolved into a series of snapshots, vignettes, flash-recorded as ministers and their Shadows were pinned, motionless for an instant in the searchlight's beam.

There was Labour's John Evans (St Helens N) asking why you had to be terminally ill for six months before you qualified for disability benefits. Well, said the Minister, Nick Scott, there were problems about telling people ...

Ah. Of course. How poignant. Government was just longing to help with a little extra cash, held back only by its concern that the patient might be upset to hear the *reason*.

And what if the early diagnosis proves wrong and the patient survives? 'Good morning Mr Jones, we're from Mr Scott's office. Aren't you dead yet? You've got till Tuesday. Otherwise that'll be £634.27, please.'

Come to think of it, why only six months wait if the Department wants to be absolutely sure? Couldn't ministers await the *only* rock-solid proof known to man that an illness is terminal? It would save on the payouts.

MPs nodded sagely when Mr Scott said (to Glasgow's Thomas McAvoy, who had asked about the young unemployed): 'I can think of no worse start to life than to begin it on benefit.' Can't you, Nick? How about beginning it *not* on benefit?

Yet more sagely did they nod after a shrewd question from Martin Brandon-Bravo (Nottingham S). Why did similar benefit offices often pay out very different levels of benefit? Mr Lloyd felt that this was partly due to 'the efforts of some officers to see that eligibility is widely known'. This means, 'Some officers don't tell people what they're entitled to.' Brief sunshine.

It flickered on the Secretary of State, John Moore, as he told Labour's Dale Campbell-Savours that he was 'trapped in utter nonsense'. This is a very grave accusation to lay at an MP's door. No Member is *trapped* in nonsense. Nonsense is his meat and drink. A bee among the blossoms would not be described as trapped.

Then somebody mentioned widows. *Nobody* is against widows, not even Nick Ridley. They mount campaigns and form organizations with more remorseless efficiency than even farmers. Their skills in moral blackmail exceed even those of the RSPCA. If an impoverished spinster is mugged by a mink-coated widow, then the only permissible Parliamentary Question is what drove the poor widow to do it.

There followed a row about pensioners' incomes. The Government claimed they had risen by 21 per cent since 1979. Labour couldn't believe it.

But the Tories' Charles Wardle was right: he meant 'income from all sources' – not just the state pension (which did much better under Labour). So Denis Thatcher's income, Robert Maxwell's and Sir Ian MacGregor's are covered by this gratifying statistic. One looks to Mr Wardle to declare that pensioners' champagne consumption, too, is at an all-time high, while more pensioners than ever own their own yachts, under the Tories. Mr Moore blinked in another quick burst of sunlight.

7.3.89

Voting floaters

DENNIS SKINNER looked roguishly around the Chamber. 'Lots of these little plots have litter on them ...' He meant the small vacant sites that Dame Janet Fookes (C, Plymouth, Drake) wanted added to the land register.

She had come to Environment Questions yesterday to ask about them. Now we watched helplessly as Skinner hijacked the question: twisted it shamelessly to his own purpose. On he went: Couldn't ministers – especially, he stressed, the Prime Minister – visit these little plots, and each bring back to the Environment Secretary a paper bag full of the litter. 'And *then* ...'

Mr Skinner paused. It must have been many years since he had recited his own poetry, on stage:

'He can bag it,
And bin it,
And stick *her* in it.'

Under cover of the general laughter that followed, Colin Moynihan managed to creep in, late, without being noticed, and sat panting. He was just in time to witness poor David Shaw (C, Dover) trying to ask a question. It was a very grave question, about the state of the beach at Deal – but MPs, in their unfair way, seemed interested only in Mr Shaw's ex-research assistant, Pamella Bordes.

'Ooh!' they squealed, and 'Aaah!' almost before he could speak.

He struggled on, putting important facts about Deal, which he had assembled, to the minister. Then he sat down with relief.

'He paid her £3,000 for that!' shouted Skinner, from a sedentary position.

Wisely, Michael Howard ignored the giggles and advised Mr Shaw that the position would improve when such things were in the private sector. 'She *is* in the private sector,' came an anonymous yell.

But of course Mr Howard had meant beaches. And beaches dominated the session. Mr Ridley struggled to maintain the tone with a lyrical tribute to the cleansing action of 'salt, sunlight, water and waves' in the disinfecting of raw sewage. One wondered only why anyone should risk the chlorinated horrors of the municipal swimming bath, when sewage-treatment plants everywhere beckon us in for a romp.

But Members were not convinced. They were soon on their feet, shouting about unmentionable things discharged, untreated, into the sea. 'You've got a lot of floating voters out there,' confided Labour's Ron Brown (Edinburgh, Leith). At least we *think* he said 'voters'.

'I have a leak,' declared Mr Ridley, and one really did fear that the depths of poor taste had been reached.

In vain did Dame Elaine Kellet-Bowman try to restore gentility: 'How do we stand in the European Clean Beach League?' she asked, hopeful perhaps of the 'Most Improved Performance in 1989' award. 'Dame Elaine and the Dettol Sisters – deux points!'

In vain did Junior Minister John Gummer lift his gaze heavenward: 'My guidance is to embrace the high aspirations but avoid the chaotic practices of Tower Hamlets.'

It called to mind those lurid pictures with which our childhood Bibles were illustrated: *St Gummer of the High Aspirations, in flight from the chaotic practices of Tower Hamlets.*

For the House's mind was elsewhere. After all, sewage was not (as Ron Brown put it) 'an issue to sniff at'.

23.3.89

Dr Glyn's chance slips by

A SMALL tragedy occurred at Westminster yesterday: slight, but infinitely sad. Dr Alan Glyn tried to ask a question. And Mr Speaker failed to see.

Dr Glyn is a collector's item. He has only been the Conservative MP for Windsor for nineteen years, yet he has a timeless quality. Small and stooped, he sports a remarkable soup-stained moustache and always sits in the same seat (on the Mujahedin bench, where Ted Heath and Ian Gilmour sit). Rare is the afternoon when Dr Glyn is not seen, but unusual the afternoon when Dr Glyn is heard. There are undoubtedly Members of whom even less is heard – but of them little is seen, either; they don't attend. Dr Glyn does attend. And listens. And listens. And listens.

They say he used to be quite garrulous. They say that in a dramatic gesture he once offered Parliament his own services (as a medical practitioner) to attend at hangings should the death penalty be restored. But these are just memories.

As the years pass, the number of people who have never seen the sea dwindles, but the number who have never heard Dr Glyn speak grows. The time has passed when the Member for Windsor needs to speak. He is just *there*.

The tale is told – in the Commons Tea Room – of an election campaign in which the good doctor decided upon a day of canvassing and stepped into one of those walk-in stand-up wardrobes to dress for the occasion. Unfortunately the wardrobe fell on its face, with Dr Glyn in it.

He was unable to get out and his cries went unheard. Nobody noticed his absence on the campaign trail until the evening, when his redoubtable wife, the Lady Rosula Glyn, found and rescued her husband from, if not an early grave, then a precipitate coffin. The story, widely believed by his colleagues, is almost certainly untrue.

Defence is his subject, and it was during a Question to the Foreign Secretary from Gary Waller (Con, Keighley) about arms reductions that Dr Glyn began to grow visibly agitated.

Dr Glyn is against arms reductions and wanted to say so. Grabbing an oaken post, he hauled himself to his feet as Mr Waller sat down. Mr Speaker did not see him and called Oldham's James Lamond (Lab) who is in favour of arms reductions. Dr Glyn's agitation increased and his moustache began to twitch. As Lamond resumed his seat, he pulled himself even more violently upright. Again Mr Speaker ignored him, and called Sir Peter Blaker (Con, Blackpool S). Sir Peter is wary about arms reductions, but not wary enough for the doctor.

A very great perturbation was now upon Dr Glyn. Up he got again, and it is fair to say that the whole House willed Mr Speaker to see him.

Cruel Destiny! The Speaker moved on to a new question about human rights. Dr Glyn is not very big on human rights. He subsided, moustache all a-quiver.

13.4.89

Dames, baronesses and pandas

WHATEVER IS happening to the Dames? On Tuesday Dame Elaine Kellet-Bowman (C, Lancaster) appeared completely to flip her lid, screeching at the Speaker, 'It-isn't-a-point-of-order, it-isn't-a-point-of-order,' for much of the afternoon as a Labour Spokesman tried to speak. She is probably the first example of a yob-Dame, or lager-Dame, except that alcohol is not the problem, sadly, or she would be better in the morning, which she isn't.

Then, yesterday afternoon, Dame Jill Knight astonished us. She sailed in wearing a black-and-white creation featuring a pattern of giant pandas. At first we thought they were tattoos. One of them covered her entire left breast. It was enormous. The panda, I mean.

I rushed, horrified, from the Chamber – sacrificing the sight of the anxious face of young William Hague (C, Richmond) as he heard a statement about dangerous baby food. Mr Hague resembles the winner of a 1950s Cow & Gate baby competition.

Over in the Lords a 'Lady Strange' was asking about schools opting out. The Baroness Strange has opted *in*, having won a long battle for the title against her three sisters. Couldn't they share the barony and attend in quadruplicate: 'The Strange Sisters'?

Replying for the Government, Lord Davidson relied alternately on a written brief and his native wit. The latter amounted to saying, 'My Lords, I was aware of that'; or sometimes, for variety, 'My Lords, I was not aware of that.' Once he abandoned routine and said: 'My Lords, yes, why?' He showed huge relish for the cut-and-thrust of adversarial politics, replying to Labour's Lord Peston: 'My Lords, the Noble Lord may well assume that. I may well assume the opposite.'

Lord Wallace of Coslany rose very slowly to his feet. If you want a sense of how old Lord Wallace is, the information that he was once *Labour* MP for Chislehurst in Kent may help. He was worried, he told Lord Brabazon of Tara (yes, really!) about the possible destruction of Oxleas Wood. This wood, Lord Wallace explained, 'leads back to the Stone Age'. He paused, casting his mind back, perhaps, to that period. How time flies! Why, it seemed only yesterday that dinosaurs roamed Bromley and there were Labour MPs in Kent.

We left Lord Ferrers, who carried himself like an Edwardian male model, promising 'to cogitate upon' Baroness Faithfull's idea that drinkers should be forcibly confined to drying-out centres, and moved to a debate on 'The Press and the People'. Lord Stevens, owner of the *Daily Express*, the *Sunday Express*, the *Daily Star* ... seemed to know a bit about the press. He greeted the demise of the Right to Reply Bill and the Protection of Privacy Bill, he said, 'with mixed feelings'. I daresay. A heady cocktail of rapture, glee, joy and triumph, no doubt.

Lord Ardwick (a retired sub-editor) seemed to know a bit about the people. 'The wages of sin,' he told their Lordships, 'is increased circulation.'

27.4.89

Downers and uppers

DRUGS DOMINATED Members' thoughts all afternoon, for which we have to blame Emma Nicholson (C, Devon W & Torridge). 'My sex,' she told the Chamber, pausing slightly to savour the expectant hush, 'being ultra-sensitive about their shapes and sizes, are also ultra-gullible to slimming drugs.' She wanted the Government to ban them. I thought I saw Teresa Gorman's limbs jerk.

It is widely reported that Mrs Gorman (C, Billericay) regularly spreads the word about a rejuvenating hormone treatment of the homeopathic kind, made from something awful taken from horses' ... well, something this sketch shrinks from naming. Certainly Mrs Gorman, who leaps around like a scalded kitten, is a good advertisement for whatever it is she drinks (or gargles, or splashes on, or whatever it is you do with it).

There is even tittle-tattle in the Members' Tea Room that attempts have been made to interest the Prime Minister in this treatment, though

Heaven protect us all from an *invigorated* Mrs Thatcher.

Douglas Hogg, the junior minister, steered clear of the controversy, remarking amiably that it was best to keep off drugs of all kinds. Greg Knight (C, Derby N) agreed: especially about slimming: 'It is better to have a healthy appetite and be overweight,' he advised. Roy Hattersley, spread across the bench, relaxed visibly.

But attention returned to Mrs Gorman when Menzies Campbell, for the Democrats, asked the Government to do something about the activities of ticket touts.

La Gorman's eyes began to roll violently, for she believes in enterprise, and it only takes about ten seconds' thought to realize that a ticket tout is simply the enterprising means by which a demand meets a supply, pointless to deplore and impossible to prohibit.

You, I, and Teresa Gorman know that: but for some reason junior minister John Patten announced that touts 'would be regarded as obnoxious by most MPs'.

Mrs Gorman shot vertically into the air as if 10,000 volts had just been pumped into her. Almost before hitting the floor again she was waving her arms and swivelling her shoulders, crackling with a passionate defence of ticket touts, 'brokers, risk-takers', heroes, galvanizers of our economy ...

Whatever it is that woman's on, I'm going straight out to get me some.

12.5.89

Question the questioners

SHE WAS simply fed up.

'The hon gentleman is talking his customary poppycock,' she told Bruce Grocott (Lab, The Wrekin). 'The Right Hon gentleman has no experience of Government,' was all she could say to Mr Ashdown. An inquiry about the economy from Mr Kinnock was tossed aside with the remark that Kinnock 'would have made a complete mess of it' himself. As for Glasgow's Jimmy Wray (Lab) who asked about money owing to the NHS – if he was ignorant of accountancy 'then I shouldn't be in the least surprised'.

There was no pleasing this woman. Fair enough. But why waste Questions on her, then? 'If *you* don't want to stand at the dispatch box,' a stern uncle should scold, 'there are plenty who do.' Tied pubs often have a 'guest beer' on tap: why shouldn't Parliament offer the dispatch box to a 'guest backbencher' every week?

How about Dennis Skinner? 'Questions to the hon Member for Bolsover,' Mr Speaker would call. A string of Questions asking Skinner to state his engagements for the day would elicit replies refreshingly different from the PM's.

No tea with the Queen, conferences with the President of Burundi or speeches to Young Achievers. 'This morning,' he would say, 'I attended a meeting of the steering committee for the preliminary shortlist of the names of citizens to be stood up against the wall and shot, after the Revolution. Afterwards I joined a 'Smash the Tories' rally at Clay Cross Town Hall, lunching at the Bolsover Colliery Miners' Welfare Club ...'

Soames could be asked to state his fox-hunting engagements for the weekend, then face angry questions from Dame Janet Fookes (C, Plymouth Drake), a former RSPCA chairman. 'Questions to Geoffrey Dickens' would probe the witches' covens he was investigating and the rings of paeodophiles he was about to smash.

David Steel could be asked about museum charges in Turin. And how we would savour Roy Hattersley's answers: 'Today I lunched on fresh whitebait, followed by Duck *aux Cerises* with a selection of fresh vegetables. Following that I encountered a generous slice of *Gateau Pithviers*, and was afterwards met by an array of cheeses ...'

Contrast Coventry's Dave Nellist (also Labour): 'I spent the morning at Cardboard City mobilizing the vagrant vote, afterwards lunching at a Salvation Army soup kitchen. The afternoon was spent discussing the poll tax with fifteen Glaswegians sleeping rough. I hope to spend the evening at Bondway Shelter.'

The nation has heard Paul Marland (C, Gloucestershire W) ruthlessly question Mrs Currie about salmonella. Now the nation demands to hear him questioned himself, fearlessly, about his alleged use of Grecian 2000; while MPs I shall not name could answer for the damage done to the ozone layer by all that hairspray.

We have had enough of these men's Questions. It is time for answers, now.

24.5.89

WANTED: shrinks, not policies

LEO ABSE, the retired MP for Pontypool, is writing a book about Mrs Thatcher's potty-training: psychoanalysing her politics through a Freudian look at her infant development. Even the *Guardian* thinks Abse has gone too far.

Yet isn't the House of Commons better explained in terms of mental illness, than any other discipline? No historian, no economist or political scientist could make head or tail of the place. Only a shrink could understand.

Witness yesterday's Questions to Mr Ridley. Everybody wanted to talk about recycling waste paper. Are the ice caps melting? Recycling waste paper would help. Are the deserts encroaching, the mountains crumbling and the rivers running with filth? Recycling waste paper is the answer!

Mrs Bottomley rose splendidly at the dispatch box. Yes, she told the Democrats' Malcolm Bruce, *all* her writing paper, and 'more and more' of her Department's total paper output, was recycled. Britain was 'the fourth largest user of recycled paper in the Western world'.

Ah, said Ms Joan Walley, for Labour, that was not enough. What was needed was an 'Integrated Waste Management Policy'. Wise heads nodded. In vain might one point out that an active woman produces twelve litres of carbon dioxide per hour and trees filter it out again. For Ms Walley simply to have a quiet lie-down would do the work of one small ash grove.

In vain did James Paice (C, Cambridgeshire SE) suggest that as trees were a crop, recycling paper might mean less trees, not more. You see, that is not what the argument is *about*.

Mr Abse knows better. Have you see those old men wandering London's streets searching the litter bins for discarded goodies? Do you have an aunt imprisoned by things she cannot bear to throw away — bits of string, broken toys?

Do you yourself suffer from a nagging desire to wash and keep plastic yoghurt tubs? Do you hoard scraps of unused soap? Then you would have understood the Commons, yesterday.

For, though environmental arguments may ebb and flow, for and against these practices, that is not the point. Such arguments are just rationalizations. We don't *want* to be told that there is no point in keeping things. It is an endemic form of mental illness, arising perhaps from early weaning.

And it gripped the House. MPs renewed the attack, led by Nicholas Baker (C, N Dorset): reduce the use of paper, he demanded. Stop 'depletion of timber resources'. Hear! Hear!

Old Frank Haynes (Lab, Ashfield) had had enough. Working up from a growl to a bellow, he began to mutter that Ministers were the last to talk about recycling paper. Confidential government memos were to be found blowing in the wind around every rubbish-tipping landfill site. By now, Haynes's voice filled the Chamber. It was time, he roared, 'to recycle Nicholas Ridley'.

25.5.89

Zen, Kafka, Thatcher

MR HARVEY PROCTOR has just opened a second shirt shop, in Knightsbridge. Can I beg Eric Forth, minister for Consumer Affairs, to go there immediately? His shirt yesterday was an outrage. Blood red, with white collar and cuffs, he wore it with a pale pink tie. What did it mean? What did *anything* mean, yesterday?

Parliamentary dialogue has assumed a Zen-like mystery. Questions and answers slide silently by each other in a verbal fog, no single idea engaging directly with another.

Harry Cohen (Lab, Leyton) loosed an East End rant at the Treasury Bench because 'top directors' are getting richer. John Major, the Chief Secretary, toyed with an imaginary Mandarin pigtail. 'I do not have and have never justified wage increases which are not justified but it is not a matter for me to determine what is and what is not justifiable in that respect.' So there, Harry!

Dr John Marek (Lab, Wrexham) tackled Peter Brooke, the Conservative Party Chairman. This relic of the Opium Wars continues to make unexplained appearances on the Treasury front bench, but never really says anything.

Marek asked a Kafka-esque question about lenders and borrowers, concluding that people with mortgages were sunk. The Ancient Warlord put down his hookah and gazed into the middle distance. 'The Honourable Gentleman is clearly broadly correct in the surmise he makes about the unlikelihood of coincidence.' Okay?

Ministers then took Questions from all directions, observing variously, that it would be a good thing if people were paid less (Norman

Lamont); a good thing if people borrowed less (Nigel Lawson); and that (John Major): 'We have never made predictions.' Asked by Labour's spokesman, Nick Brown, whether the policy of shadowing the Deutschmark had caused problems, Mr Brooke paused, smiled and replied that that was not the Question.

There was no sorting it out, so we hung on, hoping for better from PM's Questions. Some hope! Mrs Thatcher started by missing Mr Kinnock's point about commuter fares, was then unaccountably nice to Mr Heath, accusing him of 'vision', and ended by facing Stuart Bell (Lab, Middlesbrough) who had asked about the European Social Contract and been told by Mr Speaker to relate it to rainforests.

The PM replied that as far as the Social Contract was concerned we were doing our bit for the rainforests, and the important thing was 'that we are proud to be British'. Quite.

Edwina Currie reminded Mrs Thatcher that we didn't want a load of Chinamen here, thank you very much. I wonder if Mrs Currie knows a fable Sir Victor Gollancz liked to quote? An old woman dies and is sent to purgatory. While suffering there she sees an angel above, reaching down with a single onion on a stem. 'Take hold,' he says. The old woman clings on and the angel starts to pull her up. But another suffering soul grabs her ankles, desperate for a ride, then another, then another. Somehow, the onion holds. The woman looks down in terror.

'Let go!' she shouts at her hangers-on 'The stem is not strong enough for all of us!' When she says this, the stem breaks.

9.6.89

MPs with empathy bulges

LAST WEEK the shadow Foreign Secretary, Gerald Kaufman, was asked his opinion of 'Independence for Scotland within the UK'. Thinking this was an opponents' policy he denounced it: 'An irrelevant fantasy.' Gently he was informed that this was his own party's new policy. Too late! By accident he had glimpsed life from another viewpoint.

The episode proved what we know already: MPs are determined not to see things from any angle but their own party's. How could we make them try?

Well, have you heard the new American idea: 'empathy bulges'? To understand pregnancy, fathers-to-be buy a strap-on extra stomach, then waddle around until they sympathize.

The concept has wide application so why not at Westminster? No shortage of tums here but a crying need for MPs of both major parties to walk a mile in each other's shoes. So here's my plan: to compel each MP to endure just one experience that is the common lot of an MP opposite.

Bra-less and in feminist dungarees, Dame Jill Knight (C, Edgbaston) will be obliged to join Lambeth councillors in a lesbian self-defence class in Brixton. In a dingy nearby laundrette, huddled around mugs of Cup-a-Soup, Nigel Lawson will be addressing a group of single-parent mothers on 'How to Get Your Benefit Rights'.

Over on the Nelson Mandela Estate, Labour's Bernie Grant, dressed in a neat pinstriped suit with an enormous blue rosette and a *Make it with Maggie* lapel badge, experiences the lot of a Tory canvasser in Tottenham. He has a Rottweiler embedded in one heel and is trying to explain about Sterling M3.

Spare a thought for his colleague, Coventry's Dave ('Spart') Nellist, inviting questions from a board of City directors on 'Gilt-Edged Prospects for the 90s'. As he stammers, Diane Abbott (Lab, Hackney N & Stoke Newington) steels herself to take the Ladies' Excuse-Me with the Chairman of Rotary at the Harrogate Conservative Dinner Dance. Ms Abbott's shoes are killing her, and the man dances like an elephant, growling intimacies about her voting record on hanging.

Who is more wretched? Dame Elaine Kellett-Bowman (C, Lancaster), camped for three nights on Greenham Common in her 'Swapo solidarity' T-shirt and making paper flowers to weave into the perimeter fence? Or Ron Brown (Lab, Leith), judging the begonias at Chatsworth Garden Festival?

Mrs Thatcher is now in a Swansea public bar, cornered by three drunk redundant steelworkers trying to force a pint into her hand and challenging her to darts. Neil Kinnock, meanwhile, is being barracked on law-and-order at a Small Businessmen's Rally in Cleethorpes.

Mr Ridley has not enjoyed his day with carers in a Birmingham crèche. Not all the toddlers took to him. Elegant Miss Emma Nicholson (C, Devon W & Torridge) is mounting a makeshift rostrum. Horror clouds her demure features. She is to give the keynote speech to a street rally of the English Collective of Prostitutes.

13.6.89

Good-humoured nun-sense

'I THINK the North-east is *very* well placed,' said John Cope, a junior Employment minister, at Questions yesterday. This was puzzling. Beyond the observation that the North-east is placed between the South-west and the North Sea, it was hard to see how a value judgement could be made about its location. We were never enlightened and Mr Cope sat down.

'Has the Right Honourable gentleman,' squealed Labour's Eric Heffer (Walton), 'seen the pamphlet issued by the Catholic Truth Society, making the point that secondary picketing is a legitimate action on the workers' part to defend themselves from employers . . .?'

Anxious, no doubt, to coax Rome over to the Tory side, the Employment Secretary later praised what he called the 'nun-scheme' ports. We smiled to think of a Mother Superior figure, the veiled Mr Fowler, leading noviciate stevedores, *Sound of Music* style, over the meadows towards the cranes and derricks.

Hansard always spoils the fun by correcting Mr Fowler's mispronun(oops)-ciation and rendering it '*non*-scheme' ports: so Fowler probably still thinks he is getting it right. I bet his civil servants haven't dared say anything!

As he spoke, an enormous cheer went up from the Labour benches. Was this Neil Kinnock making his triumphant entry for Prime Minister's Questions? We craned over the gallery to look. Who was Labour's arriving hero?

It was Ted Heath. He ambled slowly over to the Mujahedin bench where he jostled with the other old mullahs and sat down, savouring the moment. Few could keep a straight face. Mrs Thatcher tried to, then broke into a broad grin. Ted smiled wryly.

John McFall (Lab, Dumbarton) compared Mrs Thatcher to a 'tub of hazelnut yoghurt' and rejoiced that Scotland was a 'Tory-free zone'. Mrs Thatcher replied (in effect) that the Scots were jolly lucky to have her, even if they didn't realize it – and a number of Scottish Labour MPs gave visible signs of *not* realizing it. All good clean fun.

Gigantic Labour cheers then greeted the arrival, 'desirous of taking their seats', of the new members for Vauxhall and Glasgow Central, who took the Oath, waved and shook Mr Speaker's hand, roses upon their lapels. Mike Watson (Glasgow Central) wore a double-breasted suit and the hint of a swagger, while Kate Hoey (Vauxhall), in a white lace collar, looked rather pretty for a politician. There was something of Bonnie and Clyde about the pair.

It was a sunny day. Labour are in enormous good spirits, while on the Tory side – so far – anxiety is no more than a footnote to optimism. C. G. Jung (I think?) once wrote that 'those parts of ourselves which we suppress in early life in order to achieve some cherished ambition will return, many years later, knife in hand, determined to destroy their destroyers'. The snowy-haired Mr Heath is not an obvious Jungian dream symbol, yet yesterday's sunshine caught the glint of more than one hidden blade along the Tory benches. As for Labour, they are only at the start of Jung's cycle. Ambition is paramount, idealisms suppressed, for now.

21.6.89

Bear pit shorthand

A MINORITY of sketchwriters – yours included – cannot do shorthand. We cheat. We borrow our colleague reporters' notes when we need exact quotes, and concentrate on getting down the gist of debate, mercilessly summarized, and not always in the right order. We base the sketch on that.

Yesterday, John Wakeham (Leader of the House, deputizing for the absent Mrs Thatcher) squared up to face a knockabout House. The phrasing is mine, the meaning theirs:

Timothy Wood (C, Stevenage): 'We love the Bomb. Ron Todd's a menace.'

JW (John Wakeham): 'But Nato's tops and Mrs T's brill.'

Roy Hattersley: 'What's your forecast for this year's trade deficit?'

JW: 'Not my job.'

Roy Hattersley: 'Shocking' *(splutter, splutter)*.

JW: 'The Government's wonderful.'

*(**Dr Alan Glyn** – C, Windsor & Maidenhead – indicated that he wished to rise.)*

Hon. Members *(to Mr Speaker)*: 'Call Glyn!'

Teddy Taylor (C, Southend E): 'Mrs T's fantastic ... not sucked into the socialist nonsense of the EEC.'

JW: 'Hm.'

Diane Abbott (Lab, Hackney N & Stoke Newington): *(Silence – seemed to have forgotten Question.)*

Hon. Members: 'Come on!'

Diane Abbott: *(Silence.)*
Hon. Members: 'Get on with it!' *etc.*
Diane Abbott: *(Silence. Dr Glyn still trying to rise.)*
Hon. Members: 'Call Glyn instead!'
Diane Abbott: 'The GPs don't like you.'
Sir William Clark (C, Croydon S): 'Employment's up ... Government's wonderful.'
JW: 'Yes.'
David Winnick (Lab, Walsall N): 'You're for the chop, Wakeham.'
JW: 'Sucks to you too!'
Teresa Gorman (C, Billericay): *(Gabble, gabble)* '... EMS' *(gabble)* '... exchange control.'
JW: 'Hm.'
Hon. Members: 'Call Glyn!'
Sir Russell Johnston (Dem, Inverness, Nairn & Lochaber): *(Mumble)* '... Treaty of Rome ...' *(etc)*.
Hon. Members: 'Call Glyn!'
Dennis Skinner (Lab, Bolsover): 'The SLD ...'
Hon. Members: 'Who?'
Eddie Loyden (Lab, Liverpool, Garston): 'Unemployment's dreadful.'
JW: 'There's less, now.'
Philip Oppenheim (C, Amber Valley): 'Nationalization's useless!'
JW: 'So it is.'
John Fraser (Lab, Norwood): 'Mrs Thatcher talks **** but why must it be discharged into our rivers, too?'
JW: 'P*** off.'
John Watts (C, Slough): 'That acid-house party was appalling. Something ought to be done.'
JW: 'Yes.'
Hon. Members: 'Call Glyn!'
Mr Speaker *(booming):* 'Dr Alan Glyn!'
Hon. Members: 'Hooray! Hooray!' *(Huge cheers, prolonged.)*
Dr Alan Glyn: 'I missed the party by half an hour ...'
Hon. Members: 'But it lasted all day ...'
Dr Glyn: 'It was ghastly, there were no toilets. Everyone should be fined.'
Hon. Members: 'Hear, hear! Hooray!'

28.6.89

When a 'woof' is bliss to the ears

IT MUST have been the way John Gummer yelped the 'Ip' of 'Ipswich' but, suddenly, the whole House was barking.

'Ruff,' rasped Brian Sedgemore (Lab, Hackney S & Shoreditch).

'Hragh! Hragh!' came a more peremptory bark, from the middle of the bench on which Dennis Skinner and his gang sit.

'Wrraargh ...' came something more like a growl from the middle of the Opposition.

The more Mr Gummer (Minister of State) tried to hammer out his answer (about the community charge), the more they barked. The more they barked, the crosser he got. And the more Gummer yelped, the more they barked.

For a moment there was a danger that the kennels opposite, the Government benches, would start to return the doggie noises. But, (sadly) decorum prevailed, the barks subsided, and the House returned to Question 7.

Of course the advantages of animal noises (as every schoolboy knows) is that you can make them without moving your lips, so teacher (or, in this case, Mr Speaker) cannot tell who is the culprit. It was a rowdier moment from a rowdy session of Environment Questions, yesterday. We started gently, with raw sewage, mercury poisoning and the Rhine. MPs remained troubled by the thought of sewage emissions into the sea.

Do fish excrete? If they do, then fishes must be one of the principal culprits so far as the emission of raw sewage into the sea is concerned. Perhaps there will be an EC directive on this?

Phillip Oppenheim hotted up the atmosphere by proposing the abolition of county councils. One has little doubt that this is in the Environment Secretary's mind, too, as (a dangerously honest man) Mr Ridley could think of no better reply to Oppenheim than to remark that – the Tories having just won control of the Association of County Councils – abolishing them might be thought 'odd'. 'We must give them a period to adjust to the new situation,' he added, as the walrus might, to the oysters.

It was really the lucid Robin Squire (C, Hornchurch) who calmed us down, with a question about carbon dioxide and the greenhouse effect. Ridley suggested that measures to reduce more urgent forms of pollution were actually increasing CO_2, which had become 'the Cinderella' of green politics.

Ridley certainly provided a passable imitation of an ugly sister, but is perhaps too genuinely frightening for ideal pantomime. Labour's junior Environment spokesman, Allan Roberts, fairy godmother to the orphan gas, leapt to the dispatch box with his own party's proposals.

It is a pity that John Gummer cited the local authority from Barking in his answer about rent arrears. It set them off again.

'Woof!', 'Grr!', 'Yip!'.

Oh dear, sighed Mr Speaker, 'these animal noises are *very* unseemly. It takes up a *lot* of time.'

On the contrary, Mr Speaker: it *saves* a lot of time. 'Woof', 'grr' and 'yip' are what these men and women really *mean*. Their 'arguments' are merely padding. Don't ban animal noises. Ban human speech instead. MPs would get their meaning over immediately, little that is valuable would be lost and we could all get an early night.

29.6.89

Sleeping beauty

HUGH DYKES (C, Harrow E) looks cute when he is asleep. I can say this with complete confidence, for, though I have never seen Mr Dykes asleep, I watched him for quarter of an hour during Foreign Office Questions yesterday, as he rested his eyes. His head lay gently back on the green bench, his eyes were shut, and his mouth dropped slightly ajar. An expression of Zen-like tranquillity was upon him, as the House discussed the horrors of Tiananmen Square. It was comforting to know that, should *Mrs* Dykes ever wake momentarily in the night, she will have a vision of such loveliness to contemplate.

Concentrating as he was, Mr Dykes will have heard the Democrats' David Alton (Mossley Hill) explain that citizens of the Portuguese colony of Macao (also being handed back to China) are to be entitled to live and work anywhere in the European Community – including here. How, wondered Alton, would that go down with the Hong Kong community? The Minister of State, Lynda Chalker, replied that she would be speaking to her Portuguese opposite number about this.

Fine. But what will she *say*? 'Kindly take your citizens' passports away again, Senhor: you're showing us up'?

Harry Greenway (C, Ealing N) revealed that as a teacher he had 'had the honour to teach Hungarian children who had come here driven by

45

the need to escape the tanks of their murderous regime'. Poor kids! By the skin of your teeth you escape the tanks of a murderous regime – and then you find yourselves stuck in Mr Greenway's class. Imagine all those lectures on the evils of the Brent Borough Council, the necessity of wearing a hard hat when riding a horse, and streetlighting on the North Circular ... it's a wonder many of them didn't opt for the tanks.

We all moved on to cocaine, with Mrs Maureen Hicks (C, Wolverhampton NE), who thought our EC partners should do more to combat drug-smuggling.

So did Bob Cryer (Lab, Bradford S). He felt that, as Britain seizes more drugs at her borders than do other European countries, that means we are cleverer than the rest of detecting smugglers. Well – yes, it *could* mean that, Bob; on the other hand ...

And we moved on again. Soon, Foreign Office Questions were over, and the House prepared itself for a statement from the Health Secretary, Kenneth Clarke, about Care in the Community. This is the programme for releasing bewildered, confused or inadequate people from old-fashioned institutions, back into 'the community', so they can gently readjust.

I looked down at the Chamber. Mr Dykes had opened his eyes again, now. A couple of elderly gentlemen were hobbling to and fro, and a rather batty-looking middle-aged lady was bouncing up and down on the bench as though something had excited her. Ron Brown (Lab, Leith) was opening and closing his mouth.

A question was troubling me. Was *this* the 'community'? Or was it the institution? And if it was the community, who was caring for them? Was it that nice man in black tights and a wig they called 'Mr Speaker'? And if it was the institution, how would they ever adjust to the world outside?

13.7.89

Honest soliciting

YESTERDAY AFTERNOON Mr Speaker was urged to deprecate an advertisement in *The House Magazine* (the parliamentary periodical) in which Mr Richard Alexander (C, Newark) offered himself for hire as a consultant.

The matter was raised by Dale Campbell-Savours (Lab, Workington), who said the advertisement stated that a hard-working backbench Tory MP, of ten years' standing, sought a consultancy to widen his range of activities. People were invited to contact Mr Alexander by telephone at the Commons.

Well, why not? It happens in other fields. I have always admired those men and women brave enough to place classified advertisements in the 'lonely hearts' columns of doubtful magazines. They are only doing openly what the rest of us have had to do in a more roundabout way. How many have joined badminton clubs when shuttlecocks were the last thing on their minds?

And yet we rule it 'undignified' to solicit more honestly. Imagine if builders had to find some light excuse for meeting potential bricklayers and buy them at least two dinners before anything as vulgar as a construction site was mentioned.

Yet that is precisely how most MPs look for outside consultancies. The etiquette mirrors that of flirtation and courtship. Your sketchwriter has first-hand experience to report.

Having lowered my immediate ambitions from being Prime Minister to parliamentary private secretary to a Parliamentary Under-Secretary in the Ministry of Transport and having, finally, given up that hope too, I started to wonder whether it might not be beneath me, after all, to be an adviser to some great industry.

Happily, there was a parliamentary Cupid to hand, Mrs Lynda Chalker, the then Minister of State for Transport. For, unknown to me, a very great industry indeed was looking for somebody like me. The Retread Manufacturers' Association had approached Mrs Chalker to ask if she knew of anyone who might ... well, *you* know ...

They could, of course, have placed a discreet ad in the right sort of magazine – something specializing in rubber.

But that would have raised too many eyebrows. Instead, they sounded out the Minister.

Kind Mrs Chalker knew just what to do. It would have been quite improper for her to have introduced us personally, so she simply gave the association a list of backbenchers interested in transport, and they looked up the photographs in the *Times Guide to the House of Commons*.

A discreet little lunch at a carvery somewhere near Wolverhampton, and we got on like a house on fire, the RMA and I. We both agreed that it would be best if money didn't come into our friendship. I didn't even ask for a set of discounted remoulds – and they, for that matter, didn't offer. Other Tory backbenchers found this hard to understand – but it wasn't that kind of relationship. I was just lonely, and they were – well, desperate: they must have been.

So let Mother Grundies like Dale Campbell-Savours tut-tut. Unlike Campbell-Savours, Alexander takes an unalarmed view of the world. He does not see conspiracies in every corner, spiders in every cup. He could be forgiven for being – frankly – bored: finding plenty to do (for he is a hard-working constituency MP), but little intellectual stimulation in a backbencher's life.

He's just honest enough to say so, that's all.

19.7.89

Bumping into Scotland

YESTERDAY, DURING Scottish Questions, and for the first time in my life, I blacked out.

It was during a Question from the Conservative MP for Dumfries, Sir Hector Monro, about 'beef and sheep sectors with special reference to the hills and uplands', and the EEC, and 'hill livestock compensatory allowances'. Never an orator of the inflammatory kind, Sir Hector was running through a few of the grievances of upland cowmen, sharing their worries with us – when it happened.

There is a balustrade around our gallery, which keeps sketchwriters from tumbling down into the arms of Mrs Maria Fyfe (Lab, Glasgow Maryhill). I was leaning under this for a full view of the Opposition benches beneath me.

I withdrew my head sharply, anxious to catch every nuance of the Minister's reply about the Ewe Suckler Premium. Too sharply. It struck the upper bar of the balustrade, very hard.

Chips of light danced before my eyes. The face of Scottish Secretary Malcolm Rifkind blurred and his voice was strangely distant. The whole Chamber began to spin.

My whole concern was not to draw attention to myself. Struggling to retain consciousness, I leaned back against the bench – as generations of MPs have learned to do – so that this would not be apparent.

'... Negotiations in Brussels ...' were the last words I heard. Then everything went black.

Who knows for how long? Consciousness returned with strange white shapes swimming before my eyes. They looked like great net baskets, illuminated from within by some blinding radiance. They were. They were the new lighting arrangements for the experimental TV cameras.

The walls of this place in which I awoke were of carved oak, grotesquely baroque with clusters of sculpted acorns, twigs and branches protruding from fluted panelling; and on these walls were mounted six black machines with tubes pointing outwards and oscillating slowly to left and right, looking like deathrays. They were. These were the new TV cameras.

Sweat covered my brow, and it seemed unbearably hot. It was. They still haven't fixed the cooling system to cope with the lights. And, below me, a man in black silk, flanked by two subsidiary figures, all with weird grey Afro wigs, held court.

'Mr John McAllion,' cried the principal wigged one. Was I hallucinating?

'While we're discussing endangered species in Scotland,' proclaimed this Mr McAllion, 'can I ask about tigers?' Yes, clearly I was hallucinating. Is this what acid-house parties are like?

'The Tayside Tigers!' McAllion continued. I shut my eyes again.

Too weak to leave, I remained, it seemed, for at least an hour more. From time to time new images, most stranger than the last but none stranger than Tam Dalyell, formed and melted. Questions on 'Pittenween Harbour', 'Wang Laboratories' and 'peat-burning in the Western Isles' welled up amidst shouts of anger and then subsided. 'Smokeless zones ... major intrusion into the lives of country folk ...'

'... Sul-phah di-oxide *particulants*,' moaned a wraith-like figure they called 'Lord James Douglas Hamilton'.

Only today's *Hansard* will settle the issue for a bewildered sketchwriter with a large bump on the back of his head. Was I delirious? Or were they?

19.10.89

Museum pieces come to life

'Questions to the minister for the Arts will begin not later than 3.10 pm.'

Mr Richard Luce, Arts minister and also minister for the Civil Service, was ready, at 3.10 pm yesterday.

There is a convention in public life that those with a vested interest do not conceal the fact. If, for example, you were an African elephant, your opinions on zoo funding would need to be declared.

And if you were Dr John Marek (Lab, Wrexham) or Mr Frank Haynes (Lab, Ashfield) you would not demand free public admission to national museums without mentioning your eligibility for a glass display case of your own.

Dr Marek started it, yesterday, with a question to Richard Luce. What was the minister's policy, he asked 'on compulsory admission charges to national museums'?

Mr Luce didn't seem to have one. It was 'up to the trustees', he said.

Dr Marek was furious. If you can imagine how a very angry Dalek would speak, then you have his measure. The PM was recently said to be 'fizzing' with rage. It is hard for Dr Marek to fizz as he has a lisp, but he made the sort of sound you get when steam escapes from the craters of very thick boiling porridge.

Museum admissions were dropping wherever charges had been introduced, he said. They had dropped by 85 per cent at the Welsh National Museum.

Dr Marek's indignation has a curiously soothing quality and I began to daydream. I saw him, now, in my mind's eye, behind a glass case in Cardiff, and glanced at the catalogue entry ...

'MAREK, DR JOHN, BSC (Hons) PhD MP. Born circa 1940. Lecturer in Applied Mathematics at Aberystwyth 1966–83. Labour spokesman on sundry matters. Publications: various research papers.

A very nicely preserved example of a species already in decline when this specimen was still in early prime. Of high intelligence and leftish views, the habitat was almost entirely academia and the species never really adapted to the more vulgar 'hunting pack' environment of the 1990s. Very distinctive cry: spluttering, interminable. No real instinct for the jugular, but sometimes known to bore its prey into submission. Now very rare ...'

I stirred in my daydream. Through the slumber came a great roar from the Labour benches below me. It would soon be sunset, and a

Haynes was coming down to the waterhole to drink. The other animals giggled. 'Let's have some action!' snarled the beast, 'I want to know from the minister …'; 'We don't *want* charges! I have the full backing of the Nottinghamshire County Council!' It was little short of deafening.

I pictured the exhibit's inscription at the Natural History Museum (admissions down '40 per cent', Marek had told us) …

'*HAYNES, MR FRANK, MP. Born circa 1926. Fireman on the Southern Railway, then coal-miner.*

Classic example of a species already almost extinct. Working-class soap-box orator: origins genuine, ideology confused, cry – amongst the loudest in the E. Midlands. This aggressive but loyal beast proved hopelessly ill-equipped for the hunting methods of the Filofactyls which had infiltrated its herd. A tragic loss to archaeology.'

23.1.90

The outsider

I was miles away yesterday, pondering the strange case of the MP who began to see the other man's point of view.

His name is Michael Latham; he is the Tory MP for Rutland & Melton; and he has just made one of the most remarkable statements ever heard from an MP of sound mind and healthy majority.

Quietly, Mr Latham has announced that he will not be standing at the next election. He will join the tiny band of MPs who quit voluntarily, young, untouched by scandal, and without a knighthood.

Why is he going? Let us have it in his own words.

'To fight the party battle,' he says, you must be partisan. 'It makes them tick.'

And him? This is the remarkable bit.

'Frankly,' he says, 'I have found myself thinking there is a lot to be said for other points of view.

'A certain amount of the zest one needs for this job has gone. One cannot really do the job properly without that zest and that political fire.

'I have to say that, frankly, I do not regard myself as a very good politician …'

Mr Latham is suffering from a new illness which experts are only now beginning to recognize and diagnose: ideological M.E. It is probably terminal.

On yesterday's showing at Prime Minister's Questions that is unlikely. The subject was a recent report by H.M. Schools Inspectorate.

'Hm,' replies the PM, reflectively, 'well, yes and no. As you say, Neil, we haven't ironed out all the problems. But – as you'd be first to admit – the inspectors found much to praise.'

'Sure, Maggie, but – as I know you'd want to acknowledge – they had some harsh things to say, too. Not all your fault, I realize: frankly, education began to go off the rails during the last Labour Government ...'

'Oh come, Neil. Some of it *is* our fault. I think everyone accepts we've driven the teachers spare with all the so-called 'reforms' we've been throwing at them ...'

'Too modest, Prime Minister. These changes had to come. Without your courage and resolution ...'

'Oh, it's not been down to *me*, Neil. I've got a wonderful team working for me – and the Opposition has done a splendid job, too, keeping us all on our toes ...'

You may be surprised to hear that it did not go quite thus. What *actually* happened was this ...

Mr Kinnock called the report a 'damning indictment'.

Mrs Thatcher replied that most schools were satisfactory. So sucks.

The Labour leader went bananas. Why didn't she 'tell the whole truth'?

The Prime Minister retorted that it was a 'good report'. So knickers.

And so on. Later, someone hurled a notebook down from the public gallery, aimed (it seemed) at the Chief Whip.

While I write, the air above Westminster is thick with insults as Michael Latham MP picks up his little knapsack and trudges sadly off towards the Rutland sunset.

He had become (he sighed last week) 'far too bland'.

7.2.90

A loyalty oaf

THE GOVERNMENT Front Bench at Prime Minister's Questions was a visual feast.

The PM wore a white shirt and black suit with a huge white 'Quaker' collar. She looked like the picture on a packet of oats. Beside her sat an Education minister, Angela Rumbold, wearing a cream blouse, red skirt and navy blue blazer with a silver emblem. She resembled a senior Hoverspeed air hostess.

Next to them sat two plump gentlemen with oiled grey hair, steel-grey glasses and round faces. Both wore blue ties with polka dots. One (Mr Tweedle Dum MP?) was minister for Higher Education, Robert Jackson. The Rt Hon Tweedle Dee was Kenneth Baker. Both smiled and nodded, terrestrial synchronized swimmers, while Lord Whitelaw beamed down from the Peers' Gallery like those fearsome dolls heathens use as good-luck charms.

Mrs Thatcher listed her engagements for the day, culminating in 'an audience with Her Majesty the Queen'.

'Ooh!' howled the groundlings.

Hugh Dykes (C, Harrow E) wanted us to join the ERM. His Question was so short — 'Is Britain's temporarily higher rate of inflation the last remaining obstacle?' — that Mrs Thatcher needed a gulp while she thought up another — 'free flow of capital'.

Neil Kinnock was dispatched with a swipe of the Thatcher paw.

'. . . No serious interest in joining the ERM,' he proposed.

She disposed. '. . . I was not able to join the mechanism during my first decade, but I hope to during my second.'

The Labour leader tried again, with some drollery about Mr Lawson. 'Last night,' he told her, 'you were savaged by a live scapegoat.' Anything less like a goat than Mr Lawson is hard to imagine. The Bible does not mention scape-bulls, scape-bears or scape-buffaloes.

Easier still was a question from John Gorst (C, Hendon N). In my notebook I simply wrote, 'Blah blah, great tasks ahead, blah etc.'

A hostile question — from the Liberals' Mrs Ray Michie (Argyll & Bute), about the fishing industry — helped the PM further. She knew *all* about fishing, and revealed details of recent catches.

Dale Campbell-Savours (Lab, Workington) cast his net on the other side but got tangled in the mesh. He meant (I think) to suggest that Michael Heseltine has been forced to swear an oath of loyalty, but found himself suggesting that the man had been 'driven into a loyalty oaf'. Did he mean that Heseltine's car had been in collision with Mr Gorst's? Or had he said (as some of my colleagues think) 'oilty loaf'? This was the Campbell-Savours who brought you 'Mohammed Ali' as owner of Harrods. Mrs T did not get the whole of his question, but – on the basis, perhaps, that half an oaf is better than no bread – she did her best. The Chief Whip, she said, would deal with Heseltine.

It was a good afternoon for the Tories. Cecil Parkinson dragged out a transport statement telling us that while John Prescott (Labour's spokesman) 'sits playing with his merchant ships in his bath, we get on with the business of modernizing London transport'.

Prescott, enraged, muttered something about what Mr Parkinson plays with in *his* bath.

28.3.90

The cardigan man rebels

'BECAUSE HALF a dozen grasshoppers under a fern,' wrote Burke, 'make the field ring with their importunate clink, whilst thousands of great cattle reposing beneath the shade of the British oak chew the cud and are silent, pray do not imagine that those who make the noise are the only inhabitants of the field.'

But what if the cattle should elect, from among the grasshoppers, a large and noisy one to sing on their behalf: to clink in the bovine interest? They could do no better than choose Mr Beaumont-Dark.

Anthony Beaumont-Dark, MP, could be described as the unthinking man's thinking man. Tall, bespectacled and gruffly opinionated, he carries about him the aura of the golf club lounge. His Tory constituency of Selly Oak is to Birmingham what Bromley is to London – leafy, prosperous, unfashionable, a harbour not so much for the painted sails of the intelligentsia as for the motor-cruisers of self-made men.

These are men who half think they know already what they think, but need a Beaumont-Dark to put it in a way which reassures them that they knew that all along (but couldn't put it nearly so well); men who don't know a lot about art, but know what they like; men (we might add) who don't know a lot about local government, but are pretty damn sure Maggie's got this poll tax thing wrong.

If speeches could wear slippers and cardigans, sip whisky and tap a pipe on an ashtray to emphasize bull-points, then that is what a speech by 'Tony' (as they call him in the saloons of Selly Oak) would do. Tony knows his mind. Tony says what he thinks.

Yesterday Mr Beaumont-Dark 'lashed out' (as the *Birmingham Evening Post* might have it) at the community charge. Worse, he lashed out in the presence of the Prime Minister. It was, in its way, a significant moment.

At first he was greeted with titters. Spectacles adjusted and his 'this is going to hurt me more than it hurts you' expression firmly fixed, the great man boomed out his preliminary courtesies to Mrs Thatcher on behalf of 'her many friends and admirers in this House'. Titters ceased.

'The poll tax' (how those words bring hush!) was 'friendless'. He paused for the scale of his rebellion to become apparent, then continued: 'Those who gain most do not recognize it as fair because it is not based on people's ability to pay.' Labour cheered as their unlikely ally sat down.

Sir John Stokes (Conservative, Stourbridge & Halesowen) – or, as we like to call him, 'Sir John Quixote (Empire Loyalist, La Mancha & the Black Country)' – rode to the rescue.

The man with trouser tops under his armpits renewed his famous concern over the omission of what he has called 'England's heroes' from the core curriculum.

'Is she aware that there is considerable concern about the teaching of English history in our schools today? Teaching is all about vague *themes*. Why can we not go back to the good old days when we had to learn dates by heart, and learn the names of kings and queens of England, and of statesmen, and battles, and the glorious deeds of our past?'

Hm. What Sir John might call a 'vague theme' from my own history lessons was that peasants' revolts could usually be contained: the danger sign was when they began to spread to the *bourgeoisie* – a fancy word, not the sort that Tony would use in Selly Oak.

30.3.90

Summerson finds the way

'MR SPEAKER, there are too many '*mays*' and not enough '*shalls*' ...'

Young Hugo Summerson (C, Walthamstow) is a faintly Edwardian character. Tall, dark and mustachioed, he carries his double-breasted suits with aplomb. One instinctively places him, *circa* 1903, travelling in from the northern suburbs, and (under his breath) running through Rudyard Kipling's poem 'If' with quiet approval.

Mr Summerson was chosen last year by Mills & Boon, the publishers of popular paperback romantic novels, as 'Britain's most romantic MP'. It is a curious reflection upon the British idea of romance.

Hugo has a number of pet subjects. One – upon which he tried to introduce legislation last year – was the 'nuisance of faulty burglar alarms'. He spoke (no doubt) for many. Yesterday, he spoke for many more as he introduced a new bill, his own, to oblige the owners of businesses to display the street number of their premises.

Summerson had a point. 'There must be many people in this country, Mr Speaker,' he observed, 'who on a particular day set out to find premises which they have not visited before.' Here, Mr Summerson spoke regretfully, mindful perhaps of the pain with which any gentleman would approach so distasteful a necessity.

And now he painted a bleak picture. You reach a street, he said, and 'you don't know which end to start.'

It got worse. You find a numbered address, but not the number you seek. The premises to each side of it are unnumbered. Which way is up, and which down? And are the numbers arranged, odd on one side, and even on the other? You take a guess, and walk until you see another number. Alas! You have overshot. But by how much?

And if the pedestrian's plight is pitiable, he continued, consider the motorist. 'There are people in their cars who have driven into other people in their cars because they are looking out for street numbers and unable to see them.'

As we pictured the carnage on the streets of Walthamstow, outrage mounted and the justice of forcing everyone to number his house or shop seemed irresistible.

Mr Summerson resisted it. 'My Bill does not attempt to cover houses and it does not attempt to cover buildings in the country. So, for example, 'Rose Cottage, Great Snoring-in-the-Marsh' would escape.

A silent cheer rose from countless blissful young newlyweds, loath to disfigure the rose-entwined porticos of their thatched love-nests with anything as vulgar as Arabic numerals. Cheers of a noisier kind greeted Mr Summerson's advance (bowing, as ceremony dictates) towards the Mace, carrying his Bill. He presented it to Mr Speaker, head high, moustache a-quiver.

'Aye, you've got your place in the history books, lad,' growled Dennis Skinner, a lone, irreverent voice. The rest of us — approving — were updating Kipling, in Mr Summerson's honour.

If you can keep your Bill when all about you
Are running out of parliamentary time;
Defend suburbia, when whiz-kids doubt you
And sneer at you, and shout 'Resign!'
If you can fill each parliamentary minute,
While Mills and Boon have covered you with glory,
Your prize is Walthamstow, and all that's in it.
And — which is more, Hugo — you'll be a Tory.

10.5.90

Touring historic sites

LEADING POLITICIANS will assist in the launch of a balloon tomorrow. The balloon is to encourage use of organ donor cards. What the politicians are for, you may like to guess: it is a hot-air balloon . . .

'. . . And the prospects for tourism in the West Midlands are exciting. Would my hon friend (Patrick Nichols) accompany me on a trip around the Black Country, where I can show him some of these attractions?'

Maureen Hicks (C, Wolverhampton NE) must be a desperate woman. MPs who have seen *Blind Date* on television will know that contestants choose their 'date' from volunteers invisible to them, behind a screen. The couple then open an unmarked envelope on which is written the nature of the trip they are to take in each other's company.

So female contestants face two nasty shocks: the man, and the holiday. But even malicious viewers would not inflict Patrick Nichols *and* a day-trip to the Black Country on one girl. And Maureen Hicks was asking for this.

Mr Nichols, who is a junior Employment minister, looked perplexed. He is the sort of boy that mothers encourage daughters to get to know: clean-looking and slightly churchy, with glasses. But Nichols is not unchivalrous, and (after a moment's panicky hesitation) conceded that it would be 'churlish' to refuse.

Where will Maureen and Patrick go? Surely the West Midlands' finest monuments are its MPs ...

The tour starts at possibly the last working model of late 70s' monetarism powered by Trollopean Toryism and cooled by Whiggish doubt. This bizarre contraption, sited at Wolverhampton SW, is called 'Nicholas Budgen'.

But the West Midlands is a land of contrast, and Coventry SE provides it. 'Dave Nellist' – a remarkable structure inspired by Stalinist brutalism yet of comparatively recent construction – attracts pilgrimages of militant supporters. In recent years it has drawn visitors away from what was once a rival attraction in Perry Barr, 'Jeff Rooker', now sadly mellowed by time and fortune. Pausing at Edgbaston, where a substantial and well-preserved Dame – 'Jill Knight' – welcomes viewers, we are now close to Selly Oak, or 'Beaumont-Dark country'. Here, journalists from all over the world travel – in hopes (seldom disappointed) of spotting the great man opining on one of his many chosen areas of expertise.

From the moral high ground here (for where else would Mr Beaumont-Dark be?) it is just possible on a clear day to see Sir John Stokes (C, Halesowen & Stourbridge). Voyages around Sir John need a whole weekend, for there is so much to marvel at: the monarchism, the braces ...

It is Sir John who breaks the spell and brings us back to Westminster. Yesterday he was *complaining* about tourism. 'Stratford-on-Avon,' he said, 'is bursting,' adding: 'My hon friend and I have crossed swords on this in the past.' Trust Sir John to cross swords. He has not reached muskets yet, let alone pistols.

Andy Stewart (C, Sherwood) wanted a 'British National Forest' at Sherwood. It was soon afterwards that Mrs Thatcher swept in, dressed all in Lincoln green. I do not recall that Maid Marian wore pearls.

23.5.90

That's enough bees – Ed

MOST MEMBERS of Parliament have one, or at the most two, things to say. A life is spent nurturing a bee (or two) in the bonnet. The bee is fed and watered, taken out for exercise, and on special occasions adorned with a ribbon and bow and asked to perform tricks. But it is the same bee.

In this, our MPs are no different from other people. Unlike others, however, they are paid for it. The rest of Britain is confined to writing letters to the editors of provincial newspapers. And what is Parliament if not a neo-Gothic, all-singing, all-dancing Letters Page, animated into televised pomp and bewigged circumstance?

Mr Dale Campbell-Savours, for instance (Lab, Workington) believes in an Establishment Plot. His life is dedicated to telling us about the subplots, and if upon his headstone appears the summary 'I SMELL A RAT,' that will not be far wrong.

Mr John Carlisle (C, Luton N) supports South Africa, and takes every opportunity to explain. So when, this week, he rose to question the PM on her diary, it was no surprise to learn that the engagement which interested him was her meeting with Mr de Klerk.

And this is democracy at work. Parliament succours 650 varieties of sleeve-tugger: tug – tugging at the national sleeve on behalf of their constituents – dotty and sane.

An MP's task, then, is to get a word in edgeways; and contrive to relate his own obsession to the subject discussed. One way is to lead a Debate on the Adjournment.

Thus it was that, yesterday morning, as others packed their buckets and spades for a week's recess, a little band of MPs waited eagerly in their place, a little knot of sulky ministers delayed their holidays, and a whole hive of bees buzzed importantly round the Chamber. A stack of Letters to the Editor were awaiting consideration.

Mr John Fraser (Lab, Norwood) chose the finances of housing cor-porations as his subject: but it could just as well have been the *plumbing* of housing corporations or the finances of the Coca-Cola Bottling Company. Baffled by anything? Mr Fraser will sort it out. He waited on the bench, a large man with large pink ears, a dark blue suit and tiny fawn shoes. He looked like a giant but friendly mouse.

Junior minister Chris Chope declined to endorse Fraser's reasoning. The Editor, that is, points out that opinions expressed are not necessarily those of his newspaper.

Behind Fraser queued four North-western Tories. They wanted to talk about the North-west. Michael Jack (Fylde) – speaking fluently to camera – told us about travelator links and checked-through baggage from Manchester. The minister, Roger Freeman, listened with the non-committal courtesy of a BR customer-relations officer.

The Editor, that is, will bear your comments carefully in mind.

Very last in the queue was Mr Toby Jessel (C, Twickenham). This bonnet houses two bees: the desirability of cultural heritage, and the undesirability of aircraft noise. Yesterday he attacked plans for a 'heli-port' near St Paul's Cathedral and Cannon Street Station. This, he told us, would spoil the view and make a noise. The minister, Colin Moynihan, promised to study this with care but sadly could not preempt his Inspector's report.

The Editor, in other words, is most grateful for your letter but regrets that this correspondence is now closed. He wishes you a pleasant recess.

25.5.90

Nazi war debate gets personal

'WE ARE not concerned, my Lords, with revenge.' Thus spoke the tanned and handsomely moustached Earl Ferrers. Later he was answered by Lord Shawcross with a sharpness uncharacteristic of the Lords: 'Retribution does not cease to be retribution by placing on it a label called "Justice".'

But for the moment the Earl had the floor. With lofty courtesy, this Edwardian walrus of a peer invited the ermined oysters to walk a little further with him, and support the War Crimes Bill.

He didn't sound *wholly* convinced. 'Many of your Lordships feel very strongly about this, in all sorts of different ways,' he remarked, ruefully. These were issues 'which none would have chosen to address'. But 'given the strength of feeling in Another Place' ...

Lord Campbell of Alloway rose to oppose him. In the flesh, the actual bearers of these romantic titles can be a disappointment. Expecting a kilted figure from a Sir Walter Scott novel to swagger out of a wild Scotch mist, we were confronted by what resembled an elderly Harley Street dentist; while the fearsomely named Lord Irving of Lairg, who followed, showed no flash of steel or tartan, but looked like the sports master at a minor public school.

Lord Campbell was worried about 'state show trails'. Lord Irving thought the problems would be of identification. But he did not think it right to provoke a constitutional confrontation on this.

Words like 'confrontation' caused a perceptible *frisson* of excitement. It had the elements of a pensioners' protest demo; or, perhaps, a delegation of Saga Holiday-makers, come to complain about the hotel plumbing. The unspoken thought was that peers, the soul of constitutional restraint, could nevertheless only take so much. 'The Other Place have had their bite at the cherry,' said a testy Lord (Jim) Callaghan. 'Now it's our turn.'

Later, Lord Goodman regretted that if the Upper Chamber were abolished, all the restaurants would go, too – a pity, as this was 'a very pleasant place to come to' despite having trouble with his leg. But blackmail must be resisted. 'Are we men or mice?'

Lord Mayhew spoke of the bulldozing of skeletons. Were they his family, he said, he would not now want revenge. I wondered how he knew.

Remarks like these provoked Lord Beloff to a brave, but ill-judged speech. Some of this debate, he said, reminded him of a common reaction during the war: 'Oh, the Jews are always complaining.' An awkwardness, rare in the Lords, arose, for Lord Beloff was upset. Peers do not care for this kind of thing.

Of early speakers, Lord Shawcross was effective for having been a chief prosecutor at Nuremberg – who 'wanted to prosecute more', he said. But 'crimes had been committed on both sides'.

This, he said, was something that younger people, like MPs, could not understand. At the outbreak of war the average age of MPs supporting this Bill, he said, was five. Nor could MPs understand the feelings aroused, later, by Jewish atrocities against Britain in Palestine. 'For example,' he said, 'the Stern Gang, or the bombing of ... what was it called?'

'The King David Hotel!' chorused what sounded like fifty peers. They all remembered it as if it were yesterday. It was a revealing moment.

5.6.90

Hallowed be thy name-calling

'WOOLLENS, WORSTEDS, flax and soft furnishings.' Eric Forth, junior minister in the industry department, looked an unlikely lift attendant. His interrogator, Frank Haynes, 'the snarling grandpa' (Lab, Ashfield), an equally unlikely Selfridge's shopper. Mr Forth straightened his tie. Forth was telling Haynes the (selected) good news about textile exports.

It was a positive moment in a rancorous afternoon. The rancour started as the echo of prayer died away in the Chamber.

Newspapermen are excluded from the religious ceremony. It is only after 'Prayers for the Parliament' in which Mr Speaker's chaplain leads the MPs at 2.30 every afternoon, that we journalists are allowed in. Crowding at the oak doors, pressing our ears to hear the murmured devotions, we might just pick out the words:

'Almighty God, the Fountain of all Goodness ... by whom alone Kings reign and Princes decree justice ... we, thine unworthy servants ... do most humbly beseech thee to send down thy Heavenly Wisdom from above, to direct and guide us in all our consultations; and grant ...' Or so I recall.

'Questions to the secretary of state,' the Speaker cried. All fell at each others' throats.

'... that laying aside all private interests, prejudices, and partial affections ...'

'There are a number of unpleasant features about the hon gentleman.' Junior minister Douglas Hogg was referring to Labour's industry spokesman, Gordon Brown. 'Discreditable,' said Hogg.

'... the result of all our counsels may be to the glory of thy blessed Name, the maintenance of true Religion and Justice, and tranquillity of the Realm ...'

'This arrogant little shit has not answered one question!' shouted Labour's George Foulkes (Carrick, Cumnock & Doon Valley). He was talking about Mr Hogg. Screams of protest rose from the Conservative benches.

'He will withdraw that word immediately. And do not repeat it,' said Mr Speaker, his colour rising ...

'... the uniting and knitting together of the hearts of all persons and estates ...'

'Which word?' Foulkes shouted back: 'Arrogant, little, or shit?'

'The last word,' snapped the Speaker.

'... in true Christian Love and Charity, one towards another ...'

Now it was Hogg's turn: 'This whingeing and whining from the Opposition benches is amusing and pathetic ...'

'*Further us with thy continual help, that in all our works begun, continued, and ended in thee, we may glorify thy Holy Name ...*'

'Humbug!' roared Nicholas Ridley, the Industry Secretary. 'Humbug!'

'*... and finally by thy mercy obtain everlasting Life through Jesus Christ our Lord ...*'

The Chair has the last word, here, too. Amid the hurling of abuse, Mr Speaker rose, shaking his bewigged head wearily. 'Some rough things are said in this Chamber,' he sighed. 'That's what it's all about.'

'*... Amen.*'

21.6.90

3

Junior Ministers – and their Little Shadows

Bedtime with the Bottomleys

THERE IS about Mrs Virginia Bottomley, MP, something of the blue-stocking, something of the glamorous air-hostess, and something of the hockey team.

Were she Sister on night-duty, unusual would be the patient who did not require his fevered brow to be gently mopped. Even a reprimand, from her, would be sweet. If she were Assistant English Mistress, could there be a single spotty youth in the Lower Sixth in whom she did not kindle a longing to know more of Milton?

Mrs Bottomley's evident ability only adds spice. Like those soft-core movies whose plots unfold in a dimly-lit corner of a public library (non-fiction section), one sees the camera panning from the lady librarian's desktop, up to her crisp white Quaker-collar and sensible glasses – and then slowly down, to reveal, beneath the desk, fishnet stockings, stiletto heels and a split skirt.

Not – I hasten to add – that Mrs Bottomley, Under Secretary in the Department of the Environment (with special responsibility for the National Parks) is anything but a model of modest propriety. Besides, she is married to the Under Secretary of State in the Department of Transport, *Mr* Bottomley.

And how remarkable a partnership! For Mr Peter Bottomley, MP, is just the kind of man who would have organized a protest outside the cinema where our movie was playing, parading a placard: 'This Film Insults Women'. Tall, pale and thin, with Trotsky-spectacles and a crusading ambition to extinguish sin, he regards every drink-driver dragged weeping from the court as a personal victory.

Readers versed in French history will recognize a Robespierre in Mr Bottomley. Younger readers will recognize a Richard Dreyfuss.

Both partners in this unlikely match featured in Environment questions yesterday. *Mrs* Bottomley was at the dispatch box answering a question on rats.

Harry Greenway (C, Ealing N) was worried about 'dog mess and the extermination of rats and other rodents', especially in Ealing; and this led Davyhulme's Winston Churchill to complain too: about litter on motorways.

Mrs Bottomley's eyes shone with a tender inward flame. Ah! This was a matter for Someone Else. Someone very wonderful. 'I shall have to pass that on to my ...' – and she paused, lovingly – '... my *close*, and honourable friend,' she murmured. The House chuckled, indulgently.

Readers, let us – so far as is possible without immodesty – picture the Bottomleys' marital bed, in a peaceful home at the end of a crunchy gravel drive in a leafy part of Surrey. The children are asleep.

Peter and Virginia, too, have retired, after an evening at work on their ministerial red boxes; she sipping orange juice; he, an alcohol-free riesling. The silence, now, is broken only by the hoot of an owl and the night breeze whispering in the laburnum tree.

But someone is awake.

'Darling?'

'Yes, darling?'

'Litter on the M18, darling ...'

'What about it, darling?'

'It's piling up, darling. All over the central reservation. Mr Churchill's worried about it ...'

'Set your mind at rest, Virginia. I'll get them: every motorist who drops a crisp-packet: every last one of them: I'll destroy them: I'll have them dragged in open ox-carts down the hard shoulder and spat at by the travelling public. Just you see.'

'Oh Peter! Thank Heaven.'

'As you well know, Virginia, I do not believe in the after-life.'

'Sorry, darling.' And quiet returns to the scene. But not for long.

'Virginia, darling?'

'Yes, darling?'

'There's something I ought to tell you, Virginia. It's been bothering me.'

'What is it, Peter?'

'I want ... well ... it's hard to say, darling.'

'Try, darling.'

'I want to drive a six-lane motorway across one of your National Parks.'

'Oh *Peter* ...' (long pause) 'Which one?'

Hush, readers: let us steal away before they hear.

23.2.89

The interrogation of St Edwina

EAT YOUR heart out, Lady Di. There was a crowd outside the gates of Parliament yesterday — just to see Edwina pass! Tickets for her performance before the Agriculture Select Committee? Like gold dust. *Evita* — sure — but *Edwina*? Not at any price.

So there was nothing for it but to queue. Meanwhile, MPs were already within, behind the oaken doors of the Grand Committee Room — 'conferring privately', we were told, before the public event.

Maybe so. No doubt it was only in one's imagination that the tall, dark and rugged MP for Gloucester West, Paul Marland, was applying just a touch of Grecian 2000 before the lights went up.

Perhaps it was just in idle fancy that one saw the Health Secretary, Kenneth Clarke, ensconced in his dressing-room, selecting the most double-breasted and gangsterish of his many Chicago-style suits for the occasion.

Well, how did she perform? Was she worth the wait?

The star billing was for an ex-Parliamentary Under-Secretary — the most junior kind of minister known to our constitution — in the Health Department.

The curtain-raisers were mere Secretaries of State. First came the Minister of Agriculture, John MacGregor. The chairman of the Select Committee, Jerry Wiggin, peered headmasterishly at him over half-moon glasses. Mr Wiggin's reputation is for being unnecessarily unpleasant. He added to that importantly yesterday, by being unnecessarily pleasant to MacGregor. Would he like to comment on Mrs Currie's latest statement that 'a significant number' of hens were affected by salmonella?

Mr MacGregor did not wish to comment on that, or on almost anything else of interest to the Committee, press and public. Nor did he. And he spent the better part of an hour doing it. A very skilful performance from a man who will go far, unnoticed.

Kenneth Clarke, the Health Secretary, squirmed more interestingly. He went a little beyond duty in supporting the person he endearingly called 'Edwina'.

And on it went. From time to time, some flurry at the back of the room caused all to crane their necks round — as with the expected entrance of the bride — in case it should be Edwina.

Eventually it was. And how do we sum up her performance? She summed it up for herself in her opening statement (which she insisted on being allowed to make, as a queen might, before being executed). She had had cards and letters from all over the world, she said. She was so grateful. She would be replying to all, in due course.

And that was it, really. It is true that a number of *questions* were put to her. ('Of course we are all in public life,' said Richard Alexander, hopefully.) But on the whole she could not remember the answers, or declined to reveal private conversations, or had nothing to add. Occasionally her voice would go rather faint. Someone brought her water, and she smiled graciously, wanly, at him.

Your sketchwriter suspects that she is suffering from genuine nervous exhaustion. But, if she is *not*, then this was a performance which places our young star firmly in the tradition of St Joan, Mary Queen of Scots and Imelda Marcos.

9.2.89

Ryder's big moment

IT IS every young actor's dream to be understudying Hamlet on the day that Gielgud is struck dumb by laryngitis. But does it have to be a dream?

Not for Gordon Brown. John Smith's heart attack put his deputy into the front line, where he has been jousting with no less than Nigel Lawson, to general approval. 'Better, even, than Smith,' some said.

Yesterday Mr Smith was back on the front bench, grinning amiably. He has recovered from his heart attack. Whether he will ever recover from Gordon Brown is another matter.

Tuesday saw the same chance befall a shy junior Agriculture minister. His boss, John MacGregor, had suffered a fainting fit in Brussels the previous afternoon. He was too unwell to return on the very day set down for the year's first main debate on agriculture, called by the Opposition.

Their respected spokesman, Dr David Clark, was to open. Who could reply?

Richard Ryder is not a household name. Self-effacing and quiet, he once ran Mrs Thatcher's office, where he was noted for state-of-the-art circumspection. Asked why he wore his watch face down, Mr Ryder is said to have replied that the time of day was not public information and he would give it on a 'need to know' basis. On Tuesday, after only a few months in his first ministerial job, he was to lead the defence against Labour's attack. How would he perform?

I do not know if Mr Ryder has a mother. If not, could it have been Mrs Thatcher herself who straightened his tie and checked his fingernails before he set off for Westminster that morning. 'Richard,' we can hear her say, 'this is your great day.' She smiles. 'You have always been a very polite and respectful boy. But today you must fight.' She picks fluff off his lapel. 'They will give you no quarter. Hesitate, mumble and you'll never be heard of again. So I want you to go in punching. Shout. Bang the table. Dispute anything they say. Never, *never* let them get you on to the defensive.' She pats his collar. 'Now, you won't let me down, will you?' He didn't. Mr Ryder was changed out of all recognition.

Large parts of his speech were quite obliterated by his fist hammering on the dispatch box. Poor Dr Clark had hardly begun before Ryder leapt up and berated him with Labour's previous disregard for the consumer. When Clark tried to continue, Ryder sprang up again, hurling quotations from newspapers at him.

His own speech was, well, upbeat. Heaven knows his ammunition was thin. 'Our food scientists are admired and respected the world over,' he cried. And more: the Food Acts 'have been *consolidated* by *this Conservative Government* in 1984!' ('Consolidated', here, just means 'gathered together and redrafted into a single Act, to save lawyers' time'. There is no recorded instance of consolidation curing anyone of salmonella poisoning.)

Mr Ryder's fists beat the air: 'And you ask what the Government has *done*? I'll *tell* the House what the Government has done!' One felt very certain that, over tea that night, Mrs Ryder, and Mrs Thatcher too, would be content.

25.1.89

Snapshot of a mood

WILLIAM WALDEGRAVE'S report on his meeting with Yasser Arafat was, in a modest way, a historic Commons occasion. It showed a parliament *working*: not just setting out the arguments – any newspaper can do that – but testing and giving voice to the mood of all those different groups who represent us.

Not that Britain is a major player. But if the Israeli prime minister, or the leaders of the Arab nations, wanted a sense of how Western opinion is moving, they could have done worse than watch from the gallery for an hour on Tuesday. It had a comic side: but it was more notable for a sense of atmosphere, subtle but clear, which it is not necessary to mock.

There is something old-fashioned about Mr Waldegrave's style. Not that he is stiff or stale, but that he seems to be thinking on his feet, explaining his own views in his own way. This is not a safe way to proceed and it can betray arrogance, yet it flatters the House; for members are weary of questioning ministers who are merely messengers bearing their masters' policies and their civil servants' speech notes.

With Mr Waldegrave you feel you are talking to the organ grinder. Often he stammers. Often he stops in mid-sentence and starts again. The impression is of a man responding to a real political event. It gives an edge to the occasion.

The House responds by thinking a bit, too, laying aside stock phrases. The most remarkable example of this, yesterday, was Gerald Kaufman, Labour's Foreign Affairs spokesman, who quit the pantomime in which he generally seems to be playing, and adopted a quiet eloquence instead. Mr Kaufman is Jewish; and the firm support he offered the Government, together with his clear plea to the Israelis to think again, was heard in a respectful – and interested – silence. 'It is time,' he concluded, 'to end the spilling of blood in the Holy Land.'

Jewish members on both sides contributed. People as different as Sir Geoffrey Finsberg and Harry Cohen agreed in supporting Mr Waldegrave. But how would Ivan Lawrence and Greville Janner (also from opposite sides of the House) react? They have often been the most robust in their support for Israeli governments. Both complained that he had been tactless. Neither questioned his overall direction. That silence was as significant as their complaint. A key detail.

All the old (and young) Arabists were there. Most took care not to crow. The obligatory 'As a *true* friend of Israel, I have to tell the Israelis ...' did not impute the (silent) continuation '... to get stuffed' which, from them, it often seems to.

It was Sir Russell Johnston who first mentioned Jerusalem. Peter Shore repeated the thorny question: did the PLO still insist on its return? Mr Waldegrave would not be drawn. Pointers to the great debate to come?

These occasions in the Commons are like snapshots: a changing picture captured at an unrehearsed moment, and frozen. In it are clues about the present, and pointers to the future. Perhaps Parliament used to be like that more often.

18.1.89

Two ladies and an invisible man

IT IS given to no Tory to be Social Security Secretary, to be famous, and to be loved. It would be silly to try. In that wretched post, the most you can hope for is anonymity.

Judged by this measure, Tony Newton has been an outstanding success. Any poll would confirm that this is the minister whom fewest in the High Street could identify. Even MPs forget who has that job, many believing that it is Norman Fowler, who left the post two years ago.

Why, the very *name* 'Tony Newton' is too bland to be true and has probably been made up. Of slight build, slight hair, medium height and worried face, Mr Newton would surprise few if he turned up for Questions dressed as the Invisible Man, enveloped in white bandages.

He did not go quite so far yesterday. Instead, he wrapped all his *Answers* in white bandages, concealing what little meaning they might otherwise convey.

'The increased income support pensioner premiums which took effect were on top of any transitional addition then in payment,' was his reply to Charles Wardle (C, Bexhill & Battle). Tony Favell (C, Stockport) tried to tweak the bandages. 'Some pensioners are pretty wealthy, aren't they?' he asked. 'Shouldn't we target help on the poorer?' Out came Mr Newton's muslin.

'On the latest information we have, the average total net income of pensioners has been rising considerably faster than for the population as a whole.'

With some relief, we turned to watch a new junior minister in Mr Newton's department, Mrs Gillian Shephard, make her parliamentary debut.

A Labour spokesman, Paul Flynn, had alleged that pregnant teenage girls were forced to take YTS jobs.

Mrs Shephard was only elected in 1987, yet already displays the sort of cool, unflashy competence that qualifies someone to be a deputy librarian or a rising star in Mrs Thatcher's third administration. There was 'no evidence whatever', she said with courteous finality and an accent that betrayed no trace of class, region, emotion or personal susceptibility of any sort, that pregnancy need keep a sixteen-year-old from YTS.

If Gillian Shephard is deputy librarian in charge of textbooks, Mrs

73

Teresa Gorman (C, Billericay) is the lady who wanders in off the street with seven plastic bags full of old newspapers, muttering to herself. Not that Mrs Gorman *looks* inelegant – quite the opposite – or that her pronouncements are without a certain intellectual consistency. The only thing they are inconsistent with is being re-elected. Why, she asked Mrs Shephard, should the poor carry on living in expensive areas, when the taxpayer had to shoulder their rents? Couldn't they be 'encouraged' by 'the Government' to leave Belgravia and go somewhere cheaper?

Like Billericay, Mrs Gorman? Or marginal Wandsworth, over the river? It was rather as though the bag lady had asked the deputy librarian (textbooks) for something steamy and blood-curdling from the fiction section. Mrs Shephard paused, glanced fastidiously at Mrs Gorman, and begged to 'remind my hon friend that Housing is not my department'. As to the particular axe-murder fantasy Mrs Gorman had requested: 'We have no such plans.' Still muttering, Mrs G was gently led to a place of safety.

24.10.89

I conned £42K job

'I CONNED £50,000 job' said the front-page 'Exclusive' in the *Sun*, yesterday. '**A SUPERMARKET shelf packer told last night how he fooled car giants Nissan into making him a top boss with a £55,000 salary package.**

'Bob Bell (30) was put in charge of Nissan's UK service empire a month after leaving a £95-a-week job at Tesco's ... he was given the title of Group Service Director after an interview with Nissan's UK chief ...

'With the job came **POWER** to hire and fire, a £40,000 **SALARY**, a £15,000 Bluebird ZX turbo company **CAR** and a large **EXPENSE** account.

'*He stayed at some of London's top hotels and was whisked all over the country in chartered planes ...*

'One minute I was putting cans on supermarket shelves, the next I had my name on a huge office ... I know I'm a bit of a smooth talker, but I couldn't believe how gullible some people could be. I couldn't even change a flipping spark plug.'

Readers of the *Sun* may find this surprising. But those who take *The Times* have been reading about people like Bob for years.

Mr Richard Luce (54), so-called 'Minister for the Arts', also styled 'Minister for the Civil Service', yesterday faced top MPs who have slammed his policies and accused him of massive incompetence.

Speaking from his key command post at the **DISPATCH BOX** in the luxury **HOUSE OF COMMONS**, Luce battled to persuade MPs that he was on top of his £42,000-a-year job.

The world-famous multi-million pound **NATIONAL GALLERY**, he claimed, was 'in good shape for the 1990s'. And he boasted that the multi-**BILLION**-pound British Library was 'the biggest Arts construction project this century'!

Meanwhile, the doorblocking, mega-ton Tory MP for Calder Valley, 'Don' Thompson, lashed out at the Government's miserly treatment of **BRASS BANDS**. 'We want more brass for our brass,' quipped hip-heavy Don from Yorkshire.

Still reeling from this right hook, Luce faced a crafty uppercut from Eton-educated leftie-loonie and closet aristo 'Laird Tam' Dalyell. Battling Tam from Linlithgow wanted to know how we could get our **NICKED BRONZES** back from the US unless we knuckled under to the UNESCO Convention!

On the ropes, lanky Luce from Shoreham stammered excuses. Shocked friends said later he was **GAGGED** from **REVEALING** the **TRUTH**.

In an exclusive interview with the Thunderclapping *Times*, Luce later confessed that he **CONNED** the gullible Tory top brass into offering him the prestigious, high-society, 'Arts Minister' post. And **CHEATED** his way to the respected 'Minister for the Civil Service' handle.

'I didn't know my Degas from my elbow,' jested honey-tongued Dick.

Now I'm whisked from art exhibition to art exhibition in a luxury chauffeur-driven black ministerial limousine with gold go-fast stripes down the sides. I've even kissed Kiri Te Kanawa.'

From junior businessman to Britain's biggest employer as Civil Service Minister, brazen Luce shamelessly confessed that he's done it all on **HYPE**.

'I'm not the only one,' he bragged last night. 'There's **649 MORE**, just the **SAME**, at Westminster.'

19.12.89

Offals for braces

JUST AS the exchanges on 'Mad Cow Disease' reached fever pitch yesterday, the Prime Minister stormed in dressed in stunning purple.

It was Agriculture Questions. She settled on to the green bench like an animated aubergine on a greengrocer's plastic grass mat.

David Maclean, the junior minister, looked rattled. It was too late to stop. He was just reaching his peroration.

'And Mr Speaker,' he appealed at top volume, 'it was quite irrelevant whether or not the animal's head was cut off before it went into the slaughterhouse because the *relevant offals*' (he was yelling, now) 'are removed from *all* the animals' heads!'

'Hear, *hear*!' yelled his backbench colleagues. Mrs Thatcher looked a touch queasy, a touch bemused. Mr Maclean had left so much un-answered. What *are* the 'relevant offals'? What are the *ir*relevant offals?

We know where the relevant ones go. Maclean told us. It was, he said 'a belt and braces job'. The 'offals go into the offals bag'. 'That,' he added, 'is the braces.'

Sorry, Minister, but *what* is the braces? Not the offals, surely? I glanced suspiciously at the elegant red braces of the magnificent Nicholas Soames (Crawley) sitting behind Mr Maclean. Soames seemed vast today, even for Soames. I looked again. It wasn't Soames. It was two thin Tories in thin red ties, sitting next to each other. I hope that's clear on TV.

For this was the first Agriculture Questions to be televised: and didn't you know it! Ms Jo Richardson drifted past in a sort of lavender veil. In the face of the advancing cameras, every citadel tumbles! This splendidly feminist Labour MP for Barking, who used to dress *à la Prisoner, Cell Block H*, now resembled some minor goddess.

As for the team of Agriculture ministers, their boss, John Gummer, wore neat suit, white shirt, smart tie and glasses. His hair was smoothly combed. 'Come on, duck-head,' Dennis Skinner kept shouting at him.

David Maclean wore – you guessed it – neat suit, white shirt, smart tie and glasses. David Curry – yes, right again. As a team, they looked like those squads of Bible-toting Seventh Day Adventists that rat-a-tat politely on your front door as you glower through the keyhole ... 'Not today, thank you ... No, I'm not interested in the after-life ... Just running a bath – if I'm damned, I'm damned ...'

Your sketchwriter drifted into a flight of fantasy. John Gummer was tapping on my door. Behind him, in clean white mackintoshes, were

Maclean and Curry, toting clipboards and microwave instruction manuals ...

'No thanks. I know how to cook scrambled egg already ... What's that? Bovine Spongiform? Don't care ... *Look*, if I get listeria it's nobody's business but my own. Please go away ...'

Teresa Gorman (C, Billericay) brought me back with a jolt to reality. She spoke, she said, for the chicken farmers of Billericay. Ah, noble tribune!

Chickens, she continued, come with salmonella like chickens come with feathers: so what was all the fuss?

'My hon friend,' purred Maclean, 'is a doughty fighter for the chicken industry.' Look good on a gravestone, wouldn't it?

TERESA GORMAN
1941–2041
MP for Billericay
and Doughty Fighter for
the Chicken Industry
'*And all the trumpets sounded
on the other side.*'

12.1.90

Fighting them on the benches

LORD JAMES Douglas Hamilton is a junior minister in the brave Tory Scots team. Massively outnumbered by the Opposition, the do-or-die spirit of this intrepid posse is typified by the fair-haired and plucky little Etonian boxing blue.

I watched him, my mind far from the Westminister splendour. For Lord James has just published a book (Airlife Publishing, £14.95): *The Air Battle for Malta: Diaries of a Spitfire Pilot.*

Though Lord James's book centres upon his uncle, Lord *David* Douglas Hamilton, your sketchwriter knew that the young nephew bore his uncle's tradition into a new and equally fearsome theatre of war: *The Battle for Scotland.* The odds were appalling.

As the SNP's merciless Jim Sillars (Glasgow, Govan) raked the Chamber with the ack-ack and Mac-Mac of Celtic syllables, our James crouched – a picture of bemused good humour – ducking the abuse.

Was Lord James not the reincarnation of a central figure in his book,

'Laddie' Lucas, the Spitfire pilot? Alone (well, almost: there was a handful of Tories behind him) he faced a squadron of some three score fighters on the Axis benches opposite.

A vicious Messerschmitt in the form of John McAllion (Lab, Dundee E) dived out of the sky at him on Question 2, and asked about the current level of capital spending by the Scottish Homes Agency. James adjusted his goggles and peered at the charts his civil ground staff had provided. Avoiding action!

'£356.5m ... other programmes under consideration as part of the continuous process of providing homes for the area.'

A friendly Lancaster bomber in the form of Allan Stewart (C, Eastwood) lumbered up behind and asked about housing in Barrhead.

'Scottish Homes are considering a consultants' report on the future of Barrhead,' he replied, dipping his wings. This was easy.

Suddenly, a Fokker – and a pretty silly one – came screaming out of the sun. Said Ron Brown (Lab, Leith): 'Your Government has conned people into buying their so-called homes!' *So-called* homes? What did the Fokker mean? Lord James tried to return fire but from Brown came a series of small explosions as he veered, whining, off course and hurtled like a fireball into the sea.

The heat was off Jamie as a manoeuvrable Hurricane, fellow minister Ian Lang (flying on autopilot, as usual), moved in to cover Question 3.

Wheeling out of a steel-grey cloud, now, came the Stirling 'Bomber': junior minister Michael Forsyth (C, Stirling), demolishing Thomas McAvoy (Lab, Glasgow, Rutherglen) for 'putting his own political dogma before the interests of patients'. McAvoy limped into the sunset, smoke pouring from his port engine.

As I left the war theatre, the Few battled valiantly on – numbers further depleted by the destruction of 'Kamikaze' Fairbairn (C, Perth & Kinross), who had confused a 'greenfield' with what he called a 'greenpeace' site, and crash-landed his Question amid general mirth.

This instalment of the Battle for Scotland was nearly over. Across the southern sky, from England, drifted the Crawley barrage balloon. Nicholas Soames seemed unaware of the acts of desperate courage he had missed. 'Laddie' James rested modestly on the green bench. He was not a man to boast.

7.6.90

Portillo Mk II shines

WHEN A new minister is taken out for road tests, it is a privilege to be among the observers.

Fresh from the showrooms, the air-cooled Portillo Mark II – 'Poll Tax Turbo GTI' – was driven round the circuit for the first time yesterday. Results were promising. A discreetly lively performance, road-holding good.

Over at the Department of Transport, the machine had been put through extensive trials as 'Rail minister', and reports were positive. The sleek Latin lines have, of course, been widely admired; but the Portillo's performance had been restrained. Backroom boys were impressed by this minister's information system; but the Portillo always seemed to be operating below design specifications. Answering for BR sandwich quality hardly tested this minister to the limit. This machine had still to win the hearts of the public and the plaudits of the trade press.

To do so under the 'Poll Tax' badge was never going to be easy. This is a troubled marque with a history of horrendous teething problems. Preceding the Portillo in this niche, the David Hunt (or 'Wirral Wonder') had been a smooth performer, but criticized as lacking kick. The challenge facing the Portillo was formidable.

They wheeled him in at 2.30. While a trusty Trippier raced up and down the tarmac at Question 1, final checks were made to the Portillo's paperwork and exterior trim. The minister was ready.

Performing the bump start at Question 2 was an able young mechanic, Tim Devlin (C, Stockton S). Devlin chose a safe stretch of track.

'Is it not remarkable that my hon. friend has not received the promised policy paper from the Opposition?'

That was more than enough. The minister fired first time. Brm, brrm, brr ... The Portillo was away.

'Yes, I think it is truly remarkable that they have not come up with an alternative ...'

Into a gentle bend: 'They have no "reasoned policy document" ...'

A touch on the throttle: 'There was no background paper.'

Easing up a gear now, needle creeping up nicely: 'Indeed, I suspect there was no background.'

On the straight – maybe a taste of burning rubber? 'Labour have no idea what to do about local government ...'

'Hear, *hear*!' came approving growls from the grandstand. There was an angry whine of Opposition engines, revving in the pit. Their wheels –

'alternatives to the poll tax' – long promised from Walworth Road, had still not arrived. The Portillo purred past, first lap complete.

It was time for a fast run through the S-bends. Richard Tracy (C, Surbiton) an experienced race official from the backbenches, flagged the Portillo away: would the government look at the standard community charge and the iniquitous suggestion by some local authorities that it must always be applied at the two-times multiplier?

'Of course I will look at the point.' The minister moved silkily up through the gears. 'This is an area where the government wishes local government to be local.' Rubber bit into asphalt now, as the minister tried a boost to the turbo: 'They can apply multipliers on the standard community charge up to a maximum of two.'

Chrome flashed in the afternoon sun as the minister coasted past the grandstand. The Portillo Mark II 'Poll Tax Turbo GTI' was making an auspicious debut.

28.6.90

4

Big Tories – and their Big Shadows

A conquering hero

FOR TRIUMPHAL pomp, Ted Heath's entry into the Chamber yesterday ranks with the Arrival of the Queen of Sheba.

The old boy's timing was perfect. PM's Questions being the event of any Thursday afternoon, MPs drift into the Chamber well before the curtain rises at 3.15. By 3.05 the place is packed. At about 3.12, the PM herself arrives.

She sailed in, clad in a striking garment with huge collars edged in black.

But where was Ted?

If chocolates were permitted in the Chamber, the rustle of wrappers would have been at its climax. The orchestra was tuning up, and the House was waiting for Mr Speaker to wave his conductor's baton. It was 3.14.

And in came Ted. The suit was impeccable, the hair as crisp and white as a fresh snowfall, and Mr Heath was wearing his best blue socks. His face was a composition we might entitle '*Pleasure tempered by Dignity*'. Only the dignity prevented his performing a little skip as he approached his chosen roost below the gangway. To each side of this hallowed site, senior bottoms shuffled discreetly, clearing a generous space for his own.

And, from the Labour benches, rose a great cheer.

'The next leader!' shouted Bob Cryer (L, Bradford S). Tories grinned. And Ted? No outward show, of course, but did we see the hint of a smile flicker across those noble features?

Still the cheering continued. Mr Heath half-turned to Sir Geoffrey Howe and, like one elderly field marshal to another, heavy with honours, dipped his head in soldierly salute. Sir Geoffrey dipped his head back. Mrs Thatcher studied her notes with exceptional concentration.

Neil Kinnock glanced across at her. He *knew*, we all knew, that nothing would bring her to congratulate that man this afternoon.

This, then, two minutes later, is what the Labour leader asked her to do. Mr Kinnock larded Mr Heath with as much praise as he could cram into one short question, and asked her to echo it.

Now most people in all parties here at Westminster are in two minds about Mr Heath's visit. They cannot disapprove of his rescuing hostages, but something about the spectacle it produced discomforts them.

So it did not take great cunning to devise the best response available to Mrs Thatcher. It was to offer polite praise for Mr Heath, but caution Mr Kinnock to take more care how he phrased things, lest they be misinterpreted in Baghdad. Performed with an apparent good grace, this would have taken the shine off both men's afternoon.

But she couldn't do it. She thinks he's a silly old so-and-so and she was damned if she was going to say different. So, never referring to Mr Heath, Mrs Thatcher said, in so many words, that it was good to have a few more hostages back, but it didn't alter the underlying horror. Asked a second time to congratulate her predecessor, she contrived, a second time, not to. Surrounded by a hundred public-school-educated colleagues with better manners than her, men who could congratulate the Devil himself if it got them out of a tight spot, Mrs Thatcher's own curious brand of honesty came through. She simply couldn't pretend, any more than Mr Heath can. How alike they are!

26.10.90

Bonding baby Bill

To his many domestic and international triumphs, the Foreign Secretary yesterday added a tiny victory over Japanese technology.

My bedside clock-radio was set to wake me at 7.45 am. I awoke seconds before and was gaining consciousness fast when the machine activated itself and filled the room with Sir Geoffrey Howe explaining about Europe.

I went back to sleep, as if hit by a rock. Then, renewing the struggle towards consciousness, I lunged wildly across my bed in a desperate bid to disconnect the radio. The voice swelled. 'And I think it's fair to say that all of us in the Twelve see eye to eye on this seven-point package of proposals: *firstly* ...' Arrgh! I spun, insensible, back down into the vortex. There's nothing for it but to get his taped speeches linked to my snooze button, timed to turn off when one wants to awake.

However, we're relieved to see him. Prolonged trips abroad kept him from Foreign Office Questions last week, when Mr William Waldegrave, his new Minister of State, made his debut. Many of us were concerned about this. It is well established that contact between a secretary of state and a new junior minister is especially important in the early weeks, when 'bonding' occurs.

Although Mr Waldegrave was well cared for by a kindly surrogate, Mrs Lynda Chalker, Sir Geoffrey's deputy, it's never the same. Adverse effects on the junior's development started to show last week when, with Mr Waldegrave at the tiller, Her Majesty's Government made a minor incursion into Romanian domestic policy. This will never do. Take him to your bosom, Sir Geoffrey — and Welcome Home!

I do wish Mr Nicholas Ridley would come home to the Department of Transport. Now Secretary of State for the Environment, he is sorely missed by his old pals. Look at what his replacement, Mr Paul Channon, is up to! Asked a question about the poor state of suburban rail services in Manchester, Mr Channon *actually tried to answer it*, rabbiting excitedly about attempts at improvements, effort and the like.

That would never have happened in Mr Ridley's day. 'The operational details of British Rail services are a matter for the chairman of British Rail,' he would sneer, in tones laced with vinegar. It was the answer that generations of Transport ministers have given to such questions; but what distinguished him was well illustrated, once, by his answer to a young crawler on his own side who asked whether he was aware how the London-to-Sheffield service had improved of late to be the toast, indeed, of the travelling public!

Mr Peter Walker would have taken full credit, and for the invention of the steam engine, too. Mrs Margaret Thatcher would have recited the entire British Rail Sheffield-to-London timetable, committed to memory. But Mr Ridley? He stared into the middle distance, dreaming of his next cigarette. 'I have no day-to-day knowledge of the service and reject bouquets as I reject brickbats.'

Such men come rarely into politics. Even more rarely do they stay. Mr Ridley is into Extra Time and was at it on Monday, sneaking in surprise answers in his favourite way: to Written Questions, which do not interrupt his smoking.

25.10.88

Genuine noise based on emotion

YESTERDAY WE enjoyed oratory in the finest traditions of the House. But not *in* the House. It was at the Savoy Hotel. The Parliamentarian of the Year awards were distributed by *The Spectator* and the distillers of Highland Park Whisky, in circumstances of considerable hospitality.

Lord Whitelaw gave a vintage speech. His thirty-odd years in Parliament were no record, he demurred, 'but at least it's quite a long time'. Aware that he'd better say more: 'And I had a lovely time in the Whips'

Office!' Ted Heath was '*at that time* wonderfully rewarding to work with'. Pondering, perhaps, that this sounded ungenerous, he struck out wildly for the other shore: 'Which is more than I can say for *some* things they've said later, such as "Willie is as silly as ever" and things like that.'

Did he mean Mrs Thatcher? Lord Whitelaw sensed that the whole subject was best dropped. 'And what I always say to the media,' he roared, 'is that there is a great need for all to work together for the common good!' A baffled silence suggested the need for a little more flesh on these philosophical bones. 'And people who say Parliament used to be docile are talking the most unutterable tosh.' There was a danger, here, of seeming to have raised his banner for rowdyism; so: 'But I always say that there is a difference between ...' he hesitated, momentarily puzzled by his own argument: '... between ... *genuine noise based on emotion*, and ... *deliberate* noise ...' (pause) '... to *drown out* other people.' He beamed triumphantly: 'Now it won't do any good to say all this, they'll always do it, but still it's a pity, and it ought to be said that it's a pity.' He perspired. '*And I will say it!*' he bellowed.

Some would have left matters there, but not Lord Whitelaw. Wildly (*à propos* of what, was unclear) he boomed his advice: 'They're not going to have it and therefore they won't have it and at least keep hold of nurse for fear of finding something worse.' We all felt chastened. He moved on. 'Bertie Denham (the Tory Chief Whip in the Lords) used to say to me, "It's time we were beaten, Willie."' Tories gasped. What would Mrs Thatcher say to this? Lord Whitelaw panicked. 'On some of the *little* votes, I mean, not the big ones. And it has happened and it does happen and it will happen and it ought to happen. I think I should sit down now.' And Willie, who had made a genuine noise based on emotion, sat down.

24.11.88

More bull

THE ORDER Paper for yesterday said something about 'questions' but there were no questions. Tom King, the Northern Ireland Secretary, was present to receive a number of statements from other members, but none took the nature of an inquiry.

Then came Prime Minister's Questions. Just one real question was asked during this session. It came from the Prime Minister. She asked Labour's Jimmy Dunnachie (Glasgow, Pollock) what he had just said. He repeated his statement, whereupon she made a statement of her own.

From her own supporters came contributions that could hardly even be called statements, let alone questions. It is hard to describe them, as our language lacks a single word for the extended passage of a wet human tongue over the soft leather of a lady's court shoe.

From the Opposition came Mr Kinnock's usual attempts to light a damp squib. Labour's contribution was momentarily enlivened by an alarming statement from Allen McKay about what sounded like 'wisteria in chicken'. Perhaps this is a new flowering of the *nouvelle cuisine* among yuppies.

What Mrs Thatcher referred to in her reply was 'listeria' – which sounded like a disinfectant. But then anything she says does.

Then we moved to 'none-of-my' Business Questions, where the Leader of the House received statements from almost everyone but volunteered none of his own.

The Chancellor's Autumn Statement was, in its way, a remarkable occasion. Seldom can a Chancellor have made a more relaxed, jokey speech, while standing upon shakier logical ground and facing (in Gordon Brown) such an effective parliamentary opponent.

You might think that the Government is confident of winning the parliamentary argument – but it goes further. The Conservatives don't even bother.

When the Democrats' Alan Beith protested that you couldn't just ignore mortgage costs when ordinary householders had to pay them, Mr Lawson replied that lots of other countries did. What sort of a reply is that?

Soon he was actually boasting – that 'the increase in mortgage payments will mean that people will have to curb spending on other things'.

'Like food,' shouted someone.

Had there been problems? These had been no more than 'changes of pace in the sustained upward march of the British economy'. Mr Lawson's ample frame quivered with self-satisfaction. 'We have,' he said, 'the firmest fiscal stance of any government since the war.'

It put one in mind of a disco number by a pregnant black artiste called Neneh Cherry, currently in the charts. 'We always stand in a buffalo stance' runs her mindless lyric.

'Bullish' was the pundits' word for Mr Lawson's stance yesterday, but, as he squared his considerable bulk up to the dispatch box, 'buffalo-ish' did spring to mind.

13.1.89

Poor Mr Channon

'AND I continue to press for the liberalization of cabotage.' The Rt Hon Henry Paul Guinness Channon stared at empty benches opposite in quiet despair. It had been an awful winter. Disaster after disaster. Two air crashes, three rail crashes, newspapers full of pictures of wrecked lorries all over the M6 ...

Channon had been on his feet with statements almost every afternoon last week. He cared of course – deeply. *All* the sketchwriters had remarked on his remorse-stricken demeanour. But there was a limit to how often a man could continue this grotesque ritual of tribute to the emergency services, condolence to the bereaved and pleas to the House to reserve judgement. How much more, oh Lord?

John Prescott, Labour's loud and pugnacious Transport Spokesman from Humberside, had made it immeasurably worse, blaming Channon personally for every signal the train drivers missed. Insults had been hurled of the most personal kind, insults he had never once returned. At least five times now Prescott had called for his resignation. How much more could a chap take?

And every Tory in Kent was at his throat about the wretched Channel link. Now (it was being whispered) the PM was unhappy that he'd bodged his 'presentation'. All in all, it was the most wretched Transport Questions he could remember.

Dr Michael Clark, a Tory from Rochford, had asked about expenditure on roads in the South-east. Mr Channon smiled tentatively at Clark. Painstakingly courteous, he said that spending was higher than average, and offered figures.

Clark cast his answer aside. That's not what voters *think*, he barked, as if all those carefully assembled facts meant nothing. Channon pursed his lips, and turned the other cheek. Again.

Then another Tory was on his feet: Robin Squire from Hornchurch. Squire blinked at him through his NHS pebble-glasses. Why was it cheaper to fly from New York to Washington than from London to Paris, Squire moaned?

Again, Mr Channon gritted his teeth. Yes, he said patiently, we do have a long way to go with deregulation of air fares. He consoled himself inwardly. 'Nearly through, Paul. Just got to keep the lid on for ten minutes more.'

Suddenly, Prescott was on his feet, the Mouth of the Humber tossing careless insults about safety across the dispatch box. Channon's department presided over a 'dodgy situation', he said, 'totally inadequate to enforce air safety'.

Something snapped. Mr Channon's eyes swivelled wildly. Leaping to his feet he found himself shouting blindly in Prescott's direction. Prescott was *wrong*. His department was *not responsible* for enforcing air safety. The *Civil Aviation Authority* was. 'If you had done your *homework* you would have realized that, instead of asking that *completely ridiculous* question!'

Mr Channon paused, gulped, and took one more swing: 'You've just been reading from a brief you haven't checked. PERHAPS YOU OUGHT TO RESIGN!'

Ooh, that did feel good.

14.3.89

Clamour boy

Do you know the child's game called 'pin the tail on the donkey'? The adult version for MPs is 'pin the responsibility on the minister'. CHANNON RESISTS COMMONS CLAMOUR, said the morning papers. This being Monday, the clamour had presumably been communicated by telephone: so I ventured past the Commons with earmuffs, for fear of being deafened by the real thing.

John Prescott is the real thing. Labour's Transport spokesman amounts to a clamour all on his own; and yesterday he had help from Dale Campbell-Savours. They requested a debate. They didn't get it, but they got a clamour, which was what they wanted.

Mr Prescott emerges as the clamour boy of the Opposition front bench.

Of course nothing Mr Prescott says ought to have happened would have happened any differently if anyone else — John Prescott, say, or Donald Duck — had been in charge. 'Responsibility' is purely notional. Both sides understand that.

All we need to remember is that Labour says Mr Channon did something wrong, and Mr Channon says he didn't. That is the start of the game: they have a row. The game is in how they handle it.

Prescott was off to a good start by Christmas, reacting to the *first* disaster with restraint: 'no wish to make capital out of human sorrow ...' etc.

This entitled him to a double helping of clamour now, for we cannot say that he clamours regardless. But he needed a news peg for his PRESCOTT LASHES OUT headline. He was lucky. What could be better than a 'missing letter'?

Paul Channon, however, has played a shrewd game, too – in his stammering Etonian way. True, that Mustique holiday was a bit off-track. But picture his predecessor Transport ministers handling these disasters. Imagine the ghoulish presence of Nicholas Ridley, offering sympathy to the bereaved; or the clipped utterances of Norman Fowler, dismissing it as a fuss about nothing. Channon is better. He is good at looking anguished. Fortunately, people have forgotten that he *always* looked anguished and would have announced the debut of a new British Rail sandwich with as evident a distress as he announced the demise of thirty of their passengers.

A key weapon in the Channon armoury has been to accuse Prescott of turning bereavement to political advantage. In fact, of course, if a politician can't turn bereavement to advantage, he can't turn anything to advantage, and should resign. Turning bereavement to advantage would count as a pass at elementary level – a CSE – for aspiring politicans. Making political advantage out of accusing someone *else* of turning bereavement to advantage, is the next grade up: 'O' level. Channon has passed it. Next move: Prescott.

Each has shown finesse. Each has called for the other to resign, but of course it is vital to each that neither does.

There is one thing missing in this parliamentary game. They have it in football. When transport tragedies are debated, couldn't backbenchers wave inflatable bananas (for the Tories) and herrings (for Labour) to encourage their spokesman? It would show that we took politics as seriously as soccer. Unless, that is, you think the clamour is wearing thin?

21.3.89

Making herself available

POOR JOHN WAKEHAM! As Leader of the House (and former Chief Whip) his reputation is for fixing things, smoothing things, burying things and digging things up. 'I've always been a woman,' sings Dolly Levy in *Hello Dolly*, 'who arranges things.' John Wakeham has always been a man who arranges things, and does it well. Everyone likes him. He has only one foible. He is no orator. PR boffins use the term 'fronting'. One would always choose Mr Wakeham for backing.

So when Mr Gorbachov rescued Mrs Thatcher by kindly visiting her when she would otherwise have faced another Westlands row in PM's Questions, and Mr Wakeham was deputed to reply in her place, he knew it would be a nervy session. 'Please God,' he must have prayed the night before, 'make all the questions easy; make me even more low-key than usual; and let nobody trip me up.'

It all started so well. 'I have been asked to reply,' he told a packed Chamber, 'on my Right Honourable Friend's behalf.' David Alton (Lib, Mossley Hill) asked about the persecution of Catholics and Jews in the Soviet Union, and Mr Wakeham said we were against it, and everyone said, 'Hear, hear!'

Then Mr Kinnock asked about Westlands, and everyone laughed, and Mr Wakeham said he had nothing to say, and everyone laughed, and they all sat down again. Alastair Goodlad (C, Eddisbury) asked about the economy and Mr Wakeham said it was going jolly well, and people cheered, and ... phew! So far so good.

But it got better. Why had Mrs Thatcher referred the House to a document on Namibia which was unavailable. Mr Wakeham could have said: 'She boshed it up. Sorry.' He said: 'The Secretary General of the UN has asked that the report be kept confidential' – which made it sound as though Labour was trying to be rude to Pérez de Cuéllar.

Better and better. Perhaps it was going to be all right, after all? A pause. Up jumped Labour's Harry Ewing (Falkirk E). A guileful look spread across his face. Mr Wakeham stared at his shoes. As every Leader of the House who had so far been 'asked to reply', said Mr Ewing, had been sacked or carted off to the Lords, 'Where does he' (Mr Wakeham) 'expect to be by October?'

'Now,' Mr Wakeham thought, 'I must be ultra-cautious. I must on no account try to be clever, or funny. I must shelter behind the blandest nothingness possible ...' He stared even more intensely at his shoes, thinking one up.

'I am always *delighted* when the Prime Minister asks me to reply,' he said. (Yes, an excellent little launch.) '... She has indicated to Mr Kinnock that she would not be able to be here ...' (Splendid. Something we already know. Plain sailing now, John.)

'Because she has made herself ... available, to Mr Gorbachov.'

During the longest sustained laughter that your sketchwriter can remember in the Commons, in which a heaving Chancellor of the Exchequer hopelessly failed to keep a straight face and a whole row of junior ministers giggled helplessly, we heard – twice, disgracefully – the cry 'Withdraw!' from Tory backbenchers. 'I think perhaps I have finished my answer,' blushed Mr Wakeham.

7.4.89

The liftman

AFTER SEVEN years of being punished for impertinence, it is an exhilarating experience to find myself paid for it. But the Press Gallery presents special problems for an ex-Member, gamekeeper turned poacher. When debate gets heated, the temptation to join in is almost unbearable.

'Faced by this dilemma,' I heard a front-bencher declaim, the other day, 'what should I do?'

'Resign!' I swear the cry was only a micro-second from my lips before, in the nick of time, it struck me that I was no longer a Member. Think of the ignominy. Hauled out of the Gallery by policemen, to the growls of my old colleagues and the titters of my new.

Still, it's nice to be recognized by erstwhile fellow MPs, a couple of whom (I suspect) have not registered the change either. Alistair Goodlad has only recently stopped sending me those 'Have you any spare PM's Questions Gallery tickets?' notelets.

Keith Joseph used to make the opposite mistake, as became clear during a strange ride in the lift from the Special Gallery (East) during my first year as a Member. Keith, who was in the same lift, mistook me for a lift-attendant.

'Take me to the Members' Lobby,' he said, courteous but brusque. Then a worried look crossed his face. Perhaps, I thought, he has realized his error. Better for me to say nothing.

'East–West trade,' he muttered, half to himself and then, turning to me, the only other occupant of the lift, 'By cutting the link, would we gain strength, or simply lose a potential lever?' I stammered out some half-baked reply.

Sir Keith looked at me intently, listening. 'Yes. Quite possibly . . . Ah, we're here. You can let me off. Thank you. Goodbye. I shall think about what you said, and perhaps discuss it further, next time I am in your lift.'

I suppose the story could be cited as unintended discourtesy, a testimony to Keith's absent-mindedness. To me it serves better as testimony to his intellectual openness – an unintended courtesy. Keith addressed his colleague as a lift-attendant, but was as interested in a lift-attendant's views as he would have been in a colleague's. Other ministers would address you as a colleague, and be as interested in your views as in a lift-attendant's.

10.5.89

Sir Patrick chokes

WHAT AT first seemed likely to prove a dull Monday was enlivened when the Attorney General started to choke.

It is not easy to tell when the Rt Hon Sir Patrick Mayhew, QC, MP, is actually choking, because at the best of times he approaches the dispatch box with the air of a man struggling to retain his dignity while swallowing a bad oyster. Whatever you ask him, it turns out that you shouldn't have asked it at all; or you shouldn't have asked it of *him*; or you shouldn't have asked it of him *in that way*.

Thus Tam Dalyell (Lab, Linlithgow) shouldn't have asked *anyone* about Sir Leon Brittan: especially employing phrases like 'telling lies'.

The offending oyster having slithered irretrievably down, a scowling Sir Patrick would not '*encourage* the hon gentleman' by answering this Question at all.

As for Teddy Taylor (C, Southend E) who wanted to get rid of the Common Market, the problem with Taylor's Question was that it wasn't for *Sir Patrick*. 'Mine is a versatile Office, but I am not sure that my versatility can extend to taking such steps as would *satisfy* my honourable friend.' Sir Patrick tucked in his bib and – ho, ho! – *joked* about the bad oyster.

As for Ivor Stanbrook (C, Orpington), who wanted him to condemn the Storehouse shops' defiance of Sunday Trading laws – well, that was an interesting oyster. It was just that it hardly belonged on the sweet trolley. 'I am not sure, Mr Speaker, that this Question is in order, here ...'

Sir Patrick turned, now, to tell Labour's Chris Mullin (Sunderland S) that his turn on the fruit machine had almost hit the jackpot.

Almost, but not quite, three lemons.

His Question about an alleged prejudging of three Irishmen by the press was quite in order. *Lemon 1: check, hold*. And it was asked of the appropriate Minister, Sir Patrick. *Lemon 2: check, hold*.

But had he asked it in the appropriate way? Alas! The third lemon spun from Mullin's grasp. Sir Patrick boomed that by suggesting that an Irishman could not get a fair trial here, Mullin did 'no service to the administration of justice in this country'. 'And I don't suppose he intends to.'

It was not long after this that the Attorney General began to choke. Surely the *Solicitor* General, Sir Nicholas Lyell, should have thumped him on the back?

Perhaps there is a legal precedence in this, and nobody of the requisite dignity was present to do it. So Sir Patrick had to sit down, spluttering alone.

Watching Sir Nicholas handle the next Question was to watch a mere trainee. John Fraser, a Labour spokesman, asked about a court which had (allegedly) stopped sending out Court Notices for June because they had reached the limit of their postal budget. Sir Nicholas actually promised to 'look into' this.

The Attorney General, recovered now, gave a pained sigh. Poor boy. So much to learn. Sit down for a second, and the lad had all but sold the shop.

Then, just to show he could, Sir Patrick gave a substantive answer to his next questioner, Harry Greenway (C, Ealing N) who wanted to know what qualities a prospective judge needed.

Sir Patrick had thought hard about this one. 'Judicial potential,' he announced to a stunned House.

4.2.89

New, improved Gummer

IT IS a real pleasure to bring you good news about John Gummer, the new Agriculture minister. He is getting better.

Stung perhaps by the profile in Edward Pearce's new book (*Shooting Gallery*) describing Gummer as looking 'like a hallucinogenic frog' and saying of his physique that he is 'a tragic loss to cat-burglary', Mr Gummer has studied his critics and changed his ways.

Gone is the shrill, aggrieved tone; gone the pious finger-wagging. Mr Gummer has said in his heart: 'Gum-Gum: you have made it.

'You are the Minister of Agriculture now. You are in the Cabinet. You have no need to squeal or be indignant.

'From this day forward you will be a cool dude. Your manner will be authoritative, your tone quietly confident. Remember, Gum-Gum, *you* are in charge.'

And it works!

The minister had a statement about lead contamination in cattle-feed yesterday. Calmly he rose to the dispatch box, his little face just visible, and, voice gravely lowered, he began to speak.

He spoke of Burma; he spoke of Belgium; he spoke of The Netherlands. He spoke of our friends in Europe and their failure to arrest the poison: yet without rancour, more in sorrow than anger.

He spoke of the efforts of his civil servants to spread just the right degree of alarm with all due speed. He praised the ministry vets. He commended the laboratories. He thanked the farmers for their co-operation, and assured the public that all that had to be done would be done – and more. Then Mr Gummer sat down, sustained by the gathering rumble of 'hear, hear' from all around him, covered in glory. Who would gainsay him now?

Dr David Clark tried. Dr Clark is Labour's Agriculture spokesman and the very model of informed reason. Gummer, however, had lent no wind for his sails and all he could do was agree with what the Government had done, ask why they hadn't done it faster, and congratulate the officials. This half-hearted attempt to blame the minister and praise the ministry earned Tory catcalls which, with dignity, Mr Gummer did not join.

Instead he expressed his disappointment with Dr Clark. He was mildly surprised at so churlish a response from so normally sensible a man. He hadn't, of course, wanted to mention this but he was in receipt of congratulations from no less than the chairman of the South-west NFU. Farmers approved.

Dale Campbell-Savours (Lab, Workington) didn't. Mr Campbell-Savours sees a conspiracy (usually a Tory conspiracy) in every cowshed. Was there not, he said, 'an established trade in contaminated feed'? Had the ministry not been slow to act on Chernobyl, spongey-brain disease, listeria ... Mr Speaker, familiar with the Campbell-Savours pathology, laid the equivalent of a white-coated arm gently on his shoulder, and said that that would be enough.

Surely this would tempt the new Gummer beyond endurance? Gummer's voice rose a semitone and quivered: 'If the hon gentleman really cared about food safety, he'd ... he'd ...' but – just as quickly – the storm was stilled; the old Adam restrained. 'He'd ...' (and now the voice dropped an octave and was hushed) '... he'd be *quiet* a bit more often,' said the minister, with a gentle smile.

14.11.89

Happy ever after?

WHEN, ASKED Neil Kinnock yesterday, would Mrs Thatcher see that 'this whole arrangement was a fairy tale from the start'?

He was talking about the community charge. The Fairy herself stood there, shimmering a little. She had left her wand at No. 10, in favour of more simple ornaments: green jade buttons and a gold brooch. ...

Once upon a time, children, there was a place called Hamelin in Germany. It was 'twinned' with somewhere called Westminster.

And, in this place, they had a terrible problem. An infestation of rates. Rates were everywhere: huge rates, rates with sharp teeth, slinking through people's letter-boxes and ruining their lives. The citizens begged their leaders to get rid of the rates; but the problem was, nobody could think how.

Then a man called Mr Baker with silver hair and a big smile came forward. He wore flashy wide ties and they called him the Wide-Tied Baker of Hamelin.

'I know a way of eradicating rates,' he said. 'Trust me.

'But if I do this, I want you to reward me. I want to be the next Leader of Hamelin.'

Not *everybody* did quite trust the Wide-Tied Baker but they were frantic to get rid of the rates: so they agreed to let him try.

He was as good as his word. He passed a law, saying that '*from 1*

April, all the rates are abolished' and — hey presto! — they were.

But it was at about this time that the Wide-Tied Baker noticed that the people were unlikely to make him Leader. Frankly, the elders were not giving him the nod. Younger citizens were pointing at him and snickering about some of his other schemes, like Student Loans, GCSE and the National Core Curriculum.

And, though he continued to smile, the Wide-Tied Baker grew rather impatient and slightly bitter, for he was a clever man and had really meant well, underneath. Yet there was no sign that the present Leader was planning to retire and no sign that, when that day came, Baker would be the favoured one.

And a very evil idea came to him. He called everyone together. 'With the rates gone,' he announced, 'I'll take you all somewhere really fantastic. It's a magical mystery tour to the Polltax Mountains. Not an easy journey but it'll be great when you get there; and, to lead you, my young friend Christopher Patten will dance ahead and play sweet music all the way. You'll love it, honestly.'

At this, young Chris looked a bit nervous as he wasn't at all sure he knew the way, or that people would like it when they got there. But the Leader of Hamelin told him it was his duty.

And off they all set. The Wide-Tied Baker had detached himself, now, from the throng and sat on a rock at 32 Smith Square, watching them stumble towards the horizon. A thin smile played upon his lips. 'Have fun!' he called.

As night falls, and they still don't seem to be getting anywhere, and the ground grows stonier, the path steeper, and the wind colder, cries of distress fill the air. Yet still they stumble forward ...

Children, there is a logical flaw in the plot of this story. Can you spot it? Yes — correct, David Wilshire. *The people didn't have to go to the Polltax Mountains in the first place. They still don't. They could just turn round and go home again.*

Do you think they will?

21.2.90

Pharaoh Ken

THE OLD song tells us to 'accentuate the positive, eliminate the negative', and a splendid pupil Mr Kenneth Baker has proved. For more than a week, his beaming presence has accentuated the positive side of losing 200 local government seats. This was followed on Friday by the announcement of the highest inflation figures for eight years.

'We are heading for the clearer, open sea, where the wind of public opinion can fill our sails!' chortled Mr Baker, wind of another kind filling his own sails.

History is full of bad news. Current affairs seems to admit of none. Perhaps things really have looked up. But my own analysis is simpler: the Ancients just lacked a Mr Baker.

Take the Exodus. After a formidable campaign by the Almighty, the only press release we have was that put out by His own press officer – Moses.

First, says this version, the Lord turned the Nile into blood, *'and the fish that were in the river died; and the river stank ...'* then *'the frogs came up, and covered the land,'* following which *'All the dust of the land became lice.'*

That was just before *'there came a grievous swarm of flies.'* Rather later, *'all the cattle of Egypt died,'* then came *'boils, breaking forth with blains upon man and upon beast.'* These boils heralded the hail, *'and fire, mingled with the hail.'*

Next came the locusts *'and very grievous were they.'* While Pharaoh wavered, *'there was a thick darkness in all the land of Egypt three days.'* Finally – for good measure – the Lord slaughtered all the Egyptian first-born. And off ran the Israelites, through the Red Sea.

So runs the Authorized Version. And we have no other version, for Pharaoh did not have Kenneth Baker as party chairman. Let us, though, try to imagine how Mr Baker would have handled this blip in the fortunes of Egyptian domestic politics.

Following the drowning of the greater part of Pharaoh's army, Mr Baker would have taken the initiative and called a press conference.

'I would like to congratulate the emergency services for their magnificent work,' he would have said. 'They have been hard-pressed of late; and, of course, our hearts go out to the relatives of the unfortunate victims.

'But it is a fact that defence spending needed to be trimmed and a reduction in the numbers of our armed forces was always on the cards.

This freak storm – for, despite the wilder rumours, that is what it was – has simply hastened the inevitable.

'I naturally regret the sharp overnight increase, recently, in cot deaths; but suggestions that this tragic coincidence has embraced all our first-born are pure media speculation. Likewise, the so-called "blackout" last week: it is true that we had three days of unusually poor visibility, but this was probably caused by industrial smog arising from the period of sustained economic growth we are undoubtedly entering.

'The locusts were an inconvenience: let us not try to dodge that. But agricultural surpluses were a problem. The locusts have removed them. The hail was also helpful, as was the sharper than expected natural cull of our livestock, which preceded it. I must emphasize, there is no possible danger in eating meat from the carcasses of diseased cattle.

'I must say, I am fed up with people whingeing about boils. Personal hygiene is an individual responsibility. The health service can only do so much.

'As you know, frogs are an endangered species. I am pleased to announce that, under our new Green policies, there has been an increase of almost spectacular proportions in the population of these valuable bio-indicators.

'Change brings its problems. It would be idle to deny that recent developments have been without inconvenience for some of our people. But the underlying trend is still strongly upwards. I think you will agree, gentlemen, that – under the inspired leadership of Mrs Margaret Nefertiti – things can only go up.'

14.5.90

Gerbils don't bark in the night

MUCH IS made of the lions and tigresses among ministers. One man is spoken of as an eagle, another a workhorse; there are scapegoats, poodles, running-dogs and even dinosaurs. But no one ever mentions the gerbils.

Gerbil-ministers are very important. These are the competent, colour-less men: the ones who labour at the coalface of their Whitehall depart-ment without ever becoming household names. They have greyish hair, often wear spectacles, and cannot pronounce their r's. Gerbil-ministers are those of whom it is said in bars and taxis that the PM has so outshone her Cabinet that nobody knows who the rest of the team are.

Yet gerbils are vital. It is absolutely necessary that at any one time at least half the Cabinet should be gerbils. After all, if the PM is to shine, there must be a neutral background against which to do so. Besides, there is practical work to be undertaken in government and it is not possible for famous people to do this as they are obliged to be controversial. The last thing you want, to take a difficult and sensitive bill through the House, is a controversial minister. The best person is a capable bore.

To Lady Fowler and the children and to those of us privileged to know him, Sir Norman Fowler is anything but boring. But as a departmental minister he was an award-winning gerbil. We cannot quite recall what Fowler was Minister of, but Transport, Employment and the DHSS (though not necessarily in that order) stir memories and some people believe he also wrote *Fowler's Modern English Usage*. In my view he was a huge success in each department, and my test is a simple one: during his time, each, successively, dropped completely out of the news.

Another gerbil – Tony Newton – has now been put in at the DHSS, while gerbils rule in Defence (Tom King), Northern Ireland (Peter Brooke) and Education (no – *you* guess. Can't remember, eh? John MacGregor) – a gerbil needed as never a gerbil was, to nurse a department still convalescing after a spell with a famous politician.

Gerbils hardly bite. Gerbils do not smell and keep their little nests clean. That is why they are such popular pets.

But among all the gerbils at Westminster, is there one to match Mr John Wakeham? At Energy Questions yesterday, the Secretary of State's performance was superb. He caused no fuss at all.

Checking my notes after the occasion, his name did not, in fact, appear. Mentally, I tried to recall the scene. Had he not sung at all for his supper? Had nobody commented on this? Where had Mr Wakeham been sitting and how dressed? Curious, but I just couldn't visualize.

It was then that the truth dawned. The Secretary of State had not been there. Mr Wakeham was in Kuwait. It had not been felt necessary to explain. Nobody had mentioned his absence.

Reader, do not imagine that this is meant unhelpfully to Mr Wakeham. His predecessors at Energy have made a monumental cock-up of plans to privatize electricity. Wakeham's job is now to make the best of the ludicrous structure he has been bequeathed: and sell it, fast, this year, for as much as possible and with the minimum of fuss.

If anyone can do it, Mr Wakeham can. Who knows? You may not even notice.

15.5.90

Sir Geoffrey and the Panda

IF, AT any time during my stint in Parliament, misfortune should have taken Mrs Thatcher from us, I would have voted for Sir Geoffrey Howe. I still would. Apart from the requisite qualities of skill and intellect, he seems to me to be an honourable man.

How do I know? A simple test, and a serious one. I imagine government to be in the grip of a rising Fourth Reich.

I imagine the apologetic speeches my friends deliver from the dispatch box, making what case they can for policy. They explain that, however awkward, it seems best for the moment to stay, as a moderating influence ...

It's surprising how easy this exercise proves. And depressing how few pass my final test: I ask myself — of each — if there is any conceivable point at which he or she says, 'So far and no further,' and simply quits.

I know some civilized men who would stay. But Howe wouldn't. Things would have to get bad, mind you, but that's not the point: in the end, he would quit. So he gets my vote.

Such thoughts were far away last Thursday when, crossing the corridor behind the Speaker's chair to get to the *Times* room, I happened upon Sir Geoffrey.

'Matthew,' said Sir Geoffrey, 'did you see the row this afternoon between Ted Heath and Bernard Braine? Splendid for your parliamentary sketch! You'll have fun with that.'

I nodded, wretchedly. How could I tell him? 'Spit it out,' I said to myself, '*now*. Get it off your chest, or you'll feel terrible all night.'

But I couldn't. There was no way I could blurt out: 'Actually, Geoffrey, the reason I haven't done Ted and Bernard is that it's *you* I've done. The sketch I've just sent *The Times* is all about how you fell into Hattersley's trap this afternoon at PM's Questions.' So I made my excuses and left — then sat slumped at my desk and sat there, arguing with myself.

'Well, after all, he *did* walk into it ... I'm sure the other papers will say so too ... Anyway it was only a bit of fun, nobody thinks less of him for some trivial little parliamentary joke ... Hell, it was an *affectionate* sketch. They like being teased, don't they?

'No? Well, he realizes it's my *job*, surely? It's my duty to *Times* readers to show no preferences — anything else would be corrupt ... Oh, don't be pompous, Matt: Let's face it, you're just a little ****, sniping at your old chums for a living. And you didn't even dare tell him! A pointless way of being a creep, wasn't it, when he'll read it tomorrow anyway ... I know: I'll write an apologetic note ...

'*What?* For what? Just because you saw him in the corridor? Why would it make a difference if you hadn't? A sketchwriter can't apologize every time he makes a joke. Drip! You didn't send an apologetic note that day you bumped into Dame Jill Knight when you were just writing about the wildlife design on her dress, a panda covering her bust – "a giant panda", you had written – and she kissed you – and you said nothing. Judas!'

Lord, take away my cowardice, or my conscience. I don't care which, but hurry, as I can't stand much more. And please shower special blessings upon Sir Geoffrey, and Jill Knight. And I'm sorry about the panda.

11.6.90

Door to door with Ken

'DOES THE right hon gentleman ever watch *Spitting Image?*' Dennis Skinner asked the Chancellor of the Duchy of Lancaster, *alias* the chairman of the Conservative party, *alias* Kenneth Baker ... 'And has he seen his own puppet on this show? Does he know he's the only puppet who isn't human?'

Mr Baker smiled modestly. It was not for him to call himself *super-human;* but good that people had noticed. What image had the TV chappies chosen? A Greek god, perhaps? A comet? An eagle?

'And does he know that he is portrayed as a big fat slug?'

Mr Baker sat bolt upright, shuddering with momentary affront. The party chairman's pliable little horns waved and glistened in the TV lights. But anger passed swiftly. 'One finds,' he replied, giving Mr Skinner a big fat slimy grin, 'that the more ...' he paused, '... the more ... *significant* one becomes, the more ... *trenchant* ... become the images.'

Ah. Trenchant. Exactly the word one was looking for. Mr Baker takes his place alongside Idi Amin, George III and Caligula in the gallery of statesmen who have been viewed *trenchantly.*

As pure invective, the slug caricature has its merits. But to observe the great Mr B in action yesterday, was to observe not so much a nature documentary as a lesson in door-to-door salesmanship. We started with the apprentices. First questions were to the Energy Secretary, a very low-key John Wakeham. Mr Wakeham does not comment.

On Monday he proved equal to the task of not commenting on the costs of Sizewell B, not commenting on the future of nuclear power, the disposal of nuclear waste, and global warming. He was very amiable about it, but rather vague. 'Conferences do seem to have been taking place very regularly at all sorts of places,' he muttered. His manner is rather that of a gentleman collecting funds for the village church steeple.

Ian Bruce (C, Dorset S) auditioned next, a red-haired youth with glasses and an awkward but likeable manner. His assignment was to sell loft insulation to Mr Wakeham. He stuttered something about it being the 'most cost-effective way'. Scarcely the hard sell, though we might have bought a little, out of sympathy.

So junior minister Tony Baldry showed how it was done. In plummy tones he warbled about 'minimum warmth cavity wall slab insulation'. We all wanted some immediately.

Jimmy Hood (Lab, Clydesdale) demonstrated that time-honoured Scots folk wisdom: *'If at first you don't succeed, In wi' y' boot and in wi' y' heed,'* with a bold attempt at hawking a product with an image-problem. 'Scottish coal is consumer-friendly coal,' roared the hefty Glaswegian.

But Kenneth Baker wins the cup. Using a classic salesman's double-cross he got past the front door and into the lounge under the guise of a charity worker . . .

'If you had seen that Armenian school and the outstanding contribution to a very grave tragedy . . . a great tribute to British workmen . . .'

And then sold us a dodgy Tory prospectus.

But it was time for Mr Baker to go. The man from the Prudential, Sir Geoffrey Howe, was knocking at the door. The party chairman departed leaving just the hint of a silvery trail behind him.

26.6.90

Have car, will travel

'I HAVE it in mind,' Kenneth Baker said yesterday, 'to visit Bolton.' Mr Baker is in penitential mood, but is there no limit to his craving for self-abasement? He must be curbed, before he entertains dark thoughts of visiting Wigan, Salford or even Bootle.

Mr Baker was answering (he does, for five minutes every sixth Monday) as Chancellor of the Duchy of Lancaster. Besides being an MP, this office – to which some modest emoluments, happily, attach – is his main job. Quite incidentally he is also chairman of the Conservative party, an office he holds purely as a sideline, devoting to it what little spare time remains after his onerous work as Chancellor of the Duchy is done.

In his hobby as party chairman, two other lucky coincidences come to Mr Baker's aid. Lancaster carries with it a place in the Cabinet, and an official car.

It is not, of course, that the Chancellor of the Duchy would use his place at the Cabinet table to offer an opinion as Tory chairman. Perish the thought. It is just that, while he is there – *at* the table, so to speak – *as* Chancellor of the Duchy, it sometimes happens that the party chairman's view is sought. It can only then be courtesy for Mr Baker to say what he thinks a party chairman's view might be, if he were party chairman, which he is, but not, of course, at the time of speaking. It surely makes better sense than waiting until the meeting is over, rushing out ahead of the others, and addressing them a second time, on the stairs, as chairman?

Nor should it be suggested that a minister of the Crown would use his official car for party business. It is just that as Chancellor of the Duchy a fellow has to get about a bit: and what loss is there to the public purse if the Lancaster limo, taking him to the Duchy, should pause on the motorway hard shoulder for a few moments while Mr Baker nips up the embankment to say a few words at a cheese-and-wine party? This is just an enlightened sort of energy conservation. It is Lancaster which needs Mr Baker: not Mr Baker who needs Lancaster.

So it was churlish of Tony Banks (Labour, Newham NW) to suggest yesterday that the £21,060 that Mr Baker's Lancaster limo has cost so far this year was a case of 'the taxpayer subsidizing his increasingly ineffective activities as chairman of the Conservative party', or that last year's cost (£34,000) was a similar misuse.

Denying this Baker added that, as a past Greater London Council chairman, Banks himself doubtless knew a thing or two about official transport.

Banks resurfaced, four questions later, to pick a fight with an easier target: an elderly gentleman called Sir Geoffrey Howe. Banks asked Sir Geoffrey to arrange for a bicycle mileage allowance for MPs.

Anxious to avoid incivility, Sir Geoffrey replied that the idea had merit. Anxious to avoid civility. Mr Banks retorted that Mr Baker would probably want a tandem, 'with a member of the working class struggling to do the pedalling, at the front'.

Another slur! Baker is not so dumb. He would sit the pedalling prole on the *back* seat. Mr Baker himself would travel at the front, freewheeling, smiling, waving and ringing his bell.

23.10.90

5

Leaders —
and the Leadership

Mrs Margaret Mutt

THERE IS a method of interrogation commonly known as 'Mutt and Jeff' or 'the hard man and the soft man'.

Poor Mrs Thatcher. For the hard man to turn out to be a woman is an odd reflection on us men. She is certainly the most elegant Mutt ever to press a burning cigarette into a prisoner's forearm.

I am tramping my constituency this summer on a self-imposed 'non-election campaign'. People talk more naturally when one hasn't called for anything so vulgar as their vote. My constituents keep telling me the same thing. 'Oh yes, we agree with what she's trying to do, but she's too inflexible/extreme/authoritarian/harsh/uncaring/pushy ... she should compromise a bit ... need for consensus ... slow down ...'

My typical constituent's position is sharply critical of Mrs Thatcher's, yet on closer examination remarkably derivative of it. They want the same as her, but not quite so much, so fast, so soon, or so unremittingly.

Derivative in two ways: first, she has pioneered the direction, or at least popularized it. Secondly, their preference is moderate only by comparison with the pace she is trying to force.

People cannot see this at all. They seem to think that men like David Steel and Francis Pym are 'moderate' in some objective, timeless way, in a vacuum. The thought that by pitching her tent on a far perimeter Mrs Thatcher has enabled men like Steel or Pym to move their own tents forward, yet still be considered cautious, seems not to have occurred to them.

Jeff they inform me, would be 'firm' with the unions, but not 'provocative'. They do not see that Jim Prior's approach was cautious only by comparison with rumours about what Mrs Thatcher was urging.

Jeff, they tell me, would offer the teachers 'more'. They fail to see that it takes an offer of 4 per cent to make 8 per cent sound like 'more'.

So it is the soft man for whom, after six years of bruising battle, people hanker. And until he comes, Mrs Thatcher wades on, hatchet in hand, doing a great many people's dirty work, preparing the way for successors who will be called kinder and more amenable.

They will be the binders of wounds, the reconcilers of the nation – and I do not mean to mock them. Important reforms remain untackled and may be ventured upon only by a government which commands popular affection.

Nor will there be any shortage of contenders for the post. The British establishment is packed with natural Jeffs. They are dining all over

London as I write. They are two a penny and they will come back into their own not long from now.

Not like Mrs Thatcher. She is nobody's choice for an evening at the club, or pub. Edgy, earnest, blinkered and moralizing – what a bore!

Jeff will eventually usher her out, pull up a chair with us, proffer the brandy and cigarettes, and we shall all breathe sighs of relief and say how we never really liked her all along, but hadn't thought it wise to say so.

With Jeff we shall achieve much – some of which was not possible before. To Jeff will go our gratitude. To Mutt should go the credit. She will not complain that she does not get it.

22.8.85

Priscilla the peril

TO MAKE space for her, Cabinet colleagues shuffled bottoms sideways in a series of furtive little bounces to ensure that none got too close. Upon every face was a smile but nobody wanted a cuddle. The PM sat down with a seemly gap to left and right.

Denis Healey once compared her to the deadly Upas tree. A vigorous and broad-branched tree, the Upas spreads wide; but nothing grows beneath its shade, and seedlings wither all around.

It was her tenth anniversary as Prime Minister and she was there to face PM's Questions.

The whips had put it about that the PM wished nothing to be made of the occasion, but Malcolm Bruce, for the Democrats, rather soured his own congratulations by asking her whether she would in future keep her mouth shut. Mrs Thatcher's reply – that to give him the answer he sought would be a logical impossibility – is probably the only thing she will ever say that would have pleased Bertrand Russell.

Neil Kinnock offered a dreary whine about St Francis of Assisi and his prayer. She replied – more in the spirit of Joan than Francis – that people were better off these days and knickers to anyone who said otherwise. Islington's Chris Smith (Lab) asked about the trade deficit and was told that we should be proud of Britain's overseas investments, so suck. Alf Morris (Lab, Wythenshawe) asked about the National Health Service proposals and she replied that there were more funds, more nurses, and more doctors than ever, so yah boo sucks. Jim Sillars

(SNP, Glasgow Govan) said Britain was betraying the people of Hong Kong. Mrs Thatcher replied that we weren't and anyway Sillars had asked that last time and hadn't he anything new to say, and yah boo sucks with knobs on.

Knickers, knickers, knickers. What are we to make of it? When we were young, there were two different kinds of girl who were entirely maddening in the playground. One type was horrid and contrary. She spoilt the boys' games, used rude words, carved obscenities on desks, and never, never owned up. She is immortalized in the *Dandy* as Beryl The Peril.

The other sort was the goody-goody. I remember a boyhood nightmare called Priscilla. Priscilla always got full marks for her homework and never let you copy. Priscilla used only polite language and was the only girl ever to get 50 out of 50 for presentation.

Listening to the Prime Minister yesterday, the secret of her maddening effectiveness dawned on me. Margaret Thatcher is both little girls, Beryl and Priscilla, in one.

For these last ten years she has been shouting the polite equivalent of knickers to all and sundry, without ever offending good manners, using bad words, or engaging with any serious thought anyone has ever put to her. And why not? She knows what she wants and knickers to anyone who disagrees.

Sometimes, yesterday, when they barracked her, Mr Speaker fidgeted nervily, concerned that a lady's courtesy should be so abused. For is she not the very model of civilized behaviour? Mrs Thatcher is the politest, most genteel nose-thumber in history. These ten years past have been the longest continuous nose-thumb ever recorded.

5.5.89

Ways not to treat a lady

BRITISH TELECOM have just published a booklet teaching us how to improve our telephone techniques.

Written by a psychiatrist, it tells us that all telephone-users fall into one of four human types. He defines these types, and then, to help us find out which type we are, he offers a test – we choose between images of squiggly little shapes, and these choices (apparently) give the game away. I now believe that the same psychotherapeutic analysis is needed for male MPs in their approach to Mrs Thatcher.

Englishmen have always had serious problems in dealing with women, but the advent of a woman leader is throwing these problems into ghastly relief for the 607 men in Parliament. It is quite wrong to think this is due to some defect in her; the problem is ours, and the sooner we face it the better.

At the root of the problem is the British Male's complete inability to relate to women except in the roles of little girl or big mama. Apart from the fact that this horribly confuses most men's sex lives, it can be highly irritating for the women themselves, who are for the most part neither. And it is certainly irritating for Mrs Thatcher.

It will be helpful at this stage if we define the male types with which we are dealing.

There are four: two principal types, each dividing into two sub-groups. The two principal types (as I have suggested) are those who see Mrs Thatcher as a little girl, and those who see her as a Great White Mother. We shall call these prime groupings the *Dominant* and the *Subservient* types. All male politicians incline to one or the other.

These two types split into two sub-groups, depending upon whether the male in question likes or dislikes Mrs Thatcher.

Thus we have four categories: *Dominant-sympathetic, Dominant-hostile, Subservient-sympathetic*, and *Subservient-hostile*.

Dominant-sympathetic is basically the fatherly sort. To feel fatherly about Mrs Thatcher you have to feel pretty posh yourself, so this type is typically found among the Tory knights-of-the-shires. Sir John Stokes (Halesowen) is an example, as was Sir Peter Emery (Honiton) in PM's Questions yesterday. So is Lord Whitelaw. This type speaks of (and to) her as though she were a favourite (or, occasionally, errant) daughter. Sometimes – it happened yesterday – a young whippersnapper like the Afro-bearded Jerry Hayes (Harlow) attempts the same patronizing manner.

She adopts, towards all, the withering cordiality of an old fool's favourite daughter.

Dominant-hostile is the approach of the headmaster to the silly schoolgirl. Denis Healey is the most famous exemplar: he can belittle in a relaxed, self-assured way.

This is the approach Mrs Thatcher finds hardest to handle. It is one reason why Sir Peter Tapsell is not in the Government and Sir Ian Gilmour did not last. Jim Callaghan took this sneering line with her, to great effect, when he was Prime Minister.

Neil Kinnock tried it, yesterday, but (though his question about water charges was splendid) Mrs Thatcher still escaped with her life because, at heart, Mr Kinnock is not *Dominant*, but *Subservient-hostile*.

This is basically the plaintive approach: 'Please stop whipping us, you cruel woman.' It is the theme of today's Labour Party. These men have thought themselves into the political equivalent of what Soho calls 'bondage'. Lesser women than Mrs Thatcher cater to lesser men than Mr Kinnock by sticking advertisements in telephone kiosks – for 'discipline' and the like. Though the words cry 'Stop!' the subtext cries 'More!' Mrs Thatcher gives them more.

And that leaves the *Subservient-sympathetic* group. Most Tory backbenchers fall into it. They are, so to speak, Mrs Thatcher's love-slaves. Their purpose is but to adore. Harry Greenway (Ealing N) contrived a delightful *exemplette*, yesterday, on the unlikely theme of a National Freight Corporation buyout, and fully deserved the brief, chill smile she reserves for her little helpers on these occasions.

He got it.

8.2.89

They shoot horses

THE QUESTION has to be asked: Is the Prime Minister on crack? This drug is said to produce a feeling of mildly aggressive well-being. Nothing better described Mrs Thatcher, yesterday, reporting on the Paris summit.

'The vast majority of people in the streets of Paris were cheering,' she told an astonished Chamber, 'and saying "Madame *T'atcher*, Madame *T'atcher*!"'

But who should wonder – for she projected a kaleidoscope of global certainties.

'Every free country in the world is a *capitalist* country!'

'And then we discussed the Uruguay Round ...'

'And we have some *excellent* meteorologists.'

For had she not just returned from the biggest acid-house party of them all?

These gatherings are now very common. Guests party the night away. Some think they can fly. Others that they can reduce inflation to 4 per cent by next year. Some think they can stare at the sun. Others that they can conquer the Third World debt crisis. At its wildest extreme, guests even come to believe that they can reduce agricultural subsidies.

These people need help. Yesterday, Labour's Brian Wilson (Cunningham N) tried a douche of scepticism.

'Isn't that just *typical* of the pathetic small-mindedness of the Opposition?' she retorted. 'That's *just* what they are like!'

Mrs Thatcher gave us a taste, yesterday, of her new style: a punchy but often jokey grande dame. 'Wait a moment, wait a *moment*,' she scolded Eric Heffer (Lab, Liverpool, Walton).

As for Mrs Thatcher's career, there is much partying in Paris still to come. 'Why limit your timescale?' she replied, when Dennis Skinner suggested the next election might blow the whistle.

We have a word of advice. The 'high' she was enjoying yesterday needs ever larger doses of stimulant – experts warn – simply to maintain the same level of elation. Soon she will need a mega-party in a major European capital at least once a week. How much longer can she keep up the waltz?

They Shoot Horses, Don't They?

18.7.89

Hit and run

WALKING IN Blackpool, I glanced into an amusement arcade. A young girl was playing at one of those car-chase games, where (hunched behind an imaginary wheel) trees, pedestrians and crash barriers flash at you from all directions on a screen.

She was wholly absorbed. As she opened the throttle, teeth clenched, her eyes had a manic expression. I walked on. At the newsagents the headline asked: 'Can Maggie save the day?' Later, at the Empress Ballroom, the Empress herself was to help us answer that question.

To the strains of 'Oh I Do Like To Be Beside The Seaside', Mrs Thatcher appeared in royal blue, pearls, and what seemed to be a diamond replica of a military medal pinned to the shoulder of a jacket cut in the 'power-dressing' style.

And she was away. With more poise than I have ever observed in her before, she began to extol the virtues of liberty, charity and Kenneth Baker.

Much followed. There was the fond glance at Denis as she announced the end of the 'earnings rule', which taxed elderly pensions. There was the journey of Challenger II to Jupiter and Mars, which proved the need for Mr Patten's new litter Bill. But it was when she spoke of Freedom that a strange insight dawned. Where had I seen that manic look before? Yes! The girl in the amusement arcade, on the car-chase machine!

For is our Prime Minister not the ultimate hit-and-run driver?

It was Ted who gallantly opened the car door to her. She grabbed the wheel, floored the accelerator and threw him out. Passengers counselled caution — Jim Prior, Francis Pym — and she threw them out too. Willie Whitelaw clung grimly to the bonnet as she swerved onwards.

Sometimes there was the sound of sirens. Sometimes she bounced off crash barriers, leaving pedestrians bleeding in the road. Sometimes there were flashing blue lights in her rear-view mirror. Always she hit the gas pedal and accelerated out of it.

Once, on a bend called 'Belgrano' she almost overturned. Then she lost her way and crashed straight through a helicopter factory. Did she stop? Did she heck!

Just at present the sirens grow louder, the Law closer. Chewing Polo mints and praying hard, she obeys every road sign and drops temporarily within the speed-limit — 'what, me, officer?' 'We will never privatize the NHS,' she declared yesterday. 'We were never going to!' How she longs for the open road ...

But that look in her eyes as she barked the word 'freedom'! As thousands cheered and Whitelaw, tears streaming down, bellowed like a beached hippo, I fancied her — even then — to reach in her handbag for another 50p piece, and fumble for the throttle-lever.

Sixty-four today, and the oldest girl in the amusement arcade. Just one more game, O Lord, just one more game!

14.10.89

Cool high noon

ANOTHER DAY, another scrap. Or so we thought as she sailed in for a routine skirmish on the Commonwealth. But what did *she* think? Did she know, as she entered the Chamber in dove grey and pearls – her hair perfect – that the Foreign Secretary beside her was about to become one of the shortest-lived in that post in history?

She *must* have had some foreknowledge; yet, if she did, not a muscle betrayed it.

Did *he* know, that John Major, recently Chief Secretary, recently junior minister in the DHSS, recently unknown backbencher, recently nobody, suddenly Foreign Secretary – was poised to make the most astonishing leap of all? If he did, then the slight, grey figure seated by the Prime Minister's side, nodding gently and occasionally smiling an encouraging smile in her direction, gave no hint.

Her style yesterday? Much as ever, but with refinements urged on her by the television coaches. She had notes, yes: there is no autocue (yet) at Westminster. But reporters noticed that the typescript used had suddenly magnified enormously. Thus she could manage without her glasses, leave the text on the dispatch box and speak straight up into camera, glancing only occasionally down. Her hands quite still, as the TV boffins recommend. She did it well.

So much for style. Content? The usual, with knobs on. Through the swinging doors of the frontier drinking saloon she came, swiping wildly at anything which moved.

Nothing new, there. There was one in the jaw for President Mitterrand who wanted to renegotiate the Rome Treaty. One in the stomach for Canada, which was trading more than ever with South Africa. Up yours, Brian Mulroney.

A playful pat for Sonny Ramphal by way of 'tribute' ('She's been attacking him all week,' shouted Dennis Skinner) was followed by a quick jab at Robert Mugabe and the whole lot of them, 'sitting around being entertained in the most excellent circumstances' in Kuala Lumpur, deciding who should starve.

Surely she could not have known that her own Chancellor was about to resign?

Perhaps her riposte to Mr Kinnock did betray distraction. Patiently she had taken him from sulphur dioxide to carbon dioxide via sewage, rivers, a 'global ozone layer conference' to 'the North Sea'.

Then she seemed to lose heart. 'And so on and so forth,' she said, wearily. But it was a temporary lapse.

Dennis Skinner was the first to tell us. The House was bogged down in tedious debate about the allocation of time to the Companies and Children bills (Lords), when Skinner got up.

'The Government is in a shambles,' he said. He always does. Nobody took any notice. 'The Chancellor has resigned.'

Gobsmacked is the word I'd use to describe the face of David Mellor, the junior minister on the bench opposite.

27.10.89

The sadness of Nigel Mutt

'YOU'RE LOOKING very well, Enoch!' I once said to Mr Powell. He fixed me with a baleful stare. 'The Three Ages of Man,' he snorted: 'Youth . . .' He paused. 'Middle age . . .' Longer pause. 'And, "You're looking very well, Enoch."'

Nigel is looking very well. The Chancellor of the Exchequer was in robust form at Treasury Questions. To only a few was his secret sadness apparent. The reason? Mrs Thatcher now plans to go on, and on, *and on*.

Poor Mr Lawson. He will never be Prime Minister. Still, as my mother once said when I wasn't invited to a friend's party: 'You probably wouldn't have enjoyed it anyway, dear.'

Besides, the news that has taken the spring from the step of Mr Lawson has infused with a new warmth the smiles of the next generation down – the foremost among whom yesterday sat right next to him on the Treasury Bench: Mr John Major, Chief Secretary, victor of the Treasury crusade against spending ministers.

By instinct a thoughtful and solicitous man, ambition must now have redoubled Mr Major's natural concern for the PM's health. I imagine him leaping to help her down difficult steps, tenderly murmuring advice about wrapping up warm against winter. Major it was who had to take the flak (as a DHSS minister) for not giving extra heating benefit to pensioners during a cold snap. Ironic if a sudden chill should carry her prematurely off.

Perish the thought. Mr Major's grief would be real for he is a kindly soul, well suited to play the Soft Man, Jeff, in the 'Mutt and Jeff' method of police interrogation, leaning worriedly towards the prisoner: 'Here, have a cigarette, old man, and let me explain: my friend the Chancellor has a *very* nasty temper; frankly I'm as scared as you of what he might do – but you could rescue us both by just giving a little . . .' Mutt shifted testily on the green bench beside Mr Major. He was bored. For months he had dreamed of the Foreign Office. Why, he had been standingly ovated at Brighton for his thoughts on World Peace. And now these pesky MPs were asking him about the *Economy*.

What had that to do with him? Had he not woken the Economy up, bathed and dressed it and found its satchel? Had Mr Major not tied its shoelaces while Elaine Kellet-Bowman warned it about talking to strange men? Had he not seen it off at the garden gate bright as a button? Yes, he did read the newspaper reports about truancy; and no, it was quite grown up enough to take care of itself.

So when Labour's Mr Stuart Holland raised matters of such erudition that he gasped in the middle of his own question, the Chancellor's impatience surfaced in a reply so weary that he ceased bothering to finish off his words.

It was a particularly loutish PM's Question session. Mr Major looked anxious as Mrs Thatcher reached for a glass of water. Then came the Social Security Secretary's Statement which Mr John Moore survived well, though he can hardly have guessed how much one of the final sections of his statement meant to two people on the bench with him. Heating allowances for the elderly during cold snaps, he announced, were to be vastly improved.

Mr Major glanced, infinitely caringly, at the Prime Minister.

28.10.88

Therapy for an angry lady

AND WE should be very, *very* doubtful, the Prime Minister said yesterday, 'about transferring financial control to supernatural institutions'.

Well! Fancy that! One knew, of course, about the *supra*-national institutions: they were bad enough; but the thought that Keynesian phantoms might be tampering with our money supply was unnerving. A shriek in the night, a slight prickling along the back of the Chancellor's neck, and – *pouf!* – a mysterious jump in the retail price index and no clue but a faint whiff of cologne . . .

Cologne? Could that have been the reference to what Mrs Thatcher kept calling 'the *boondies-bank*'? It sounded spooky, especially when she linked it to someone called 'Otto'. It was all very mysterious.

Last week, this sketch accused the Prime Minister of treating the House to a demented rant. Well, it must have been nerves before Madrid as she prepared to do battle in the spectral world − for by yesterday calm had been restored, and she was a model of quiet lucidity.

I'm afraid we did have a little relapse with Neil Kinnock, but the provocation was intense. Whenever Mr Kinnock mentions inflation, something in Mrs Thatcher's brain seems to snap and she starts to holler.

'TWENTY-SEVEN PER CENT!' she yelled at the cowering ginger-nut opposite. She was referring to Labour's record in government, but the volume control had gone haywire.

In the next course of therapy we are devising for Mrs Thatcher, in a darkened room, she is to be shown slides of Mr Kinnock while she practices not shouting. As her resistance builds up, a looped tape of his voice saying − softly at first, then louder − thing like 'society', 'care' and 'community' will be played, while she tries to perform simple tasks without visible sign of distraction. The final stage will be a wall-to-wall screen of moving images of the Labour leader accompanied by the perorations from his speeches, with 'The Red Flag' playing insistently in the background. The Prime Minister will be asked to maintain a fixed smile and gently read from the Prayer of St Francis of Assisi.

30.6.89

Those in peril on the sea

AN EAGER young new boy once enthused to Churchill that it was a thrill to sit on the Government benches, surveying the enemy opposite. 'No sir,' Churchill is said to have retorted. 'Across the floor are the Opposition. The enemy is all around you.'

Mrs Thatcher sat, yesterday − tense, composed − facing an Opposition attack from shadow chancellor John Smith.

He welcomed the new Chancellor. Mr Major, he said, had been 'Kuala-Lumpured' as Foreign Secretary in October, only to face being 'Strasbourged' as Chancellor next month. We glanced at Geoffrey Howe, badly Bruged in a Continental road accident last year.

Mr Smith's greatest good-fortune yesterday was Mr Robin Maxwell-Hyslop (C, Tiverton).

All but skewered by a demand (from Northampton's Tony Marlow) that he list Labour's conditions for entry into the ERM, Mr Smith couldn't think of any, on the instant.

He didn't have to. Maxwell-Hyslop started a series of disruptive 'points of order' and, while the House bayed, Mr Smith wrote out some policies on an envelope, then read them – despite, he said, 'organized wrecking tactics from the benches opposite'.

I must advise Mr Smith that Robin Maxwell-Hyslop is a *dis*organized wrecking tactic.

Major got better as he went on. But he did go on – and on. He was best when sparring with substantive interventions, answering figures with figures, for which, happily, Mr Major seems to have some kind of a facility.

'Why,' shouted a Labour heckler, 'did Lawson resign?'

And in due course, Mr Lawson rose to speak.

Grim, pale and strained, he stared around the Chamber. 'That article,' he said – he meant the offending article in which Mrs Thatcher's adviser, Sir Alan Walters, had called the European Monetary System 'half-baked' – 'that article was significant' (and he paused) 'only in that it represented the tip of a singularly ill-concealed iceberg ...' Mrs Thatcher turned her face, expressionless, towards him ... 'with all the destructive potential that icebergs possess.'

You could have heard a pin drop.

I scanned the Government benches. The tips of a dozen singularly ill-concealed icebergs heaved gently in the swell. The rounded surface of Ted Heath rose and fell on the forward bench. Near him a jagged pinnacle they call Ian Gilmour spiked through the waves. John Biffen, innocent above water, lethal beneath, lay behind. And – right over to one corner – Michael Heseltine, the ultimate hazard to shipping, glinted in the television lights – razor-sharp with all the destructive potential that *he* possesses.

How is she to navigate a passage through all this? Can she trust her first mate, Sir Geoffrey Howe? Can she rely on her new pilot, John Major? Was that a smooth rock, just under water on the other side, or was it Kenneth Baker? And where was Douglas Hurd? Sitting on the steps, some distance away – plenty beneath the surface there ...

Some of these could sink her, now. And, all around lesser perils bobbed up and down in the waves: backbenchers she had disappointed, and the flotsam and jetsam of discarded junior ministers.

A sea of troubles. Ah for that trusty old ice-breaker, HMS *Whitelaw*! Why ever did they decommission him?

1.11.89

After the event

THERE NOW *follows a review of this morning's Press.*

Following his shock victory in the Tory leadership election over the weekend, Sir Anthony Meyer has gone to ground. Senior Conservatives, however, have been talking freely to journalists and their comments dominate the front pages of today's papers.

It appears that Sir Anthony was far more widely admired than had been suspected.

The *Daily Telegraph* leads with an exclusive interview with party chairman, Kenneth Baker. 'I always said,' comments Baker, 'that this election was a distraction. And what a marvellous and helpful distraction it has been. It is no secret that many had doubts about the previous leadership. What I think Anthony did was to focus those doubts and courageously to resolve them.

'In this great purpose, Ant will have guessed, I know, that he has had my quiet support throughout. I should be honoured to serve him.'

A number of junior ministers, previously thought to be hostile to Sir Anthony's ambitions, have emerged through this morning's papers as supporters. The *Independent* quotes Michael Howard, the 'dry' water minister, as backing Meyer's opposition to the poll tax. 'I always said,' says Howard, 'that only loyalty kept me from mentioning my doubts about this farce.' Every minister interviewed praises Meyer, most referring to secret doubts about the previous leadership.

The Times quotes a speech pre-released by Michael Heseltine, hailing Meyer as 'English visionary and European prophet'. 'Anthony dreams dreams,' Mr Heseltine will say to the Henley Dyno-Rod operatives' annual dinner tonight. '*We* must awake and make them reality.'

In *Today*, Norman Tebbit puts it more bluntly, under the slogan: 'TURN TO TONY!' 'Tone and I,' he says, 'are very different blokes. He's a philosopher. I'm a kicker of backsides. I always said we need both. Tone knows that.'

From elsewhere on the backbenches the unanimous chorus of approval is maintained. Beneath the *Daily Mail's* banner headline THE IRON DONKEY, influential Tory backbencher Anthony Beaumont-Dark (who had earlier described Meyer as 'not so much a stalking horse: more a stalking donkey') clarifies his thoughts: 'This magnificent beast,' he says (referring to the donkey), 'is rightly celebrated for its iron will and endurance. Yet it is also famous for the gentleness we respect in Tony, too. Naturally I voted for him.

'His first task will be to bring new blood into the ministerial ranks. I always said ...'

The scoop of the day, however, goes to the *Guardian*, which carries an anonymous eyewitness account of the vote in the Tory 1922 Committee. Apparently the vote revealed a small majority for Sir Anthony.

The announcement, says the *Guardian*, was accompanied by a vigorous and unanimous thumping of desks. Committee chairman Cranley Onslow explained this seeming about-turn: 'It is not always easy – even for the MP himself thumping the desk – to know at the time whether it is a hostile or friendly thump. Subsequent events have helped us to clarify. I have always said ...'

Sir Anthony himself, apparently, was carried out – too shocked to speak.

28.11.89

Taking no part

THE STAIRCASE outside our Westminster room has a dustbin-alley air. Overshadowed by the black metal caging of an ancient lift, it is cluttered with bins of old papers. You don't expect to meet the Prime Minister there.

So, walking to the stairs just as a colleague asked me how many rebels would surface today, I flung open the door with a confident declaration. 'Sixty,' I said. And stared point-blank into Mrs Thatcher's eyes.

I felt myself blushing. What do you *say*? I was seized with an absurd desire to sing '*green bottles, hanging on a wall, sixty green bottles ...* – Oh! Good afternoon, Prime Minister. Fancy seeing you here!' ... but suppressed it, and stood mute.

Mrs Thatcher glanced at me for a micro-second, and – almost on the instant – addressed her Parliamentary Private Secretary: 'Ah, Mark, I think it's one floor further down.' I heard her voice trailing down the next flight of stairs: 'It's *such* a labyrinth ...'

She was on her way from casting her vote in the Committee Room above, whither your sketchwriter quickly scarpered.

Like small craft scattered and bobbing in the wake of some great ship, the journalists who had gathered there were still agitated by the Prime Minister's recent passage. They were interviewing each other, notebooks and pencils in hand.

'What did she say? Did *you* hear anything?'

'Would you say she looked worried? Or would *dignified* sound better?'

'*Tense but composed*, old boy. Did you catch what Ted said a moment ago, when we asked how he'd voted?'

'Yes. "I always accept my responsibilities." At least we think that's what he said. It was a bit plum-in-mouth.'

'What are we saying he meant by that?'

'The consensus up here is that it was like Heseltine's "I will take no part in this process." It's what we call a "Bush" remark.'

'Hear, hear!'

'Ah' (pause). 'And what are we saying is meant by a "Bush" remark?'

'We aren't saying.'

'Maybe we mean a "*beating* around the bush" remark?' I piped up. Withering silence.

'Did you hear about Dennis Skinner?' (I took out my own notebook.) 'Came up here earlier on, poked his head into the Committee Room, came out and announced that he'd seen a Tory filling in his ballot-paper in front of the 1922 Chairman. Said it proved they're being bullied.'

'Are we believing that?' I asked.

'On the whole we're sceptical.'

We fell silent at the approach of Alan Haselhurst, who had just voted. Journalists circled in like vultures. Norman Fowler hove to.

'You're all ticking us off as we come out, aren't you?' he exclaimed, in genial admonition. And it was true: we did appear to be trying to conduct some sort of exit poll and it struck me as somehow unseemly to be part of it, having myself been a Conservative MP until not so long ago. I left.

Denis Healey passed me on his way to the Committee Corridor, eyebrows beetling famously: 'I want to vote in the Tory leadership election. Where can I apply to join? *You* should remember.'

I returned to the *Times* room. 'How would you have voted?' someone asked me.

I wonder.

6.12.89

In combative form

ON LONDON'S South Bank, the political event of the week was about to occur. Mr Brian Walden was about to withdraw his support from Mrs Thatcher's leadership.

How would she react? I watched the occasion on television, forming so clear a view of the Prime Minister's performance that there seemed no need to check my recollection against that of others.

Or so I thought. Then came yesterday's newspapers. '**Resolute**,' said the *Financial Times*.

'Hm,' one thought, 'well, the *FT* does need to maintain a certain dignity. But perhaps the *Guardian* will sock it to 'em ...'

'**Sticks to tough line**', read its front page.

'True as far as it goes', one thought, 'but what about the really interesting thing? Perhaps it will be in *The Times*?

'... **Showed commendable good sense**' – no, not there. The *Telegraph* perhaps?

'**In combative form**' – nor there. I waited for the London *Evening Standard*. '**Confident and characteristically assertive**'.

I sat down in bewilderment. Was Sunday a dream? Was I plagued by delusions from which the rest of the world was free?

Had I just *imagined* that I saw a woman going completely crackers?

It took me back to an unhappy encounter I once had in a number 77 bus with an elderly lady who thought I wished to make an indecent approach. She was in combative form (*Telegraph*) as she swung at me with a plastic bag, screaming accusations.

I denied them. Sticking to her tough line (*Guardian*) she repeated herself half a dozen times and told me to get off. I said it was she who should move but she was resolute (*FT*). I challenged her to substantiate her accusations but, showing commendably good sense (*Times*), she refused to be drawn. Finally, as we reached Vauxhall Bridge, she moved off to berate one of the other passengers. She was confident and characteristically assertive (*Standard*) to the end, when they took her away.

31.10.89

Cat on a hot tin roof

As WE go to press, a dramatic rooftop protest continues. On the roof of Number 10 Downing Street one of the most hardened inmates the place has ever known, a certain Margaret Thatcher, is still refusing to come down. We are looking at a desperate woman.

She came from nowhere in 1975 and scaled the perimeter fence of a crusty old political party. In a daring raid in 1979 she snatched the keys from 'gaoler' Jim Callaghan and stormed the country.

But then in 1981 she seemed to be cornered. Having laid waste large sections of manufacturing industry and with no relief in sight, a whole artillery of menacing opinion polls had Thatcher at bay.

How she gave them the slip, no one can quite remember but (like many a convict before her) she sought her fortunes abroad and distinguished herself in a foreign war. By 1983 there was no restraining her and she stormed the country yet again.

From 83 to 87 she laid low. There were a few hairy moments – most notably when she took on another battle-scarred street-fighter by the name of Scargill. But she saw him off. Indeed there were few who could stand up to her. One by one, the senior officers most experienced at dealing with this offender retired or were fired. 'Warder Willie' (who had talked her down from many roofs in his time) was transferred to a gaol down the road with red leather benches. 'Gentleman' Jim Prior was already there – as were two old lags from her foreign adventures, Carrington and Pym.

'Paddy' Jenkin joined them. Patrick had never entirely recovered from horrific wounds inflicted when she used him as a human battering ram ('Secretary of State' she called it) in her successful break-in at County Hall, London. In each of these attacks she had personally been triumphant, but each had taken its toll on her followers, and comrades-in-arms were usually mutilated beyond recovery.

One key comrade, a fellow they called 'Tarzan', noticed the fate of all who fought with her and did a runner. He grassed – turned Queen's evidence – on one of her worst capers. This had happened at a helicopter factory through which she smashed her getaway car. A passenger, now known on the Continent as 'Commissioner' Leon, was maimed; but the woman herself escaped. And again she stormed the country in 1987.

By now you would have thought that her appetite for adventure was satisfied. Not so. A shootout in the nation's schools was closely followed by a showdown with the nation's nurses. Then she attacked the doctors, took a swipe at some lawyers, flogged off a swagbag of water companies and pitched into some ambulance workers.

There seemed to be no stopping her. Yet again, there were costs. One of her oldest partners in crime, a man they called 'the Chingford Strangler', had already wearied of aggro, and hung up his jemmy in a late bid for respectability. Ken 'The Bouncer' Clarke won the GPs' and ambulance workers' scraps for her, but he won't bounce again for quite some time. And when 'Bully' Lawson quit – fed up with her habit of shin-kicking her own mates just for a laugh – she lost a heavyweight.

It looked bad to her followers too. She had started with a fair number of fans. The woman was a gangster from the start, but gangsters can be popular – when they're winning. Yet with every run-in she made new enemies. At first it didn't matter. But as nurses added to teachers, added to dons, added to civil servants, added to ambulance workers ... the followers grew more ragged. And the team grew more ragged too. Nearly all the old fighters were gone and those who remained were wounded.

Yet at this point she launched her most outrageous assault of all. She picked a fight with half her own team, local authorities, householders across the nation, and tens of millions of her fans, all at the same time.

Battle has been raging now for more than a month. Our heroine is on the roof and chucking tiles in all directions. She is surrounded, at bay, and yet defiant. Megaphone in hand she assails the crowd below with statistics, Biblical quotations and ritual abuse.

One by one her original army has deserted her. Some slipped quietly away before she emerged on the roof. Others have been talked down by teams of pollsters and political commentators. Only a few remain.

There is John Major – though some see him more as a chaplain and psychiatrist. There is Chris Patten – though rumour has it that he is as much a hostage as a willing combatant. There is Douglas Hurd – though he is suspected of being a law officer under deep cover, sent in to relay messages to and from the real world. There is Geoffrey Howe, and of course there is old Nick 'Scarface' Ridley, faithful to the end.

What are the odds? Roofs don't come hotter – yet this cat has nine lives.

My own guess? I'd say it was the eighth. The Prime Minister is on her penultimate roof.

13.4.90

Mild turns to bitter

ALL ALONG the rabbit warrens inhabited by journalists at Westminster, a tannoy system crackles occasionally into life with urgent information. At ten to four yesterday came a warning hiss . . .

'*Attention! Attention! In view of Sir Geoffrey Howe's personal statement, there will be no four o'clock.*'

We looked at each other, incredulous. Our deputy prime minister (resigned) – the mildest of men – has never been suspected of so much as wrenching petals from a marigold, let alone hours from the day. Colleagues explained. At four o'clock, Bernard Ingham (Mrs Thatcher's press secretary) gives a briefing for lobby correspondents. They expected as much, yesterday, but it seems that Sir Geoffrey's personal statement to the House (scheduled for 4.15) had intervened.

It was only the first of Mr Ingham's disappointments.

'*Oi! Bernard!*' – one of the journalists, leaving the press gallery after Sir Geoffrey's speech, called across to the PM's press secretary – 'that certainly got *her*, middle stump!' Mr Ingham stormed forward, wordless, his face like thunder.

What a pity the word 'devastating' has been drained of meaning by journalistic overuse, for it was never so apt as yesterday. When can so much powder have been kept so dry for so long? Outsiders sensed, as much in the gasps of the packed chamber as in Sir Geoffrey's words themselves, how much greater was the impact on a House which knows the unvarying low-key style this man has adopted over the last twelve years. The urgency of feeling reminded your sketchwriter how seldom the quality of earnestness is sensed these days in the parliamentary performances of any but the mad, or impotent.

Mrs Thatcher started with a look of tense composure and a faint smile. The composure held, the tension grew, and the smile disappeared. As for her senior colleagues, they were trying to remain expressionless, often with difficulty.

John MacGregor, John Major, Kenneth Baker and Norman Tebbit were all to be seen with hands raised to mouths, chins, and (in Mr MacGregor's case at one point) eyes, too.

Michael Heseltine sat, strained, watchful. A gentle smile flickered across Ted Heath's relaxed features, while Sir Geoffrey spoke of Mrs Thatcher's 'nightmare' vision of 'a continent positively teeming with ill-intentioned people, scheming . . .' Poor Mrs Thatcher could have looked around, across, behind her and above – and reflected that the nightmare was closer than Calais. And she was not dreaming.

That will teach her to take a fellow's country house away. If this wasn't Mrs Thatcher's Waterloo, then it was undoubtedly her Clapham Junction.

14.11.90

First ballotah

TORY LEADERS used to 'emerge' but now we have democracy. Democracy among Tory MPs, as Julian Critchley has explained, is the system under which the common will is least likely to triumph. Events of the past week prove it.

Half the Tory backbenchers you talk to subject you to a private harangue about how much nicer it would be if Mrs Thatcher could be surgically removed and somebody cuddly put in her place quickly, before the next election.

'But would you vote that way?' one asks.

'On the second ballot, yes,' they reply.

'What about the first ballot?'

'Ah.'

Ah. We could summarize the problem as the *first ballotah* dilemma. How to get from here to the second ballot without passing through a first ballot on the way. The crocodile has been goaded into the shallow water, but who is to stick in the knife? The first lunge might not kill; she might make it back into the deep water; her teeth are sharp and her memory is long. Legs could subsequently be bitten. So they all stand gingerly by the edge of the pool, muttering about 'loyalty' as the sharp-toothed one thrashes around on the mud bank.

Mr Critchley, I think, would like to go back to the old system, but nostalgia is pointless.

Nor is it reasonable to accept the existing system but ask the MPs to be braver. If they were brave they would not be MPs. An MP has been selected, elected and promoted for his circumspection. All his political life he has been punished for any tendency to say things that elements of his audience may not wish to hear.

My own proposals go with the Pavlovian grain. At present it is up to the prospective candidate to decide whether or not to stand. He 'lets his name go forward'. Why? That attracts unnecessary odium. Why not enter the name of anyone who has been proposed and seconded, regardless of whether he *says* he wants to run. We know he wants to run.

My second proposal goes further. Voting among MPs for the leadership is by secret ballot, and that is as it should be. You see who wins, then let it be discreetly known that this was your choice too, protected by the cloak of secrecy. Why, then, deny the candidate that cloak? Why can't Tories stand secretly for the leadership?

I can guess what you are thinking, but you are wrong. In the first ballot, MPs do not need to know for whom they are voting: they only need to know for whom they are *not* voting. The ballot paper would say '1: *Mrs Thatcher; 2: Not Mrs Thatcher; 3: Another Not Mrs Thatcher ... etc.*' If No 1 did not gain an overall majority there would be a second ballot and numbers 2, 3 etc. (who would have been voted for randomly) would be invited to say who they were. If we hadn't guessed already.

10.11.90

Standing below the parapet

IN THIS column on Saturday I floated the idea that Tories might stand for the leadership without revealing their identity. My telephone answering machine in Derbyshire has been working flat out to record the enquiries now being addressed to me.

Michael, from Henley, asks how it will be possible to mount a high-profile media campaign without telling people who you are. Easy, Michael. Discussions will be conducted like interviews with terrorists on TV: in the dark, so that no more than a silhouette can be seen.

Geoffrey, from Surrey, seems worried that 10 Downing Street might take reprisals. Chin up, Geoffrey. After a long association with a difficult or violent partner it is not uncommon to feel beset by irrational fears. Ask yourself what is the worst she can do. Has she not already done it?

Ken, from Mole Valley: Yes, if you have a problem about appearing in person without AutoScript, then you can give evidence on a video screen. You mastered that technique well at Bournemouth last month.

Chris, from Bath: Don't hang back! Even were you to attempt no disguise at all, she would be most unlikely to recognize you. After all, when did you last have her full attention?

Norman from Chingford asks how it will be possible for a candidate with a naturally abrasive manner to convey the full charm of that polecat quality from beneath the cloak of anonymity. May I suggest a stocking mask?

Douglas, from Oxfordshire, raises a personal concern. 'I am not too worried about being noticed while canvassing for myself,' he says, 'once I have got the difficulty of the crinkly hair straightened out. My problem is my funny voice. People do seem to recognize this. The PM herself certainly would; and would be displeased, I suspect, to know of my candidature, as I am – of course – running her own campaign.'

Easily solved, Douglas. Everyone knows your voice but nobody has seen you smile: so maintain a fixed grin and don't speak.

Edwina, of Derbyshire: You ask about concealing your own identity. Forget it.

Now, more thought needs to be given to the mechanics of the final contest itself. I am working at present along the lines of Cilla Black's *Blind Date* format. The candidates would sit, unlit, behind a screen. On the other side of the screen would sit – perhaps with Cilla herself – the chairman of the 1922 Committee, Cranley Onslow, asking the questions. But wait, my phone is ringing . . .

It is John, from Huntingdon. John is troubled by the possibility that a stint in a relatively high-profile job in recent months may have rendered his face and manner familiar to the public at large.

No worries there, John.

And who, now, is this on the line? Margaret from Finchley? *Anonymity*, did you say? Too late, Margaret. Far, far too late.

12.11.90

Call for Mrs Thasseltine

ONE AFTER the other they rose. Members of the party which, beneath the cloak of anonymity and in the shadows of Room 12 the evening before, had plunged in the knife, stood now in the light of the afternoon to congratulate their leader. With one voice they cheered her to the rafters as she entered the Chamber.

'Hear, hear, *hear*!' they bellowed.

One hundred and fifty open mouths in round faces; one hundred and fifty expensive suits; three score waistcoats covering three score plump stomachs; gold watch-chains, gold tie-pins, silk handkerchiefs billowing from top pockets ... the Tory party was marching behind its leader, every shiny shoe in step. It was a magnificent sight.

Of course 'hear, hear' has a certain anonymity. 'Hear, hear' is a noise, not an undertaking. 'Hear, hear' is not contractually binding and does not constitute an offer. So there was no shortage of mooing and yelping and growling in Mrs Thatcher's support yesterday.

Getting up to speak is rather different. You are all on your own, then. You have stood up, and you will be counted.

So when the Prime Minister had finished her statement, reporting the CSCE summit in Paris ('hear, hear!'), what could be seen differed strangely from what could be heard. The usual crowd – the place-men, job-seekers and fair-weather friends – sat motionless. And in their place rose a small and eccentric platoon: the men still willing to be numbered in her company.

They are best not named, for there were some brave supporters, careless of their own advantage, but there were also fools, ignorant of danger, and creeps so inured to creeping that they have forgotten the purpose of sycophancy.

More depressing to Mrs Thatcher even than the sneers of her enemies must be to observe the calibre of much of the band that still count themselves her friends.

For each, the Prime Minister had a word of gratitude. If we had not known that she was facing political death, nothing in her manner would have suggested it. Dressed in a mustard suit edged in black and pinned with a brooch shaped like a panther leaping, Mrs Thatcher's own expression was not unpantherlike. She looked as ready as ever to leap.

She delivered her statement like a robot, as usual, but sprang to life under hostile questioning, most notably from Tony Benn about war in the Gulf. Mrs Thatcher has never been comfortable dealing with the new 'moderate' Labour party, and flew at this representative of the old, familiar enemy with practised passion. They would miss each other, if she had to go.

She may, and everyone knows it. The search is on for a new leader. We do not yet know the identity, but we already know the qualities. The Tory party is looking for Mrs Thasseltine.

Mrs Thasseltine will be soft on Europe, but hard on parliamentary sovereignty; sweet on industrial partnership, but sour on government spending; warm on inner-city initiatives but cold on quangos; high on rhetoric but low on taxes.

Mrs Thasseltine will abolish the poll tax without restoring the rates. Mrs Thasseltine will give every backbencher a job. Mrs Thasseltine will not be Mr Heseltine. Mrs Thasseltine will not be Mrs Thatcher. Most important of all, Mrs Thasseltine will win the general election.

In the event that it proves otherwise, you may be sure that the next leader comes with neck already marked by an encircling dotted line in ballpoint pen: 'Cut here.'

22.11.90

Charmingly astray

ON THE stairs at the Savoy, yesterday, I found myself alongside an old friend on the Tory backbenches.

'Why,' I asked, 'did you vote for Douglas Hurd as party leader? You do not agree with him on Europe; you intensely dislike the Foreign Office; and you advocate a rigid monetarism which none have ever associated with Mr Hurd.'

'Douglas's views on almost every subject are anathema to me.'

'Then why,' I persisted, 'did you vote for him?'

My friend paused. 'It is plain,' he said, 'that a Tory leader's task is to lead Tories astray. But if I am to be led astray, I want it to be done stylishly. Of the candidates on offer, I took the view that Douglas would betray us with more intelligence and charm than the others.'

We continued our walk together, for we were going to the *Spectator* 'Parliamentarian of the Year' luncheon. The recipient of the award was Mr Hurd. He gave one of the best speeches of its kind I have heard: stylish, intelligent, charming. With a hint of self-deprecation he beguiled us, teasing his enemies in an always gentlemanly way; and taking us just a little – never too far – into his confidence. One departed filled with an approving glow for this polished parliamentarian.

Mr Hurd had left slightly ahead of us, to field Foreign Office Questions.

Tam Dalyell (Lab, Linlithgow) asked about the ecological disaster threatened by war in the Gulf but Mr Hurd's reply was most persuasive: if we were to funk our duty to resist aggression when the aggressor showed the capability to do great harm, even a Hitler would have gone unchallenged.

'*Hear, hear!*' – But, hold on: was that *quite* fair to Mr Dalyell? Tam's case is not, after all, that no aggressor should be resisted but that it is worth doing the sums before deciding to pick a vast oilfield as the place on which to fight. Perhaps he deserved a slightly less generalist argument in reply?

From Tony Marlow (C, Northampton N) on his own backbenches, Mr Hurd listened to the argument that others should contribute more, because their dependence on Arab oil was greater. The Foreign Secretary found this coarse.

'If we'd been concerned with oil,' he said, soothingly but ever so slightly affronted, 'we'd have settled a long time ago.' An early deal with Iraq would have secured supplies.

The Tory side liked that. They had not realized that we were quite so noble as to be *forgoing* oil in the cause of valiant little Kuwait.

'*Hear, hear!*' But, hold on: was this argument entirely honest? Is this dispute only about Kuwait and existing oil supplies? Is it not also about Saudi Arabia, and future oil supplies? Mr Hurd spoke of principle, but, when Iraq was gassing Kurds, was he much exercised? Ah, perhaps he was not Foreign Secretary at the time.

I watched Mr Hurd: deft, nimble, assured, 'safe hands', 'bottom', gravitas, decent, courteous ... we have heard the thesaurus.

But was he *right*? And did he *believe* all this? And, if he didn't, how would you know?

29.11.90

All is safely gathered in

THE JOURNALISTS' church of St Bride's in Fleet Street should hold an additional harvest thanksgiving service this week, for media people to offer gratitude for the windfall of the Tory leadership crisis.

What a bonanza! '*Potosí!*' as Spaniards exclaim – referring to a Bolivian mountain composed entirely of silver. This yuletide there will be turkey galore for us all.

If a leadership crisis did not exist, it would be necessary to invent one. Maybe we did.

Can we spin it out to a third ballot, do you think? Three more days of views, opinion polls and comment? Three more days of rumour and gossip?

'I've got some good stuff from the Major camp,' I heard one lobby correspondent greet another in a Westminster corridor last week, 'discreetly rubbishing Hurd. I'm getting back to the Hurd camp for something to balance it, discreetly rubbishing Major. Should make a nice little piece.'

In the predatory pack that we media folk constitute, these, the lobby correspondents, are the big players: the condors of the team. If some great political beast seems to be limping or breathing hard, these are the ones who first dart in for an exploratory peck, while the rest of us hover at a distance, watching.

Should the beast then stumble, should its herd not gather to protect it, the lesser predators move in. Mongrels from the tabloids, jackals from the Sundays, pedigrees from the quality magazines converge. Magpies from the diary columns squeak and dive.

The beast is down and bellowing. In this, the last stage of the kill, the beast's fellow-beasts have retreated entirely, trampling her with their own hooves as they gallop over the skyline in a cloud of dust.

And now ground and sky are thick with scavengers. Some of the front-line predators turn to snap angrily at lesser tormentors trying to steal a share of the action.

Others are bigger-hearted. One such, remembering my own Christmas, handed me a South African radio interview the other day. 'Here,' he said, giving me a Johannesburg telephone number, 'have this. Leadership crisis.'

For I am part of the second wave, as much scavenger as predator. A sort of rook. Preening my glistening black plumage, I am conveyed in taxis from radio station to television studio to radio station ... Microphone on? Red light. Cue? Green light. And we're away with our profound thoughts.

'Mrs Thatcher is in deep trouble.' How deep? 'Very deep.' Terminal? 'Possibly.' Green light off. £20 plus VAT. '*Ping*,' goes the cash register. '*Taxi!*' Off to the TV studio.

Cameras rolling? 'Mrs Thatcher is in deep trouble.' *Ping!* £50 plus VAT ... Radio down-the-line telephone interview? Maybe; what time? 7.30 am? Do you pay? Ah, yes, well, I do have a phone by the bed. Give me a ring beforehand to wake me up, would you?

7.30. *Ring, ring*. 'Hello? What sort of man is Mr Major? Quiet, classless, blah, blah ... Heseltine? Showy, presidential, blah, blah, vote-winner, blah ... Hurd? Safe pair of hands, assured, blah, blah, establishment candidate, blah ... Who do *I* think will win? Who knows? *Ping!* £15 plus VAT. Roll over and go back to sleep.

Lord, send us a new Tory leader, but not just yet.

26.11.90

The Tribe

THERE WILL be people who will portray what has passed in recent days as an embarrassing lapse. Such people speak of chaos and confusion, of panic and self-destructive anger. Soon they will be referring to these past few weeks as an awkward wobble, when the Tory party temporarily took leave of its senses, then recovered its nerve.

Nothing could be further from the truth. As in some tribal folk-mystery, the Conservative party has suffered a great internal convulsion, triggered as much by the collective unconscious of the tribe as by any conscious plan to contrive its survival. They have not, as individual men and women, known what they were doing, but the tribe has known what it was doing, and has done it with ruthless efficiency. The instinct to survive has triumphed.

Not that they were aware of that. All they knew was that they were heading for disaster. Each had his own opinion as to why. What they concurred upon was the imminence of danger; and when they concurred on that, the convulsion began.

At their conference in Bournemouth, a strange, flat despair gripped the occasion. We all noticed it, but none of us knew how to interpret it. Then they began to fight. They lashed out at the media, they lashed out at Europe, they lashed out at the opposition, and they lashed out at each other. The tribe was in turmoil.

Michael Heseltine – as much, by now, a totem of dissent as a person – found members of the tribe dancing around him and chanting. He responded. The media took up the chant. Michael Heseltine started a teasing dance: was it a war dance? Nobody knew. He did not know himself.

At this point their leader took on the dervish character. Saddam Hussein said she was 'possessed'. In a series of sustained rants she stunned the Chamber, alienated half her party and scared hell out of most of us.

There followed a short silence, and then the murmurs began. They grew until an extraordinary thing happened. One of the elders of the tribe, Sir Geoffrey Howe, began to speak. He spoke almost in tongues: he spoke as he had never spoken. He poured down imprecations upon the head of the leader.

Around Mr Heseltine the dance now reached a pitch of excitement that demanded answer. He rose, took the dagger and stabbed her.

What happened next is folklore. With the leader now wounded, but still alive, her own senior tribesmen drew back with one accord and left her. Suddenly alone, she hesitated a moment, then staggered from the stage.

The tribe mourned her departure. Not falsely or without feeling, they wept. Then, last night, the final twist occurred. The tribe fell upon her assailant, Michael Heseltine, and slew him, too – with many shouts of anger. Real anger.

All drew back, and the new leader, already blessed by the old leader, clean, apart, and uninvolved, stepped forward. With cries of adoration, the tribe gathered around him.

It could have been done as a ballet. It had all the elements of a classical drama. Like Chinese opera or Greek tragedy, the rules required that certain human types be represented; certain ambitions be portrayed; certain actions punished. Every convention was obeyed: every actor played out his role. The dramatic unities of time, place and action were fulfilled. It started in autumn 1990, and ended in the same season; it started in Committee Room 12 at Westminster, and ended there.

It started with an old leader, who was assassinated as she deserved; then her assassin was assassinated, as he deserved. Then the new leader stepped forward; and here the ballet ended.

And the tribe danced. As I write, they are dancing still.

28.11.90

Boring us out of business

A GROUP of reporters and political sketchwriters sipped tea yesterday in a Commons cafeteria. Despair gripped us. It was 3.40, just after Prime Minister's Questions. One spoke. He voiced the mood of all.

'If people are going to be moderate, reasonable and fair-minded, they have to be got rid of. They are no use to us.'

Yesterday was John Major's debut.

Mrs Thatcher had arrived first, in papal purple.

Opinion divided sharply among the press corps as to whether she was early for Prime Minister's Questions (3.15) or late for Prayers (2.30). One faction among us noted that waiting until other MPs had arrived (and the public gallery had filled) guaranteed the cheers she got.

The other faction speculated that she would have wanted her new life to start with devotions. Missing Prayers might arise from having been caught in her first traffic jam for eleven years. Now she knows what all those stationary cars are doing.

When she came in, Mr Heath's front seat was empty.

'Don't let Heath get that place!' came the helpful call from Labour's Dennis Skinner. Mrs Thatcher smiled and shook her head, occupying a more modest position near the back. She sat next to Mrs Elizabeth Peacock (Batley & Spen), a known second-ballot *Heseltinista*.

Next, at 3.11, came Mr Heseltine himself. He strode in to scattered cheers from both sides and plonked himself down next to Chris Patten, who gave him an encouraging pat on the arm – as well might a minister who had just handed his successor 'an unexploded time bomb' (if Mr Patten's description of the poll tax is to be believed).

Then, thirty seconds later, in walked the Prime Minister.

There was a huge cheer from the government benches. Mrs Thatcher smiled – her face a tug-o'-war between pride and anxiety: like a gym mistress watching her young star pupil approaching the vaulting-horse in his new leotards.

3.15. They were away – with a planted question from Roger King (C, Birmingham, Northfield) of a type of which we all fervently hope Mr Major's fixers do not intend to make a practice.

And what, you ask, of the main event?

What indeed! It was dull. Mr Kinnock asked a routine question about the poll tax, Mr Major gave a holding reply about the need for 'refinements' and Kinnock (luckily for Major) did not enquire how exactly you do refine an unexploded time bomb.

A series of the usual crawling questions from the Government benches, and the usual insults from the Opposition left both the strengths and the weaknesses of their target untested.

Apart from the intriguing hint of an underlying petulance, Major kept a cannily straight bat. He looked intelligent but nervous and sounded like the whine of a chainsaw in a distant forest. He does not, yet, command the Chamber naturally. Achieving that took Mrs Thatcher years.

'Resign,' shouted Labour hecklers at him, without enthusiasm. 'Resign,' came the returning shout back at Neil Kinnock from some Tories. From others, more interestingly: 'Don't resign.' It was, in short, a day like any other. If this was Thursday, that must be John Major. If this was Prime Minister's Questions, that must be the Prime Minister.

30.11.90

6

Performers –
Conferences, Cameras
and Occasions

A man's-eye view of woman-power

GRANDER PERSONS reached Westminster on Tuesday by State Coach. Your sketch writer took the number 69 bus to Plaistow tube station. Dimbleby, commentating, would have described me descending from the bus, looking 'tense but dignified', watching for the first (if not only) time that day, female power.

She was dressed in a severe little black number, relieved by a flash of yellow on the epaulettes and cap. She was a traffic warden, involved in an unhappy exchange with a lady parked on a zebra crossing '... I don't care if you *are* waiting for your kids. I've got kids too, ain't I? But I've got a job to do ...' She looked tired, not frightening at all.

The Embankment offered a second vignette. At the wheel of a parked vanful of men, this woman wore a sharp-cut dark jacket and skirt, with a white blouse and a chic black-and-white checked silk cravat. Encircling her matching hat, a slim band picked up the same chequered theme. She was a Metropolitan police officer. A backward glance found her off-guard, yawning, hat off, her curly brown hair shaken out and caught in the wintry sunlight. She looked rather nice.

Early for the State Opening, I looked out from the Lords gallery over a sea of rather different uniforms. The Guide to the Ceremonial read bewilderingly. Black Rod we recognized, but which was the Rouge Dragon Pursuivant? Where was the Woman of the Bedchamber, and what distinguished her from the *Lady* of the Bedchamber? Perhaps the Woman cleans under it and the Lady lies on it? Unwilling to speculate, one looked up to the Visitors' Gallery. Carol Thatcher, in scarlet, with a floppy felt hat, resembled an upmarket Paddington Bear. The Lord Mayor of Westminster, Elizabeth Flach, wore a tartan two-piece suit, neat hat dwarfed by a vast bow. She looked like a British Caledonian air-hostess. We all rose as the Edwina Currie of the Royal Family, Princess Michael of South Derbyshire – sorry, *Kent* – wandered in with some other princesses.

Then a hush, a fanfare of trumpets. In walked the Queen. Eat your hearts out, traffic wardens. Her crimson train, with matching pageboys, her gown, studded with jewels, were all just an underpinning to the Crown itself. The only known case, perhaps, of clothes and wearer being accessories to the hat.

She spoke. An admirable thing about our Queen is her complete inability to pretend that she is enjoying herself. She fails to be taken in by her own role. Her Majesty reminds one of the little girl who didn't *want* to go to the party but has been persuaded that she simply must, dressed up in her party frock, and dispatched, gritting her teeth and grimly clutching the birthday present – the Queen's Speech. She ploughed dutifully through such poetic phrases as 'My Government will provide for the sale of the utility functions of the water authorities' with as weary a dignity as she could command. Then she and the Duke of Edinburgh left, holding hands. They looked not so much awesome as sweet.

And what of the Prime Minister? Trailed by a hundred backbenchers (including Bernie Grant in Ashanti morning dress and Keith Vaz in a restrained little Nehru suit) she marched fiercely back to the Commons chamber. Dressed mostly in black, crowned by a sort of junior hussar helmet, Mrs Thatcher wore the outfit of a dowager Cossack and the expression of a B-52 bomber. No uniform, this. Our Prime Minister, alone among the power-dressed ladies of our day, has long ceased to *wear* a uniform, for what is worn can be removed. She has *become* the uniform: the woman and the office are not separable.

Outside the Lords, in the Victoria Gardens, is a tender, unself-conscious, English sculpture: of Emmeline Pankhurst, observed mostly by pigeons.

On State Opening Day I could see from there over to Millbank, where a bus-conductress stood with binoculars. Why? She had been watching the Queen, she said. One uniformed lady watching another uniformed lady, through binoculars! I wonder if Mrs Pankhurst could see them?

23.11.88

No policy, or three

'I AM deeply sorry for the unkind things I said about Liverpool,' Disraeli is reputed to have quipped. 'I had not seen Leeds at the time.' Looking back to the (Liberal) Democrats' conference here last week fills me with remorse for the unkind things I said then. Compared with this lot, they were all so *nice*.

Why are Labour delegates so physically unattractive? Why do they all have spots? Why is their hair so horribly greasy? Why is their gaze reproachful, their speech a surly monotone? No disrespect to the genuinely disabled, but it must be said that if one didn't have a limp naturally, one would feel under pressure here to develop one. And why do they never laugh?

Mr Gerald Kaufman (Labour's spokesman on foreign affairs) does have a sense of humour but rarely lets it show. Often compared with Kermit the Frog, there is an air about him (though he is properly fed and dressed, and spikily confident) that makes you somehow want to look after him; construct for him a little pond of his own with water lilies, safe from predators and stocked with gnats and succulent flies for him to pounce on.

By the end of today's debate Mr Kaufman must have longed for such a haven. The day had started awkwardly as he boasted on the radio that the world's ambassadors are queueing to meet him. It sounded a little plaintive: like the slightly confused lady who lives up the road from me who keeps telling everyone that 'Ivor Novello's boys came to my wedding, you know'. As a strategy to impress it has its limitations but it is not without impact in the launderette.

Mr Kaufman found himself discussing foreign affairs, this afternoon, in a launderette of truly vast proportions. He didn't actually mention Ivor Novello but he mentioned almost everybody else. He was off to Moscow shortly to see the people in the Kremlin. He was on the best of terms with Mr Peres in Jerusalem who had *assured* him that Israel would gladly talk to Arabs who renounced all their claims. He had spoken to absolutely everybody who mattered in the Middle East — he had spoken, in fact, to more leaders than Sir Geoffrey Howe *or* Mr George Shultz ... the list seemed endless. One felt more and more confident that at Mr Kaufman's wedding — whenever that happy day should occur — *all* of Ivor Novello's boys will be there.

Mr Kaufman turned momentarily from this to dispose of the slight problem of Labour's defence policy. It would be best, he argued, not to have one.

Alan Tuffin, the next speaker from the floor, thought we could have three. Yes, we could have multilateral disarmament. Yes, we could have bilateral disarmament too. *And* unilateral disarmament. Why skimp? Why not have the lot?

Dizzied by the richness and diversity of the world that was opening up, my imagination took flight. The baroque and gilded patchwork of panels that arch across the ceiling of the great hall at Blackpool began to blur — until they seemed to become one of those huge, comfortable, heavy old eiderdowns of our childhood. Far away, now, I heard the words 'I will now call Ron Todd.' I refocused sharply. Mr Todd stood before us waving his arms. In his excitement he had stumbled in his text. 'The North Sea Divide!' He shouted above bewildered cheers: 'The North Sea Divide ...'

God, we recall, rescued the Israelites from a seemingly hopeless position by just such a means. Perhaps He will do the same for the Labour Party.

7.10.88

Not bonkers after all

MR ROY HATTERSLEY has to his name one success and one signal failure. The success is to have realized that Labour needs a new philosophy. The failure is not to have been able to think of one. Of course everyone suspected that he had nothing to say when he chose, last year, to write a whole book saying it. But suspicions were confirmed yesterday morning, at Blackpool.

People are not free or equal, he argued, if some can afford things that others cannot. Delegates looked puzzled. That would be an argument for equality of incomes, or universal state provision: yet Mr Hattersley was billed as urging Labour to embrace the free market ... all right, not exactly 'embrace', perhaps, but a manly handshake, surely? It was unclear. The vote (about five million to nothing) enthusiastically endorsed him.

So why didn't they applaud? Surely the applause should be brought into line with the block-voting system. It is wholly unjust that someone with only one vote should be able to make as much noise as someone wielding millions. Machines can simulate applause. Block voters should be provided with them, volume regulated to reflect the exact size of the block.

But such irritations aside, Mr Hattersley had won a 'crushing' victory. It is not surprising that some of the media are seeing in this the 'basis for a final sweeping away of the ideological cobwebs'. This week, it is said, Labour may emerge as a modern party.

I have to inform you that this is not to be. To expect *denouements* in the Labour Party would be like reading Garth in the *Daily Mirror* in the belief that, today, all will finally be sorted out.

It won't. It is vital to the future of the party that the hard left keep losing, of course: but it is absolutely essential that they are not routed. If they're routed they can't keep losing, in which case what battles are there left for the leadership to win? For years now Mr Kinnock has been bravely repelling the forces of blind dogmatism. It is the thing he does best; some believe it is the *only* thing he does. Why take it from him now?

Imagine a world without the 'Leftist Threat'. *Three years* of Mr Hattersley reading extracts from his book about freedom . . .

No. Without the flanking menace of Mr Scargill and Mr Skinner, how would John Smith continue to appear the wise old owl? Without the scowling bulk of Mr Heffer, where are Mr Hattersley's claims to slim rationality? Who would fly to the arms of a Kinnock, except from the claws of a Benn? If God has made us slightly daft, we are rescued only by the comparison with men who are completely bonkers. Labour should give thanks that the week opened amid fears that the Party might go totally berserk; and pray that it ends in tears of relief that they are, after all, just a little confused.

4.10.88

High moral picnic

OF COURSE the question everyone at Brighton is asking is: Does *she* have the body search? Does Mrs Thatcher submit to the patting and prodding that the rest of us endure whenever we enter the conference centre? Opinion is divided. Some say there could be no exceptions. Others, that nobody would *dare*. But I can guess: she will have been offered exemption but will have insisted on being treated like everyone else – and made a frightful to-do about it.

For I remember her of old. As a backroom boy when she was Opposition Leader, I was preparing the Shadow Cabinet Room – when in she sailed, hours early as usual. What happened next took us all by surprise. Without explanation, she kicked off her shoes, climbed on to the armrest of a leather armchair, and stood there precariously on tiptoes. Then she began running her fingertips along the top of a picture frame. 'It's the way a woman knows whether a room's been *properly* cleaned,' she announced, chair wobbling violently.

Richard Ryder (then her Secretary, now an Agriculture minister) begged her to come down. 'The cleaners will do that,' he protested.

She fixed him with a gimlet stare: 'We are *all* cleaners, Richard,' she said.

There was more to be cleansed yesterday than litter. A delegate from Scotland, of Presbyterian demeanour reminding one of those men in ties who call uninvited at your home to sell religion, told the conference that massive resources should be committed to 'a regeneration of moral values'. Quite how Mr Tony Newton, to whom the debate was addressed, was supposed to undertake this challenge remained unclear until the speaker explained that, swooping 'from the moral high ground', we must clear the streets of slot-machines.

I've never actually been to the moral high ground. The view must be terrific. One pictures an Alpine scene (but without cowpats) where Mrs Thatcher and John Gummer picnic on alcohol-free wine. It must be such fun that really one wonders why they come down to visit us, on the moral low ground, at all.

But there she was, floating six inches above her seat as a delegate told her, voice trembling with excitement, how 'there are times when our Party just ... just *transcends* ordinary politics.' The Prime Minister, who also transcends ordinary politics, and almost everything else, gazed especially transcendentally at us all.

Mr Brooke made a good speech. Indeed, so good that a delegate and I turned to each other and said, simultaneously: 'I wonder who wrote that?' For he had launched a series of hard-hitting one-liners.

But he sounds such a decent old stick that one no more supposes him capable of real harm than one supposes that Paul Channon, the Transport Secretary, who told us urgently that 'we *must* release the spirit of enterprise', is capable of releasing a pet budgerigar. If only that could be said of the delegates. They looked like Moonies.

The sound system was the best, the lighting subtle, the decor pastel, the autocue discreet, the huge video-screens to either side of the dais hypnotic. 'We must lay the foundations of morality and build upon them with the cementation of citizenship,' the Presbyterian droned, hijacking a debate on inner cities and demanding to be flown straight to the moral high ground ...

'Look at the ministers,' a delegate whispered to me: 'They couldn't care less what we think.' Heavens to Betsy, I hope he's right.

12.10.88

146

Two seaside performers

IT WAS more than an ovation. It was more, much more than a standing ovation. It was a *leaping* ovation. It was a running, jumping, raving, waving ovation.

But she deserved it. She and I had both been working hard on her speech since before dawn. She because she was going to deliver it, and I because that would occur shortly before this sketch has to be ready for the printers. So it was necessary to anticipate what she might say so that one could guess what one might write if she said it.

It is more than pleasing to record that, over dinner with a Tory agent, the outline I drafted for her proved in almost every point correct. 'There'll have to be a Green bit, of course.' the agent said.

'Yes,' I agreed, 'but with a little more flesh on the bones, this time.'

'And Europe,' he said. 'She'll do the Little Englander thing again.'

The Fight Against Inflation, we agreed, was a must. We agreed, too, that an expression of confidence in Mr Lawson was needed: 'Warm,' said my friend. 'But not ecstatic,' I warned.

Nurses? You bet. Home Office? A tricky one. Mr Hurd's historic pledge – 'We shall grub up the roots of crime' – lacked a certain ring. 'She likes education,' said my friend.

'But she doesn't like Mr Baker,' I reminded him. We concluded that the marginal note 'that's enough about Education – M.T.' would appear fairly early in her speechwriters' drafts.

And jokes? 'Oh yes, as many as her advisers have time to explain to her. They've got all night. That's about one joke.'

'But where's the Moral High Ground?' I said.

'Oh, quite right. An extended passage on social obligation, don't you think?' I fixed him with my best Thatcher glare: 'There is no such thing as society. They are renaming it the Royal Community for the Protection of Cruelty to Animals.'

'Sorry old man. *Active Citizenship*.'

'That's better.'

I leaned over the table: 'Aren't we both forgetting the big one?' 'Foreign aid!' he exploded. 'The centrepiece of her speech. I don't think ...'

Then off he went to the Conference Ball. A great many other people did, too. I went to a drag show in a basement off Preston Street.

I must have looked too much like a junior minister. 'You do realize what sort of a place this is?' a young man at the door asked. Remarking that one glance at him had left me in no doubt, I went in. I'm afraid there were a great many conference delegates there, all trying not to recognize each other. The artiste wore something made out of green net curtains, it seemed, and false eyelashes. He was called Maisie Trollette.

'*Memories*,' sang Maisie. '*Like the corners of my mind: misty water-coloured memories, of the way we were.*'

Then, turning to his audience: 'Is it anybody special's birthday today?'

About a third of the audience stared at their feet and tried not to remember that it was indeed the birthday of a rather different sort of Artiste; whose rather different sort of performance they would be cheering not many hours from now.

15.10.88

Women in hats

MRS THATCHER has a new voice; warmer, gentler, and even more caring than the last one, this is the 'healing' voice. As it slid between the marble busts and trickled from the wooden rafters of Guildhall yesterday morning, like a soft rain of cough linctus, I reflected that, where lesser persons might welcome a foreign statesman in a new hat, new gloves or even a new Daimler, our Prime Minister could bestow upon her guest no greater honour than to show him her new voice.

For her guest was Mikhail Gorbachov. For his benefit, London was putting on its finest performance: a selection of our 900-year-old ancient traditions at their vulgar best. The Hall itself, whose origins might appear shrouded in some timeless Gothic mist, was in fact designed out of the shell of the previous building by Sir Giles Gilbert Scott in 1954. Scott also designed the red public telephone box.

Taped music somewhat in the style of a piano-bar repertoire played by an RAF band floated over the assembly while some men in pith-helmets upholstered in feathers ushered in the audience. Dominating the guests were a group of elderly gentlemen in red nighties – Aldermen of the City of London, apparently. The ordinary Councillors had blue nighties.

The other guests were women in hats. Whenever you have women in hats, you know you have an event of no practical significance.

The taped music quickened, then ceased. Heralds blew their trumpets, and in walked the platform party.

How is Mrs T's and Mr G's relationship developing? Her press office called their earlier meeting 'extremely wide-ranging, good-tempered, solemn, and enormously frank'. I often feel like that on the bus, don't you?

The Lord Mayor took off the black Cornish pasty he had been wearing on his head, and welcomed us, in English. I listened to him on my headphones in Russian. It was more interesting, though I could not understand it.

Then came the speeches. Vulgar *reporters* will tell you that this was effectively the beginning of the occasion. Your sketchwriter avows that it was the end. The fun was over. Nothing was said. Besides, if it had been, the women in hats could not have heard it as the hats stopped them putting on their headphones. One of them ingeniously wore the headset like a bonnet-strap, under the chin, but the others were concerned not to upset their milliners, and did without.

They missed only – perhaps – a slight redefinition of socialism, which was, said Mr Gorbachov, no more than 'social provision, justice and humanism'. We looked to the future, he said, in a mood 'associated with hope, but tinged with alarm'.

Then came Mrs Thatcher's new voice. In terms that would have served her well in an audition for the voiceover in a nature documentary about the nesting habits of voles, the puniest of the Great Powers addressed the mightiest of our potential adversaries; and told them to keep trying. Mr Gorbachov glanced at her with a look associated with hope, but tinged with alarm.

8.4.89

Lions exit left, pursued by lambs

'I'VE WORKED for this for years,' said a Labour MP to me yesterday. He was talking about the new party image, with bland policies to match – Edam socialism: socialism for people who don't like socialism. Two young men with narrow ties and narrow briefcases quick-marched past us, blow-dried hair quivering in the sea breeze. 'And now we've got it I don't think I like it.'

The change has been unbelievable. 'I wanted to abseil,' Debby Epstein told the conference during the gay rights debate, 'but the security people took my rope away.' She added that she would rather be sat on by Sue Lawley than Neil Kinnock.

Your sketchwriter can testify that this preference transcends sexual orientation.

Where *has* the old Labour party gone? Those hordes of smelly, spotty, greasy-haired people waving placards and angry fists, where are they? Vaporized?

To look at Dennis Skinner, you would think so. Offside all his political life, the Beast now carries the referee's whistle. He occupies the chair at Brighton, keeping order. Full of wise utterances, the MP who wrecked countless parliamentary debates and terrorized successive Speakers now nods, smiles, sips water and presses buzzers as his officials bring him notes and ordinary delegates stumble through their speeches in dread of Mr Skinner's ruling.

Were he to turn up tomorrow in wig and black breeches, few would wonder. Is it really the Dennis Skinner who at Westminster called Dr Owen a 'pompous sod', who now at Brighton leans over to an elderly, disabled delegate, whose speech is out of order, and rules 'I'm awfully sorry, but you'll have to go'? Weep ye sons of Bolsover: grieve o ye daughters of Clay Cross!

In fact it did not matter what a speaker said. More and more, the conference seems seized of Lord Melbourne's remark: 'Gentlemen: it does not much matter what we say, but – mind – *we must all say the same thing.*'

Witness David Blunkett's impressive speech yesterday morning. One has already forgotten what was in it (always a good sign) and remembers only the sensation of having dozed off and woken up in a Tory conference: measured tones and circumspect commitments being punctuated by regular, polite applause – at which Mr Blunkett would smile his shy smile. They say butter wouldn't melt in his mouth. One would need to be sure that ice would.

Mrs Gwynneth Dunwoody, MP, would only need to look at an ice cube to dissolve it. She has had her problems, but when she was voted off the NEC this week, most people recognized the loss of a strong and brave political intellect from the right. Few said anything. She held the fort for a decade but she hardly fits the new image: it is not easy to imagine Mrs Dunwoody using a Filofax, except as a weapon.

One NEC member tried a tribute to her. He was greeted with a ripple of derisive laughter from the left. Anonymous. Drifting around the hall. Like the smile on the face of the Cheshire Cat, all that is left of the left.

There was a moment when I thought the conference had reverted to type. Watching the press room TV, I heard a conference voice:

'Comrades, the eyes of the country are on this party,' and glanced at the monitor to see a man with three albino ferrets coming out of his trousers. My joy was short-lived. Someone had switched to *Playbus*.

6.10.89

Battle for the loonies

'WOE UNTO bloody Lichfield!' cried the first Quaker, George Fox, awoken from a nightmare in which he saw the town punished in blood for its heresy. He fled barefoot.

Like Sylvia Heal, Labour's candidate? I searched.

Through the window of a hairdressers, I saw seven women sitting under driers. They *all* looked like Sylvia Heal. When I arrived too late for her press conference, the room was empty. There was no trace. Just a faint smell of vanilla.

I would go, then, in search of the real battle, the battle for third, fourth, fifth, sixth, seventh and eighth place. The battle for the hearts and minds of the nation's freaks, free spirits and loonies.

I never found Lindi Love. Her NICE (National Independent Correct Edification) posters bore a crimson declaration: 'Love Is All You Need.'

Searching for the Green Party I blundered into the command post of the MRLP, in the King's Head, Lichfield. 'You've missed Lord Sutch,' said the barman. 'He's gone to London for two days before his rock concert here.'

'OFFICIAL MONSTER RAVING LOONY GREEN TEETH CANDIDATE,' said the posters. Don't be fooled by other loony parties! Sutch deserves to win for posing the best question of the century: 'Why is there only one Monopolies Commission?' Beneath a Monster poster, talking earnestly, three Green Party activists rested from canvassing for their Robert Saunders.

'You've come to write about how the loonies are doing, haven't you? We are doing fine, thanks.'

'A group of pagans came to our meeting last night,' one told me, 'and warned us the general election will be this November. They read tarot cards.'

I mentioned that the photo of the National Front candidate resembled Buddy Holly. 'He doesn't look that good in the flesh,' said one of them;

then (gloomily) 'nor does Buddy Holly, now, I suppose.' Holly has biodegraded.

But at La Terrazza, near Safeway's car park, Liberal hope springs from a renewable source. Tim Jones (its candidate) was organizing a 'motorcade' through Rugeley.

'No red or blue cars,' said his bubbly agent, unbelievably named Candy Piercy. Jones looks like a mouse: a nice mouse, with bright eyes and little whiskers.

A nasty cat of a journalist asked: 'Is the bandwagon starting to roll?' The Mouse flinched. '*Continuing* to roll,' it squeaked; 'polls can underestimate a position.'

The Cat pinned with a cruel paw: 'What are *your* figures, then?'

'We're not disclosing our figures,' wriggled the Mouse.

The Mouse's special guest, painfully decent Robert Maclennan, MP, shrugged off the indignity of finding his name spelled wrongly two different ways on the leaflet, and spoke of 'buoyancy and optimism' on the streets of Rugeley. I fled. And stumbled, late, into a huge applauding crowd at the Eton Lodge Hotel. Buoyancy in the SDP camp? It was a Tupperware party.

Upstairs, for an audience of five journalists, John Cartwright, MP – greying, honourable – was supporting the SDP's large, blinking and genial Ian Wood. Mr Wood is Daffy Duck to Mr Jones's Mickey Mouse.

'The Liberal candidate,' a journalist said to Daffy, 'says he's going to win. Is he talking out of his ... (pause) hat?'

The reply was swift: 'Depends where he positions his hat.'

20.3.90

Vision, regulation and the Liberal Party

'As LONG as humankind retain their civilization; as long as birds sing in unclouded skies; so long will endure the power of the compassionate spirit.'

63. Never use bleach, chemical cleaners or toilet fresheners in the lavatory.

Here at Blackpool we received the first quotation from Charles Kennedy MP, speaking as incoming Liberal Democrat president. The uplifting moment occurred on Tuesday. I encountered the second remark yesterday, in the Liberal policy document *'What Price Our Planet?'*

'Liberty is the vital question of the future,' said Mr Kennedy.

4. Compost all garden and household waste which will rot down — says the policy document.

'. . . nothing short of the systematic demolition of the current apparatus of British politics.' – Mr Kennedy again.

32. Turn down heating thermostats a little.

'It was the joy of fresh thinking aloud.'

49. Try to keep noise levels down.

'We will enter the campaign with a sound and united philosophical base . . .'

5. Avoid plastics wherever possible. Re-use yoghurt and margarine tubs for plants and seeds.

'. . . an honest and realistic political strategy . . .'

73. Make a small pond for frogs and toads.

'. . . and, our greatest asset, a determined membership of genuine goodwill and compassionate spirit.'

55. Report any noise in everyday life which you find unacceptable.

Right. Can I report Simon Hughes MP? Mr Hughes was onto a new theme in a new debate: global warming. He was making a significant contribution, to the phenomenon if not the debate.

'Wild swings in temperature, droughts and typhoons may become commonplace,' he roared. '. . . small islands like the Maldives could disappear altogether.

'Plankton population could also be severely affected . . .' Mr Hughes had hardly started. I began to fear that, ere he sat down, the Maldives would have long gone, soldiers would be sandbagging the Isle of Man, and the Irish Sea would be tipping down the steps of our conference hall. I fled to higher ground.

When I returned to the conference hall, Mr Hughes was still speaking.

'I give you this historic pledge. Tackling the environmental challenge is going to require major changes in the way we live . . .'

52. Keep pets under control. Do not let your dog foul the pavement or grass area.

'Yes!' cried Des Wilson, the party's campaign manager, in a rallying speech before lunch, 'There is an alternative!'

80. Use natural fertilizers (e.g. animal manure, liquid plant manure, bonemeal, hoof and horn).

'Yes! We the Liberal Democrats are ready now!'

53. Avoid slamming car doors, revving car and motorbike engines, and shouting in the streets late at night.

'Yes! You can believe again!'
36. Take your litter home and encourage others to do the same.

20.9.90

Wider yet and wider

How Wonderful Thou art!
How Wonderful Thou art!
Mrs Thatcher cast her eyes modestly down. The chorus rose on the
wings of a thousand Tory voices to the rafters of the great conference
centre at Bournemouth. We were singing hymns before the talking.
When I in awesome wonder
Consider ...
Heavy with golden chains, the 'Worshipful mayor of Bournemouth,
Councillor Wycliffe Coe' glanced worshipfully at the PM, considered,
in awesome wonder, the extraordinary pantomime in which he was now
to play a part, rose, and – enjoying a privilege granted to few – exercised
his right to three minutes of Margaret Thatcher's undivided attention.

You were frisked, sniffed and geiger-counted; and led down a maze
of plywood corridors in an underground car park. From this purgatory
you emerged into a carpeted foyer where people with silk scarves and
metallic voices greeted each other, European-style, 'M-*wa*, M-*wa*'; big,
furry, bobbing BBC microphones dangled from rods, like bait; and ex-
MPs in search of winnable seats hung around the bottoms of escalators,
hungry for eye contact.

'Charles, how splendid! Are you up all week? M-*wa*.' I think the
enthusiasm of these people for the ERM derives from some notion that
the Continent consists of millions of people rushing around going M-
wa M-*wa*.

And into the hall itself. The programme had yet to start. From
loudspeakers came the cocktail lounge tinkling of a piano. *When I'm*
64:
'Will you still need me,
Will you still feed me?'
The Prime Minister, not yet 65, had still to enter.
This she did, to the strain of *I'd like to teach the world to sing. ...*
'in perfect harmony' – remember that Coca-Cola commercial? – 'I'd like

to take it in my arms/And keep it company.' The Real Thing having arrived, we rose.

'God grant us the serenity to accept what cannot be changed,' prayed the Rev. Roger Hall, eyeing Mrs Thatcher warily, and interrupted by interference over the loudspeaker from a police message.

'Oh praise ye the Lord!' we sang. The press, confused as to whether joining a hymn amounts to joining the Party, put in a ragged performance.

Attention wandered from the distant podium to the huge screens on each side, where the podium's tiny occupants are projected — their images blown up to poster size. Each screen is a bank of smaller screens. Together these comprise the whole picture, sectioned into internal squares and seen as through a sash window. During our devotions we were offered a window cleaner's view of an enlarged Mrs Lynda Chalker.

Gaining in the poster version, Trade Secretary Peter Lilley delivered an excellent speech, undismayed by Gallup's findings that two per cent of the public recognize him. I could see him doing an effective TV advertisement for a bathroom freshener. In time he may resemble a Secretary of State for Trade.

The morning ended with a classic performance from Kenneth Baker. It was shameless. 'My friends ... as storm clouds gather ...' He turned to Labour. 'There is a credibility gap, Mr Kinnock, and that gap is the widest gap in British politics!'

During the applause that followed, Mr Baker's open mouth gave some clue as to the second widest gap.

10.10.90

A myth is born

YESTERDAY AT Bournemouth we were present at the birth of a myth.

It was 16½ minutes of sweetly choreographed ecstasy. Eyes were filled with tears. Speeches were filled with standing ovations. Mrs Thatcher's hand was kissed twice. Prominent persons from the new Eastern European democracies were led to the rostrum to pay their respects to Mrs Thatcher, praise the Conservative party, and receive small plastic ornaments featuring Mr Baker's Tory flame of freedom, redesigned to look less like an ice cream.

While the video screens showed the Berlin Wall collapsing — and Mrs

Thatcher – and Lech Walesa – and Mrs Thatcher – waves of emotion swept us all. A foreign prime minister saluted our own PM, a Polish professor kissed her hand and a smashing Czech brunette offered a personal thank you. Eat your hearts out, Labour.

So moving was the spectacle that we lost track of the reason for it. This was lucky, for the whole show was founded upon an illusion.

The illusion was outlined by a Mr Michael Teale, speaking (from the floor) about the flame of freedom which had burnt behind the Iron Curtain. 'It owed much to Mrs Thatcher,' he said. 'British resolve played a vital part during those dark hours.'

Mrs Jackie Nilsson was less grudging. 'Without your great leadership,' she told our PM, little would have been possible. Change, freedom, the fall of the Berlin Wall – 'We see proof in these miracles. Who did this? Margaret Thatcher.'

Too generously, though, Mrs Nilsson also gave a little credit to the foreign leaders on the rostrum: 'Kind gentlemen with beautiful manners. These are the people we need ... so polite to Mrs Thatcher.'

If, before lunch, poor John Major had realized the scale of gratitude that would be offered to the PM after lunch, he would hardly have volunteered his own paltry effort. Indicating his ministerial team rather as a sultan might point to a posse of superior eunuchs, he turned to Mrs Thatcher. 'I'm grateful to you, Prime Minister, for giving them to me,' he said.

But it was otherwise his most accomplished conference speech yet, and the representatives warmed to him.

And it was gently done. I suspect that the Chancellor has been advised not to raise his voice, for his throat tightens to a strangled monotone, like a distant model aeroplane engine. He began, however, by shouting. About a third of the way in, looking more assured by the minute, he remembered to drop his voice and started to vary the pitch and speed. The speech improved immensely.

Mr Major tried one of his shy Princess Diana smiles: a great success. He dropped his voice yet further. The effect was stunning, but it was now becoming hard to hear what the Chancellor was saying.

The PM led the standing-up for his ovation. She then led the sitting-down. Mr Major's prospects are improving.

But why was Mrs Thatcher smiling? As the Foreign Secretary sat down, word reached me that Mr Heath is going to Baghdad. Saddam Hussein should be advised that, while a certain lady's finger is on the button, this is one human shield whose interposition might provoke the missile it was intended to deter.

12.10.90

Pomp reigns, ermine ghosts cry

CIRCUMSTANCES BEING unpropitious, pomp reigned at the State Opening yesterday. With cupboard and Queen's speech bare, ceremony was all that was left for the Lords. They camped it up a treat.

I am fairy Buttercup,
Come to dance and cheer you up.

The song and dance routine was led not by the main act at all. Not by Black Rods, Lords Chancellor, trumpeters, rouge dragons pursuivant ... not even the peers of the realm. From bobby's helmet to monarch's crown, all are uniformed attendants to the spectacle. The real stars in this show are the amateurs: the only members of the troupe who design their own uniforms: the peers' wives.

Lady Stevens of Ludgate was magnificent. She came as a fairy. In black satin with lace frothing from the cuffs and a huge Elizabethan ruff fanning up behind the neck, she wore a tiara of diamonds and azures. Our Titania — a *good* fairy, with a lovely face — was flanked by ladies sprinkled with sparklers, resembling bridesmaids of the maturer sort.

Over on the other side of the Chamber was Lady Strange. This substantial hereditary baroness, more *Space Odyssey* than *Blue Fairy Book*, had stuck a silvery aerial on top of her head, as though in radio communication with lighter nymphs.

After a State Opening, what do they all do next? There are no other parliaments being opened. Sad to have to take it all off before lunch!

Other peeresses in their own right were less spectacular, being obliged to wear standard-issue scarlet, with ermine. The lords do the same, earls enjoying the accessory of a long cape with white ermined sections, like a polecat's tail. Dr Runcie was covered entirely in white fur and resembled an intellectual sheep. If we could but see them, the ghosts of tens of thousands of ermines must teem, shrieking up the walls, on State Opening Day.

After the ladies come the diplomats. Their excellencies appear as an illustration from the *Arabian Nights*. There were black men in white fezzes, white men in black fezzes, two Lawrences of Arabia, and the Papal Nuncio in a red biretta.

Men with lace cuffs walked in. 'Ooh!' whispered an expert behind me, 'the purse-bearers have arrived. Minor royals are imminent.'

But the Major Royal was imminent, holding hands with Prince Philip and heralded by a posse of men with white sticks, of uncertain function. Her Majesty is the only person who is not ludicrous on such an occasion. She is plainly not enjoying it, and so keeps her dignity. To enjoy being a monarch would surely be evidence of personality disorder.

Proof of sanity, Her Majesty's awkwardness is immensely reassuring. She fumbled in her handbag and put on her glasses, a green flash from her crown striking me sharp in the eye. The Queen was fidgeting, and breathing quite heavily. The Lord Chancellor, knocking 'em cold in black and gold, handed her the Gracious Speech, which was without content. She read it without enthusiasm and left.

The Soviet ambassador talked earnestly to the Nuncio. 'You think *you've* got problems!' he was perhaps saying.

Guessing what people were saying was half the fun. Directly beneath my seat, nodding in whispered conversation, was Neil Kinnock's head. One was reminded of the temptations to which a pigeon is exposed. My view of the Prime Minister was on to her hat: a wide black brim ringing a plain white crown, a negative photo of a Polo mint. What was she saying?

Framing her reply, perhaps, to the anonymous Labour voice which, in the hush following Black Rod's arrival in the Commons Chamber to the chime of a bell outside, had stage-whispered: 'It tolls for thee, Maggie.'

And *was* it Dennis Skinner who looked the buckled and breeched Black Rod up and down and growled: 'I bet he drinks Carling Black Label'?

8.11.90

Wild about Harry

IT IS a brutal letter. 'The unfortunate reality', writes the 'CMB Image Consultants' managing director Mary C. Spillane, to MPs, 'is that the impression you make on TV depends mainly on your image (55 per cent) with your voice and body-language also being very important, accounting for 38 per cent of your impact.' Then, the pitiless blow:

'Sadly, only 7 per cent depends on what you are saying.'

I am still reeling from the shock of reading this. What? All those hours, all those nights spent when I was an MP, attending Standing Committee A (Transport Bill) (1982) waiting to speak, while the late Harry Cowans filibustered on the subject of 'the Maltese breast-stroke'; all my thought-provoking interventions on the privatization of the British Airports Authority – do these count for nothing? Seven per cent, says the heartless Ms Spillane.

'What you must appreciate,' she adds, mercilessly, 'is that some fine-tuning to your appearance would serve you, your constituents, and your party, well.' I still remember dear Harry Cowans, the shrewd, kind-hearted Labour MP for Tyne Bridge, described in Andrew Roth's *Parliamentary Profiles* as 'bulky waddler, specs'.

Sweaty, hopelessly overweight, rucked suit, pasty face, hair (what there was of it) all over the place ... there was no 'fine-tuning' Harry's appearance. Even a major overhaul – points, plugs, filters, check all oils – would have been pointless.

The voice? It was Geordie – doubtless not a 'favoured' regional accent. The body language? The air was blue with Harry's body-language.

Yet those who knew him would have found it hard to vote for any other. In his last election, 11,693 more chose a bulky waddler (specs) than the alternative.

Harry is now demonstrating the Maltese breast-stroke in celestial waters.

What would he have made of Mary Spillane's letter? I picture him now, chuckling as we study the points on which she offers help. In a one-and-a-half hour session, she says, 'You will learn: which colours (for shirts, ties, suits) make you look healthy, and which shades to avoid.'

Nothing would have made Harry look healthy. He wasn't.

'How to combine suits, shirts and ties with confidence and flair.'

Harry only ever wore a tea-stained NUR tie. Little combines with this tie to yield confidence and flair.

'If you need a new hairstyle, and where to get it.'

Harry needed new hair.

'The most useful suiting weights for inside and outside the Chamber.'

Harry did not change suits to enter or leave the Chamber. Harry did not change suits at all.

'How to build a flexible, coordinated wardrobe.'

Harry was a railwayman, not a joiner. If they had asked him to build wardrobes, he would have had the lads out.

'Personal grooming tips to deal with any problems (double chins, shiny heads, florid complexions, circles round the eyes, etc).'

I do not know what the Geordie is for 'personal grooming tip' but, when provoked, Harry certainly had a few at his command. You would have heard a selection had you suggested he put talcum powder on his bald patch.

'A complimentary shopping trip can be scheduled after the consultation to help you learn "how to shop" as well as to buy whatever few items might be needed to improve your appearance immediately.' A razor, for instance, Harry?

'The investment in yourself will ensure that your message is heard and that you *always* look your best.'

Well, Ms Spillane, Harry never did look his best. Perhaps you are right that a TV assessment that's 93 per cent image, voice and body language would have been unkind.

I just prefer to remember the seven per cent that depended on what he was, not on how he looked. And I'll pit 7 per cent of Harry against 93 per cent of your new-look MPs, and bet confidently on the outcome.

I'm backing the bulky waddler.

4.11.89

Forbidden to the cameras

WEDNESDAY WAS a happy day for the nation's parliamentary sketch-writers. We are to retain our pre-eminence; Parliament is not to be televised after all.

Admittedly you do have to read between the lines of the report published yesterday by the Select Committee on Televising of Proceedings of the House, to realize that this is their real message. On the face of it, they set out what they call 'Rules of Coverage' under which cameras will be allowed in.

The penny drops, however, during the third paragraph of these rules. Television directors, says the report, 'should have regard to the dignity of the House, and to its function as a working body rather than a place of entertainment'.

What? 'Dignity'? '*Working* body'? *Not* a 'place of entertainment'?

Sorry, readers. Let me compose myself. Let me shut my eyes and contemplate the dignity that is Anthony Beaumont-Dark (C, Selly Oak), the decorum that is Dave Nellist (Lab, Coventry SE) – 'A militant is just a moderate who has got off his knees' – the sheer gravitas that is Colin Moynihan, the small-is-beautiful sports minister.

Let me remind myself of what a truly 'working' body we were on those long summer nights on the Transport Bill committee, when dear old Harry Cowans filibustered as only a Labour Geordie could, for two hours, on the subject of the 'Maltese breast-stroke', while Nick Ridley smoked outside.

Let me curb my tongue and immerse myself in the certainty that 'entertainment' plays no part in our proceedings at Westminster. Does Dennis Skinner seek to entertain? Surely not. His little poem, recited recently to the Chamber (and, most particularly, to Mrs Thatcher) about the dustman with his rubbish, who can:

'Bag it, and bin it
And stick HER in it!'

– was intended for GCSE students of public affairs to dissect and comment upon, not, surely, to entertain? Does Nicky Fairbairn (C, Perth & Kinross) wear his frock-coat, Bill Walker (C, Tayside N) his kilt, or Anthony Marlow (C, Northampton N) his Black-and-White Minstrel Show stripey blazers, to entertain? Banish the thought!

Did that prima donna of the Labour backbenchers Shakespearean actor Andrew Faulds (temporarily 'resting' in Parliament), grow his enormous beard only, or even mainly, to become the hairiest chorus girl in the House? Indeed no. It is worn to give added authority to Mr Faulds' many important reflections on world affairs.

So, suitably chastened by these improving thoughts, we read on into the select committee's report: 'In no circumstances should close-up shots of members' or officers' papers be taken.' Aha! Carry on writing your Christmas cards, boys and girls, and signing all those fund-raising constituency round-robins: viewers will never know. And, as for those notelets that pass continually between ministers at the dispatch box, and their civil servants in the gallery, we are not – after all – to be let into the secret of whether they say *'for God's sake how do I answer Meacher's point about elderly dependents' supplementary heating claw-back? Quick!'* – or just *'winding up soon: a large whisky & dry ginger back in the office, ready, please.'*

'The standard format for depicting the member who has the floor should be a head and shoulders shot, *not* a closeup.' Pity about that. Viewers would have enjoyed seeing Mrs Thatcher grinding her teeth, as Mr Kinnock rumbles on.

'The camera should normally remain on the member speaking.' Readers, at any given moment, the *least* interesting thing in the chamber is 'the member speaking'. Nick Budgen (C, Wolverhampton SW) interrupting, Ted Heath snoozing, Frank Haynes (L, Ashfield) snarling, Simon Hughes (Dem, Bermondsey) bleating, Dame Elaine Kellett-Bowman screeching, Roy Hattersley digesting ... *these* are the stuff of which Parliament is made. The nation is not to see them. Sketchwriters will lie easy in their beds, tonight.

18.5.89

Censoring the giggles

TODAY'S SKETCH will show (using italic script) which bits of yesterday in Parliament you would be barred from seeing when the Commons is televised – the bits the select committee have just proposed be kept off the screen.

Ken Livingstone asked about the Government's reaction towards American sanctions against businesses in Northern Ireland which do not employ enough Catholics.

Merlyn Rees (Lab), a former Northern Ireland Secretary, shook his head at his colleague. The Opposition front bench looked embarrassed at Livingstone's apparent satisfaction at the harm being done.

James Kilfedder (UUP, Down N) said the sanctions campaign had links with the IRA. *Clare Short (Lab, Birmingham, Ladywood) muttered angrily and tried to catch Mr Speaker's eye, to speak. After many attempts,* Ms Short was called and denied the 'lie' that there were links. *Tory back-benchers shook their heads disbelievingly at her.*

Ken Livingstone decided not to stay for other Members' questions, and left.

James Pawsey (C, Rugby) asked approvingly about the scheme to encourage schools which 'bridged the sectarian divide'. *William Ross (Ulster Unionist, Londonderry E) folded his arms and stared grimly forward.*

An exchange followed about the Anglo-Irish Accord. *More by grunts and gestures than by what was said, it was clear that this opened up divisions on both sides of the House. Ian Gow (C, Eastbourne) in particular looked stony-faced. A little group of Tories who oppose the Accord muttered mischievously among themselves, throughout. Unionists on the Opposition benches shook their heads and tut-tutted whenever the Accord was mentioned.*

Sir William Clark (C, Croydon S) rose to congratulate a local government candidate in Northern Ireland who had won election on a 'Conservative' ticket, and the Secretary of State, Tom King, replied that 'the jury is still out on this one'.

There was a ripple of laughs, grunts, and raised eyebrows on the Government side which suggested that Tories are still bemused by the idea and unsure how to react. The Labour Party enjoyed this discomfort.

With fifteen minutes to go, MPs were coming in for the next performance: PM's Questions.

People started chatting among themselves, laughing, checking their papers – clearly oblivious of the Northern Ireland business. From time to time Mr Speaker called 'Order' *but nobody could interest the Chamber in Ulster. Mrs Thatcher, when she arrived, did not listen either.*

There was a discussion on the use of plastic bullets *but interest had evaporated. There was much giggling on the Tory side. One backbencher walked along the benches trying to interest colleagues in signing the yellow forms on which Parliamentary Questions have to be submitted.*

It was a sunny day outside and some time since anyone on the mainland had been blown up. Ulster was sinking under parliamentary indifference.

The bits you will be able to see on TV will not tell you that.

19.5.89

Box hits wardrobe

YESTERDAY THE TV cameras came to the Commons.

'Hold on!' called Mr Speaker to Dame Elaine Kellett-Bowman, 'We haven't started yet.' I stared in disbelief. Mr Speaker has had his wig dry-cleaned. She rose again. Disbelief grew. Dame Elaine has bought a new dress!

'Now we are going to be televised,' she said, could 'prayers, at least, be in no circumstances recorded by the camera?'

'Or could they point at the sky?' asked David Ashby (C, Leicester NW).

All around us hung what those who know the tropics recognized as vast mosquito nets, circular muslin cages radiating an eery, acid white light. It was a dummy run for the televising of the Commons which starts with the new Parliament next month. Robin Maxwell-Hyslop (C, Tiverton) wore snow glasses.

Above the back benches, rows of suspended black cameras on remote control swivelled silently like security scanners in supermarkets. Donald Thompson (C, Calder Valley) lay back spellbound by these devices, his head following them hypnotically round. Giggles of excitement and the hum of conversation filled the air.

Shouldn't somebody have told them that this was not for broadcasting? It was the *technicians* who were rehearsing, not the Members? This was supposed to be an ordinary day. Yet on what ordinary day would Sir Peter Emery (C, Honiton) wear puce socks? And why had Sir John Stokes (C, Halesowen & Stourbridge) chosen a black tie with white moons scudding across it, tucked into trousers worn just beneath the armpits?

Nobody was taking in a word that was said, of course. Apparently this was 'Questions to the Education Secretary' (and Mr John MacGregor's debut) but I can only tell you that he wore a neat suit with shiny shoes and conservative tie, because I was concentrating on Dennis Skinner's hair. Does he or doesn't he? Blow-dry, I mean. Tony Banks (Lab, Newham NW) clearly had, for the occasion. And *where* did Dale Campbell-Savours (Lab, Workington) get that apricot shirt with white collar? His suit, which has been slowly crumpling over three parliaments, has uncrumpled at a stroke. I can't remember whether he said anything as I was thinking how nice Douglas Hurd, the Home Secretary, would look in a little red fez, with a tassel.

Simon Hughes (Lib? Dem? LibDem? – Bermondsey, anyway) brought out his camel-hue mohair suit, cream socks, white shirt and tan shoes for the cameras. He looked like the youthful operator of a Soho clip joint and glanced at Rosie Barnes (SDP, Greenwich) in burgundy tights. And two things that we thought would never happen have come to pass: Jeremy Corbyn (Lab, Islington N) has combed his beard and Dr Alan Glyn (C, Windsor & Maidenhead) has had his suit darned.

Clare Short (Lab, Birmingham, Ladywood) said something quite lost on those of us transfixed by her new dress, an abstract cotton print in lurid swirls which on Ms Short looks like an infra-red heat map of the Pennines. Near her, in scarlet blazer and white blouse, Joan Lestor (Lab, Eccles) seemed ready to hand one the keys to an Avis Rent-a-Car.

I was just admiring a junior Education minister's courage – for Angela Rumbold (C, Mitcham & Morden), with carrot-tinted hair, to wear electric purple takes guts – when something in the Strangers' Gallery caught my eye: a visitor looked on in a luminous green T-shirt. In fact all the Strangers – I nearly called them 'audience' – seemed smarter.

Perhaps they thought this was *Blind Date* and they were expected to applaud? MPs reacted by sitting up straight and not sniffing under their armpits or cleaning their ears.

Then Mr Speaker explained about the new flashing digital clerks. Or clocks. These 'clocks' he said would 'operate the clerks ... Sorry. The clerks will operate the clocks.' They would 'flash, intermittently'. I think he meant the clocks. I'm not sure. My attention wandered.

For Nicholas Soames (C, Crawley) had come in. Can't remember what he said, but have you *seen* his socks?

18.10.89

A forbidden city's Last hours

YESTERDAY PARLIAMENT was prorogued. It was the last day of the last Parliament to be closed to the TV cameramen. From a near-empty press gallery, I watched a private ceremony as might an infidel in Mecca, conscious of the poignancy, conscious that this was not – yet – public property. Not quite yet.

I gazed at the Tory side.

Mrs Thatcher was there. Downing Street describes her as 'dressed in emerald green crepe, by Aquascutum' but I describe her as looking very tired. Near her were Geoffrey Howe and John Major, one serene, the other frisky. Every human type was there.

On the backbenches, Richard Shepherd (Aldridge-Brownhills), lonely hammer of the Secrets Bill, representing valour and truth in a naughty world;: and representing the naughty world, wily, charming Tristan Garel-Jones, the Deputy Chief Whip and 'soft man' of that band of brigands; near him, like a nightclub bouncer, hard man David Lightbown, a bulky figure of a whip. Nick Ridley was there, in case anyone should wonder why we need whips.

For the rising junior talent there was the coolly courteous Peter Lilley, fresh-faced Financial Secretary; and, not far behind, resting between press releases, Harry Greenway (Ealing N). Brooding in his customary corner was Dr Alan Glyn (Windsor & Maidenhead). Our secret until today, soon these will adorn every parlour.

A knock at the oaken doors and in came Black Rod, bowed, walked four paces, bowed, walked two paces, bowed and said:

'The Lords who are authorized by virtue of Her Majesty's Com-

mission to declare her Royal Assent to Acts passed by both Houses and also to declare the prorogation of Parliament, desire the presence of this honourable House' (and here he bowed once to each side) *'in the House of Peers: to hear the Commission read.'*

All rose. But where was Neil Kinnock? Normally he walks with Mrs Thatcher over to the Lords. Today he was absent – busy, perhaps, learning the pronunciation of foreign cities: we reached Leipzig last week when it all ended in tears. Mrs Thatcher made do with Jack Cunningham, Shadow Leader of the House, leaving the Leader of the House, Sir Geoffrey Howe, in the position of Right Honourable Gooseberry. All exited, chatting amicably.

It left me wondering about their hats. For the State Opening next week the women wear hats, if only to give the TV commentators something to fill the silence with as MPs process out of the Lords. '... And for this occasion, the Premier has chosen a dignified purple toque ...' But now the cameras will have to follow them into the Commons, too. More space to fill. So isn't it time the men wore hats, too?

Neil Kinnock I picture in one of those rapper's caps – a baseball cap worn backwards. Roy Hattersley should have a velvet turban, *diamanté*; Douglas Hurd, a little red fez.

I picture tawny-haired Tom King, the swashbuckling new Defence Secretary, in a Davy Crockett hat, with raccoon tail behind. Mr Ridley needs a Latin-master's mortarboard, like 'Chalky' in the Giles cartoons; and Chris Patten cries out for a college boater. Geoffrey Howe would only look right in a Wee Willy Winkie nightcap and slippers.

Naturally, Paddy Ashdown would have a tweed cap: but what shall we do for Labour's menacing John Prescott, Transport Shadow? A stocking, surely, worn over the head, bank-robber style. It would complement Michael Meacher, from the chilly Left, in surgeon's cap, mask and rubber gloves. A woolly Rasta hat would suit Tottenham's Bernie Grant and joker Tony Banks (Lab, Newham NW) would enliven the scene in jester's cap, with bells ... How viewers would love it!

Speculation was interrupted by the MPs' return. Mr Speaker proudly read a list of achievements (British Railways Penalty Fares Act 1989 ...) and declared the show over. Everybody left.

Last to go was a quiet fellow, Nicholas Baker (Dorset N). On leaving he turned to glance behind. Above, cameras already installed were waiting. It was the Forbidden City's final hour.

17.11.89

Hallelujah!

DID YOU see it?

Breathless at the novelty, I watched Parliament in my jeans, coffee by my side and cat on my lap. It was hard to believe that Mr Speaker could not see me and would not disapprove.

Hallelujah! Pen poised to sneer, I stayed to cheer. Television works!

A dozen carefully prepared jokes about twiddling the colour-control until Mrs Thatcher went green and purple, trying Neil Kinnock with the sound off, and getting the lovely Mrs Virginia Bottomley on horizontal hold, went into the bin. It's no joke: the House of Commons is seriously watchable.

First came the ceremony. Ceremony is a matter of taste, and in this your sketchwriter freely admits to having that part of his brain which enjoys ceremony unaccountably missing.

'And now the Cushion is being handed to the Queen's Bargemaster,' breathed a reverential Dimbleby voice ... 'The Crown is now being put on to its larger Cushion and handed to Lord Cholmondeley ... Colonel Ross takes the Cap of Maintenance from its Staff ...'

I flicked over to BBC 2: *Why Some Food Goes Bad* and watched two cartoon mice: '"What shall we have for supper, Spick?" said Span ...' While they decided, I flicked back to the Royal Procession '... and the Papal Nuncio you can spot there with a pink cap on his head ...' I flicked back to the mice, became wholly absorbed in an account of how a lump of cheese decomposes, and missed the rest of the State Opening. It's the Queen I feel sorry for, as I don't think she's interested in it, either, and she doesn't have the option of flicking over to the mice.

But even the mice went out of the window as the cat and I watched the debate on the Queen's Speech, yesterday.

Tradition dictates that two government back benchers, one senior and one junior, open the debate lightheartedly. They are, as it were, warm-up acts.

Ian Gow, the senior choice and MP for Eastbourne, was for me a litmus test of Commons television. Dry, funny and terribly British, his humour works well in the intimacy of the Chamber; but would it work on television?

It certainly did. Gow joked about his resemblance to a famous alleged murderer, Dr Bodkin Adams, joked about 'grocers from Old Bexley' and joked about his bald pate reflecting the camera-lights.

Beside him the pink head of Gerald Bowden (Dulwich) shone, a rising moon to Mr Gow's setting sun. It was compulsive viewing.

Mrs Thatcher got better as she relaxed and took interruptions in good-humoured, knockabout style. She seemed warmer, less formidable and correspondingly more human on the screen.

Neil Kinnock defied predictions with a performance which was humorous without being lightweight.

Both of them, though speaking at length, kept my cat's and my attention throughout. It was genuinely good television.

22.11.89

D.I.Y. Commons TV kit

FIRST, A word to people without TV sets. The (largely untelevised) *Spectator* Parliamentarian of the Year awards, sponsored in style yesterday by Highland Park Scotch Whisky, were fun. Neil Hamilton (C, Tatton) accepted the 'Wit of the Year' prize, remarking that Parliament was full of 'what Dr Spooner would have called "shining wits"'. John Prescott (Labour's Transport spokesman) praised 'the team who made it all possible: Paul Channon'.

Nigel Lawson – 'Speech of the Year' (his resignation speech) – hoped future winners would find a less painful route to the prize ...

And that's enough offscreen talk. Over to viewers.

Hello viewers. Here is an experiment you can carry out now, in your own home, without any special tools. All you need is this newspaper, and a pair of ordinary kitchen scissors. Fetch them, would you, and return to your armchair. Hold the scissors.

Sitting comfortably? Right. Now, cut a neat rectangle all the way round the edge of these first five paragraphs. Remove the scrap of paper you have cut around.

Done that? You should now have *The Times* minus a small hole in the back page. Yes? Good. Next, hold the paper about a yard from your face, back page open so that this sheet blocks your vision.

Finally, close one eye, peering through the other, at the view through the hole you have cut, into the room on the other side of the sheet. What can you see?

Not much, eh?

But what's that you say? You can sweep to left and right so that the entire picture passes across the little hole? No, viewer: sorry: that's not allowed. You must keep your peephole trained upon the head of whoever in the room is talking. The one alternative permitted is to retreat backwards down the corridor till the room is so distant that it all comes within the margins of your peephole.

These are the two views permitted: none other. Oh, and one optional extra touch: frame the hole, if you like, with the drawing of a television cabinet: legs, an aerial, and knobs along the bottom. Now, would you like to watch Commons TV without the expense of buying a TV licence?

Then come along to Westminster bringing your *Times* with you, sit in the Strangers' Gallery with the newspaper over your head, and watch the debate through the hole. No cheating, mind! No peeking at other MPs snoozing as Sir Bufton Tufton explains the effect of the EC Hill Cow Suckler Premium upon his constituents.

I tried the experiment briefly yesterday during the Industry Debate. Nicholas Ridley spoke first.

Behind him (on *my* screen) was a remarkable backdrop: two groins and an expansive stomach. If I tell you that the tum belonged to Nicholas Soames and the groins to David Harris and Tony Baldry then you will know that I cheated and executed the taboo 'up-body scan' – at least that is how I *hope* you think I knew.

But should I award constituencies to these groins? (Crawley, St Ives and Banbury, respectively)? Sketchwriters normally do, but does the bottom half of a person really *have* a constituency, properly speaking? Heaven help the first Member who forgets to zip up.

23.11.89

MPs that bloom in the spring

IT WAS the first of May, the sun was shining and the ladies looked like herbaceous borders. MPs were the waiting blossoms, TV cameras the wandering honey-bees.

Your sketchwriter has remarked before on the stunning effect of television upon MPs' dress. Though it took the plant world eons to choose the best blooms for attracting insects, it has taken MPs only twenty weeks to learn which colours stand out brightest on TV. Never has natural selection been fast-forwarded at such alarming pace.

All around the Chamber, clinging to oak-panelled walls, the big, black, electronic bees whirred and swivelled their lenses. Upon whom would they alight first?

Michael Foot shambled in. This great man has altered nothing for the cameras. The electronic bees swung their lenses away in distaste and scanned the Chamber. What was that on the Tory benches? A hydrangea bush in full flower? No. It was Dame Jill Knight (Edgbaston), in a vast floral design of blue, turquoise and pink. How could the cameras – or Mr Speaker – resist?

'Dame Jill Knight,' he called, as the cameras spun.

The hydrangea bush questioned the Health Secretary about doctors' pay. Kenneth Clarke revealed this to have risen from £12,230 in 1979 to £33,280. The Bush resumed its seat, ample blossoms trembling.

We awaited the entrance of the Prime Minister.

At this, Edwina Currie swayed so enticingly that it seemed that if the cameras would not come to Mrs Currie, Mrs Currie would come to the cameras. Maybe she has forgotten the King of Siam in *The King and I*:

> To fly from blossom to blossom,
> The honey bee must be free.
> But blossom must not ever fly
> From bee, to bee, to bee!

Over on the Labour side, two by-election victors had burst into flower. Sylvia Heal (Mid Staffs) was in a floral print of greens and blues, while Kate Hoey (Vauxhall) was a slender spray of star-like little crimson flowers, on a black field.

The camera chose neither but – though the hydrangea bush was bobbing again – preferred a billowing bunch of big red poppies called Emma Nicholson (C, Devon W & Torridge). The poppies wanted the PM to know that more paid the community charge, so it must be fairer.

The pollen count was high and rising. And we have passed over a bed of orange and crimson nasturtiums in a blue jacket. Mr Speaker noticed it, though, and so did the bees.

'Dame Peggy Fenner,' he called; and the nasturtiums (representing Medway, in the Conservative interest) rose, petals upturned in a colourful plea: would the Prime Minister list the five councils with the worst record on Education, the five (*lost in hubbub*) and the five (*howl!*)

Where another woman might carry with her a tin of Elastoplast or a spare button, in case of sudden need, Mrs Thatcher carries a list of the five authorities with the worst record on anything-you-please, in case a passing MP for Medway should be caught short just before a local election. She produced it, leaving the now traditional pause after each name, for the Tories to chorus 'Labour!'

Ted Heath shook his head, aghast at the vulgarity. The nasturtiums grinned, the Speaker sighed and the bees − for whom this whole show has been contrived − whirred happily around the Chamber.

2.5.90

High on hot air and hype

THE QUEEN Elizabeth II Conference Centre rose, sun-kissed, from a dark sea of black Mercedes cars. On their bonnets tinpot flags fluttered, while number plates like VEN 1 proclaimed their authority.

This was the class the little people in Africa call the *wabenzi* − the Mercedes Benz people: the people of which any good Third World jamboree consists: the rich from poor nations, come to blame the poor from rich nations.

The first law of political pantomime is that every fatuous 'initiative' should spawn at least two more, of equal futility. The Prime Minister's speech to her UN drugs conference yesterday spawned nine, each more specious than the last. It was a deserved success.

From the outset, the auspices were good. Your correspondent knows two signs that an occasion will lack substance. One is the appearance of women in hats. The other is the appearance of common nouns in capital letters. At 'The World Ministerial Summit to Reduce the Demand for Drugs and to Combat the Cocaine Threat', hats would have been superfluous.

'Over here, Mrs Thatcher, look this way!' *Snap, flash, click, pop ...* 'Shake hands again, Prime Minister, for the cameras!' Encircled by corded rope in mid-foyer (where you might once have placed an extravagant display of flowers) was an island of tripods and cameramen, waving like tropical palms.

The AutoCue glasses glowed cool blue in the dark. All at once a taped disco-style fanfare filled the hall. And hidden projectors beamed a picture of the UN flag tangled up with the Union Jack. A ripple of applause signalled the entrance of the Great Ones.

From the Prime Minister, or, rather, her AutoCue machine, came a cornucopia of initiatives. There was the 'Pompidou Group', 'Crimestoppers', 'Drug Command' and 'Crop Substitution'. There was a new charity, 'Business Against Drugs' ('BAD'?), money for Colombia (ha!) and a new UK 'Taskforce' to advise foreigners how to 'reduce demand for drugs' in their own countries (no joke!). There was a protocol with Finland.

Mrs Thatcher wore shimmering blue and pearls, she who once spurned the politician's addiction to hot-air summitry. No longer. If 'initiatives' do for the PM what a sniff of cocaine does for some of her citizens, then on yesterday's showing, this woman needs help.

10.4.90

7

Strange Countries

In a coca field in Bolivia

I AM sitting in the sun in the middle of a huge coca plantation in Bolivia. By the time this appears in *The Times* I shall be at the Liberal Democrat conference in Blackpool. I lose track of what is real.

On balance I think it is the coca. The young seedlings look robust – millions of slender shoots, closely packed in rows of deep and steeply raked little terraced trenches, like the upper circle at Covent Garden. Apparently you can get four crops a year, better than the 'substitute' peasants are encouraged to grow: passion fruit. I ask you! I have yet to see a passion fruit vine here. Coca is five times as profitable.

From the hill behind me comes the sound of drums, trumpets and a Sousaphone. The town of Chulumani is rehearsing for the day of its patron saint, Bartholemew. Dancing troupes in costumes and headdresses that owe much to Indian folk culture but something to Yankee drum majorettes are high-kicking around the main square. It is stifling hot.

As I sit here, with tropical birds shrieking from the hillside at a peasant preparing a trench with loving care, my mind goes back to Mrs Thatcher's keynote address to the world ministerial drug summit staged by the United Nations in London in April. The meeting was held with much pomp in the sumptuous Queen Elizabeth II Conference Centre and cost millions of pounds. The press got free clipboards, cakes and coffee and a special lounge to relax in. Maybe they should have invited a few peasants.

By mistake I had been ushered into the delegates' gallery and found myself mingling with ministers and presidents from many nations as, lit in a blue spotlight, Mrs Thatcher emerged – to taped music – on to the rostrum. She spoke in her especially sincere voice about the scourge of drugs, and how we must all do our bit, and what a splendid effort was being made by the producer countries to stamp it out.

I assume that our ambassador in La Paz had told her what is actually going on here. I watched her carefully throughout that speech, and she never winked. I wonder why. If I have learned one thing from her it is that no regulatory force in the world can come between a willing buyer and a willing seller. Official obstruction only raises the price. Higher prices encourage new efforts at production. I think this is what Adam Smith called 'the invisible hand'.

Really, then, the resilience of the world drugs trade is a magnificent vindication of Thatcherite economic theory. I salute this; but I do wish, just occasionally, that she would wink.

17.9.90

Down and out on Tyneside

As a Tory MP in 1984, invited by Granada Television's 'World in Action', I spent a week tasting life on the dole in Newcastle ...

YOU CAN forget leather armchairs and Socratic dialogue: there's nothing like physical discomfort to challenge intellectual certainty: and I'm cold.

It's snowing outside and I've just come in from dealing with the frozen corpse of a stray cat – a kerbside victim of feline hypothermia. I had not realized their tails went so stiff. Fumbling for a 50p coin for the gas meter, it occurs to me that perhaps poverty is as good a test of a Tory's commitment to conservatism as is prosperity of a socialist's commitment to egalitarianism.

I run, mentally, through the tenets of the Free Market Philosophy, repeating them to myself a little desperately, seeking (as did Saint Theresa or Pooh Bear, in moments of spiritual or physical peril) the reassurance of a familiar recitation.

The Market must decide. Yesterday's industries must be allowed to die if room is to be made for tomorrow's. Gosh that sounds harsh, but I still believe it. Even as I stare at the sad, empty shipyards, or talk to the unemployed men who used to work there, I cannot waver from that, and nor do many of them. Unrealistic though some of them are about what the Government can do, they glumly acknowledge that there is no point in pouring billions into loss-making industries.

Regional aid distorts the market and props up inefficiency. The state has no more business choosing the geography of investment than choosing the type. I'm less cocksure about that than I was a few days ago. Millions of people are settled here; must they move to the jobs – or cannot industry be prodded into coming to them? No – come to think of it – no: on the economic argument it is wrong to interfere. But on the social argument? I'm less sure ... but then so is Norman Tebbit, so I cannot be all that wet. If we cannot transform the North-east, perhaps we can at least help let people down gently? Or do I really mean 'die with dignity'?

People should move to where the jobs are. It has just struck me, and struck me hard, that Adam Smith is not saying that at all. I've been muddling him up with Sir Alfred Sherman. Smith was not a moralist. Smith would say that people 'will' move to where the jobs are. Sherman would say that they 'should'. It is the difference between the priest and the scientist and why Sherman is offensive and Smith is not. The fact is, of course, that people do move, without needing instructions from any of us. People are quitting Newcastle at a faster rate than the economy can absorb, already. There is no evidence of a shortage, anywhere in the country, of middle-aged, unemployed ship-workers, created by the disinclination of these gentlemen to leave Newcastle.

I see why the moral imperative in that word 'should' is gratuitous and therefore offensive – but I see, too, why it is important to those who use it: it comforts them. It implies that the distress of the unemployed is somehow self-imposed, unnecessary – their responsibility entirely.

We must not stifle energy and initiative. Fear not, Prime Minister. That famous British drive and ingenuity is alive and well in Scotswood, Tyneside – and emerging in ways which are not quite what you, or I, had in mind. Curiously, I find that rather encouraging, if reprehensible. Far worse would be to see people's spirits broken ... but one had better say no more, for fear of being thought to condone fraud or vandalism.

Less controversially, it could be put like this: I worry most about those who do *not* riot or become barrack-room social security experts, but passively accept their fate.

I am meeting many such people. For those in middle life, unskilled or skilled only in the trades whose industries are declining in Newcastle (and everywhere else), the chances of a job are poor indeed. You could (my hard-line colleagues are right) push them into seeking the unskilled broom-and-shovel jobs for which school-leavers already vie, at rock-bottom wages, by reducing the family benefits, which create the 'poverty trap'; but what would be the point, when unskilled work is already as sought after and as badly paid as it is in the North-East? Alternatively you could, as more 'imaginative' politicans often argue, try to train people for new careers. We do this for some, but to do it for all would cost the earth, produce mixed results, and offload on to the jobs market hundreds of thousands of middle-aged men to compete with apprentices and college-leavers for jobs which there is already no difficulty filling.

So what else can these men do? Is it practical to urge that they take their families and rise, like a flock of birds, heading for the Home Counties? Of course not. The Government rather depends on their *not* doing so – not, at least, all at once. They are well and truly stuck.

What is there to say to them? When I protest that Mrs Thatcher is doing as much as anyone is able, this is met with incredulous jeers. 'Why are we being punished?' is the question I have been asked everywhere. In that sense the residents of the estate where I am living are deeply unrealistic. I keep telling them so. But (it occurs to me) am I, too, living in a fantasy world, believing that there is any way to lead them away from such delusions? What is more bitter than the thought that your problems are nobody's fault at all, but just your own bad luck – that your region is a victim of some kind of economic road accident?

Is there any way you can tell a man that his industry, his job and his family are necessary, even glorious, casualties in the battle to transform the British economy and revolutionize social attitudes – and make him feel good about it?

Five years ago, scolding a Conservative parliamentary candidate who had got into hot water for writing a rude letter to a complaining council tenant (a Mrs Collingwood), Auberon Waugh wrote:

'... The truth of the matter is that something rather nasty *is* going to happen to the Collingwoods of this world and ... the least we can do is imitate the Walrus:

> '*I weep for you,*' *the Walrus said,*
> '*I deeply sympathize.*'
> *With sobs and tears he sorted out*
> *Those of the largest size.*

The best idea might be genuinely to feel sorry for the things that have got to be done.'

The parliamentary candidate in question happened to be me. After five years in the House of Commons and three days in Newcastle, I rather think Mr Waugh was right.

23.1.84

Doorstep contrasts

Out of Parliament and freed from the Tory whip, I go knocking on doors for all three parties.

STARING TOO intently at an underwear advertisment on the Piccadilly line, I was once recognized by a constituent from Belper. The incident still burns in my memory. That, however, was the only time London ever caught me out, so strikingly unmemorable is my face. The risk of apprehension was never great. And now, no longer an MP, the penalty, too, has been removed. What forbidden fruit, what secret gardens, what half-lit rooms and exotic company await?

I was shocked at the plan forming in my mind. Why not see what it is actually like *canvassing for the Labour Party*? And the Alliance too? Why not all three, and compare the experience? The local elections would provide the ideal opportunity.

It was easy to arrange. A gentle start seemed best: with the Tories in Fairfield ward, Wandsworth, held by Labour in 1978, against Parris, M. (Con) by a majority of 13 votes and fought, now, for the Conservatives by Massood Qureshi, a bright local shopkeeper, and Brian Graham, an accountant of the agreeable sort.

How little had changed! The same steward of the same constitutional club showed me up to the same committee room. Same old table too, but dear Mrs Saunders had passed away and presided no longer, as had the redoubtable Mr Pavovich. Mrs Pavovich, however, remained firmly in control. First, a little chat with everyone (no Conservative committee room is complete without it).

A cup of tea? No, get to work while it's still light: 'They don't answer the door after dark on the Wendlesworth Estate.' Oh God! Not the Wendlesworth Estate! 'Binstead House for you, Matthew.' Oh Lord! Not Binstead House!

'Yes, certainly, Mrs Pavovich.'

Binstead House had not changed much either: a depressing brick-built, medium-rise council block. But the entryphones were new and I quickly perfected a technique which served me well for all three parties. Press any bell:

'Crackle-crackle ... Who is it?'

'I'm (mumble-mumble) local council. I've got a leaflet for you. Can I come up?'

It never failed!

'What? The *Conservatives*? You must be joking. You've trebled the rent.'

'Yes, but look at the rates: cut to half what they are in Lambeth.'

'Keep your voice down! I don't want people to know I'm even *talking* to a Tory.'

A Conservative canvasser in Binstead House feels rather like a preacher among unbelievers, looking for outposts of the receptive. He does find them, though. Tory Wandsworth's policy of selling council flats and houses brings a couple of new votes on every staircase. At one flat the lady refused to speak, but mouthed, and gestured, that she would support us. 'I don't want the neighbours to hear,' she whispered as I left. She might like to know that the neighbours vote Tory too.

Not all of them, though: 'Of course I won't be voting. I hate this bloody government.'

'Well, goodbye ...' I exited. In this case abstention was the best one could hope for.

There were many West Indians but few seemed to vote anything but Labour. These were, without exception, among the politest 'no's I got. Nor is it true that young people are especially rude. Of the three really nasty responses I got, all came from old, working-class white men.

Canvassing later, for Labour, I found that old middle-class white men were rude as well.

The similarities, in fact, were remarkable. I gulped as I rang for Flat 5: the committee room for West Putney Labour Party. Peter Hain, the prospective parliamentary candidate for Putney, had sent me. I wondered how I would fare and whether the gap would be unbridgeable.

In I walked. But where were the Trotskyites with their rimless glasses? And where the pale Marxists with sunken eyes? The candidates, Madeleine Campbell, Niki Cartwright and Mark Hagger, looked the kind of people one meets at supper parties: bright and distinctly unmenacing. There was a slightly less chatty, more determined atmosphere than a Tory is accustomed to.

A yellow sheet of paper listing the likely questions ('Are the Tories *really* running Wandsworth so badly?'), the recommended answers and some hints on canvassing would be less common in Tory committee rooms. But the differences were not profound. I stuck a red and yellow Labour sticker on my green jacket (grey shirt with a red T-shirt beneath – the flash of crimson hinting, I thought, more at excitement than danger) and set off.

It was a similar estate to Wendlesworth and my canvass returns showed a similar preponderance of Labour voters.

The nicest thing about canvassing for Labour is perhaps also its most serious problem. The more hopeless or unsuccessful a voter seems – the thinner the hand or the shabbier the furniture – the more likely he is to vote Labour.

'Labour d'you say? Oh yes, don't worry, I'll be there!' The little man in the threadbare cardigan, his anxious-looking wife hovering in the passage, added that he felt worried about extremists: 'But Mr Kinnock does seem to be doing something about that.'

'He certainly is!' I replied. 'There are no Militants in the Putney Labour Party.' The arguments, oddly enough, come quite easily. One just seems to throw a switch in one's mind and new circuits are engaged. What is harder to alter is the almost unconscious association of certain types of doorknob, floor mat, household and householder, with 'friend' and others with 'foe'.

By the end of an hour, at last, I was beginning to realize that 'bad' areas were now 'good' for 'us'. I was beginning to see the three little ragamuffins hanging on the grubby skirt of the harassed mum as tokens of probable support rather than ill omens; and to approach the polished open-air door with a brass knocker and 'welcome' doormat with the reservation that I was as likely to be *un*welcome!

Canvassing for Labour is heart-warming because you feel that your voters really need you. Conservative voters often exude such self-confidence that the candidate feels redundant. I am not, here, arguing whether it is wise or in the national interest to provide help on the scale that a Labour canvasser is wont to offer: only pointing out that it is humanly very pleasant to do, and good for the canvasser's self-esteem.

I must not exaggerate. Equally interesting is the undeniable fact that Labour is clearly regaining some support among the more genteel types of voter.

'Well, I switched to Mrs Thatcher last time,' a retired schoolmistress told me, 'but now they're doing something about Derek Hatton I think I'll vote Labour. I'm worried about all these lesbians though ...'

Where one did meet stiff resistance was among the group Brian Walden calls 'strivers'. Young husbands, doing well at work and buying their flats, were politely 'not interested'. 'Where would the money for all your schemes come from?' said one tenant who was hoping to buy. 'Besides, the Tories have cut the rates to half what they are in Lambeth.'

'But they've trebled the rents!' I retorted, quick as a flash. Useful this political double-life.

Quite without doubt, it is Liberal canvassers who have most fun. Perhaps Anne Winfield is untypical, but everyone, or almost everyone, in the Little Ilford ward in Newham seemed to know her. She had been the sitting councillor but her husband Rif was standing in her place along with Tommy Humfrey and Clefene Skyers. Their daughter was called Storm. What odd names Liberals seem to have. And, yes, there was a barrel of muesli in the cluttered kitchen that seemed to double as committee room and Liberal club.

I agreed to wear an enormous orange rosette in return for their agreeing not to photograph me, and set out with councillor plus Storm. My classic Tory 'Can we count on your support on May 8' soon faltered as I heard the agent, Peter Guest, at one door ('Are you pleased with the work Anne's done? Yes? Oh good: then you *will* display this grand orange sticker, won't you? Here, I'll help you – just drag that stepladder over, dear. Scissors please, Storm. Sticky tape!') and Anne at the other ('How's Ada, my love? And little Freddie – shingles, wasn't it? Yes. I'll get that guttering removed.').

At first I wondered whether the householders had been specially set up for me: but there were just too many for that. I began to gather confidence myself: 'Conservative? But it's a wasted vote in Newham – only we can stop those awful Labour councillors. Do think about it, dear!'

Now at last I was really beginning to enjoy myself: 'Look at that dripping cistern, love! Those Labour people just don't care, and the Tory cuts make it worse. We'll have Anne on to that right away.'

Again, I make no political argument. I understand perfectly well that Anne doesn't have to balance the council's books . . . I'm just saying it's more *fun* to be a Liberal, that's all, and not denying that it's hard work, either.

More fun, anyway, than the one incident which I have yet to relate. It happened outside Binfield House. A couple of smiling faces looked down from an upper floor:

'Who are you?'

'I'm from the Conservatives.' I grinned too.

'Wait a sec.'

I waited. Splash! Bucket of water emptied on to my head. At least I think it was water.

5.5.86

A passage to Pemba

'I, MATTHEW *Francis Parris, British subject born in Johannesburg on 7 August, 1949, and holder of passport number B171432, declare that I intend to travel by dhow from Mombasa to Pemba and that in the event of mishap I shall not hold the Captain or the Government of Kenya responsible for my safety.*

Signed. . . . . . . M F Parris

Witnessed. . . . District Commissioner, Mombasa,

18 September, 1989.'

It wasn't a dhow, really, more a sort of tug with a mast. But it was the first thing leaving the Old Port in Mombasa that week, and I had only four days left. My only map – which, being of the entire continent, lacked detail – showed Pemba as a rather small speck in the Indian Ocean, about 100 miles southeast-ish of Mombasa and somewhere above Zanzibar. This information exceeded that possessed by the Captain, as events were to prove.

The tide rose and the sun set and still the Captain had not come aboard. Instead, more passengers kept arriving in canoes. Our boat was only about fifteen yards long, powered by a small four-cylinder Lister diesel engine: but, by midnight, it was carrying forty-nine Africans, one Asian, me, no lifeboat, no lifebuoys, and one inflated inner tube – which was perhaps for the Captain.

He arrived at midnight – a sort of black Captain Bligh plus spectacles and minus shoes. We sailed.

Then the waves hit us. Surf and spray streamed over the side of the boat. As if with one accord, all the Africans placed blankets over their *heads* – their heads alone, their bodies being left uncovered – and lay down on deck to sleep.

All through the night we pitched and rolled. I slept as best I could, but there were too many bodies and not enough space. I finished up parallel with the side of the boat and pinned against it by four pairs of legs, the forty toes of eight black feet digging into me.

Dawn brought ginger tea boiled on an open wood fire at the stern of the (wooden) boat and served in a single, communal, tin jug. Dawn also brought the sight of land. Land? But it was on the wrong side! 'That is the port of Tanga, in Tanzania,' said the Asian, pointing. My map suggested that Tanga, on the African coast, was not on the way to Pemba. So did the Captain's expression. It was at this point that I realized there was no glass in the frames of his spectacles.

We did a 90-degree turn to the left and headed out to open sea. As we did so, the colour of the ocean changed from deep blue to speckled turquoise. Lumps of coral and patches of sand swam into vision beneath us. All the passengers started leaning over the side and shouting advice as to where the deepest parts might be. For half an hour we weaved through the shallows until the water turned dark again and everyone relaxed. The sun came out and I slept.

When I awoke, no land was visible in any direction. We were chugging into an empty horizon – towards which the captain was peering anxiously.

Lunch was served on an upturned dustbin lid. It was a heap of solid maize porridge, sprinkled with fried fish heads. We all washed our right hand in a bucket of sea water, squatted round, and tucked in.

Then the Asian spotted land – far, far away, just a speck, about 30 degrees off the course we were steering. The Captain was on the toilet at the time – two parallel planks jutting out over the side, shrouded for modesty by a knee-high screen of coconut matting, so that head and shoulders alone were visible, and licked from beneath by the icy crests of passing waves: a sort of natural bidet.

The Captain affected indifference. There being no game of bowls to complete, he completed his toilet instead. Ten minutes later, when he thought no one was looking, we swung round and headed where the Asian had pointed.

And it did turn out to be Pemba, where they grow cloves. You are enveloped, as you arrive, in a warm haze which owes something to baked apple and something to the dental surgery.

It was wonderful to arrive. It proved almost impossible to leave. But that's another story ...

30.9.89

Bounced Back to Oujda

THE PLAN was to cross the Sahara by Land Rover, ending up in East Africa. Well, Morocco was easy. In a blistering heat we drove out of the last Moroccan town you pass – Oujda – before the Algerian frontier on the fringes of the Atlas mountains. I have done it before. The four-hour queue at the Algerian post was two hours shorter than last time. It was less entertaining, though, for last time we helped a Chinese lady from Hong Kong who had spent three days being batted backwards and forwards by suspicious Moroccan and Algerian officials across a fly-blown no-man's-land. In the end, the Algerians let her in.

But now there was no such drama, just a boring wait. Unusually I had the right documents, and I presented them confidently to a uniformed officer.

He beckoned me to follow him into an adjoining room. Strange. Why?

The next thing I knew, I was being yelled at by an Algerian official. 'Madame Thatcher no good!' he bellowed. And he threw our passports down on the table.

I sprang to an impassioned defence of Mrs Thatcher, as you do. It was no good. The *Chef du Poste* was even ruder. We returned, to a sympathetic shrug of the shoulders from the Moroccan side.

A Moroccan telephone kiosk is not the easiest place from which to make international calls, but I reached a friend in England, who reached the night duty officer at the Foreign Office, who told him that this was not a matter for the Foreign Office. The Algerian embassy in London felt that this was not a matter for them, either: 'It's a different ministry, border posts,' said their man, helpfully.

Our embassy in Algiers sympathized, explained that there was a dispute over immigration practices between Britain and Algeria, that the Algerians were taking it out randomly on British travellers, and that our chances were slim. Could I call back soon? At that point, all lines out of Morocco were cut.

So we motored two hundred miles down to Figuig, a desert border post where (we hoped) the news that Mrs Thatcher was no good might not yet have got through. It had. Returning, the Moroccan officer caught sight of my elderly map, showing the Western Sahara (which is claimed by Morocco) as Spanish.

'*Ça touche la monarchie*,' he growled, which, freely translated, means 'I like that map.' So mapless and miserable we drove back across the desert to Oujda. And it was there, wilting in the shade of a pavement café, that I learned about Thomas F. Garnett Jr.

A worried-looking young Arab approached our table and shook our hands with courteous timidity. Could we help him understand something? A letter, he said, unfolding a grubby piece of paper and explaining that he had heard there were vacancies for carpenters at American military establishments and had written to inquire. This was the reply. It was in English which he could not speak. Could we translate?

It was from the Office of the Assistant Secretary of Defense, RCE Management and Personnel, to Mr Cherifi Hichham of 2 Rue Tiznit, Oujda.

I took down every word. 'Employment programs within the DoD are decentralized ... tailor recruitment efforts to varying skill and professional intake requirements ... doubtful whether there will be openings matching your interests.' Cherifi's face fell as we explained.

'This Department is bound to observe Presidential Executive Order 11935 which was issued on 2 September 1976. In essence ...' – *En essence*, we explained to Cherifi.

'It is hoped,' the letter concluded, 'that this information will be helpful.' It was signed 'for' Thomas F. Garnett Jr, Director, Workforce Relations, Training and Staffing Policy.

We looked at Cherifi. Cherifi looked glumly back: hostages, all of us, to the insolence of office.

21.10.89

Felines and freedom fighters

WHAT STRIKES one about Algiers is the smell of cats. Cats everywhere. Cats in the alleys, as you climb the steps from the harbour, cats in the avenues, promenading in the sun; cats in the corridors of the posh hotels. The sleekest of vagabonds, they belong to no one. Accepted with a shrug, they prosper and multiply.

It was a short holiday. On Boxing Day my parents and I were welcomed at Algiers airport by a friend – Walid – from the embassy of the Saharwi Arab Democratic Republic.

Britain has yet to recognize the SADR, though we know their cause is just. Even by the standards of a cynical age it was an outrage for General Franco to sell a whole country to the King of Morocco. For many years the people of the Western Sahara have been fighting to recover their territory: and they appreciate what friends they have – even mum and dad and me. They smoothed our path through Algiers and saw us off next day, bound for the Algerian Sahara and the oasis town of Ghardaia.

The cats had got to Ghardaia first. Our hotel was showily modern and faintly grubby. There is something comic about a snooty head waiter tripping over a miaowing stray. He classed me with the stray: probably because I had lost my smart clothes when the airline lost my suitcase. But I still had one jacket.

I lost that next. My fault, of course. It was sunny by the pool and the jacket came off. Nipping inside. I forgot it and became absorbed by the pool rules, committing them to my reporter's notebook. 'The dangerous Games is forbidden in the Swining pool', I read. 'Deep: 2m towards the plimge end of the bath.' I returned to find the jacket gone. Silly, really, to have left my passport in the pocket.

Everyone was very upset. Frankly I found it hard to match their agitation, for I had lost little, and the sun was warm. 'He seems too calm,' whispered an officer in French to his mate at the *Gendarmerie*. But he typed a report (in Arabic) on a backwards typewriter. I telexed the British embassy. We stayed.

Ghardaia was fascinating. We watched a Muslim rally from the roof of our hotel. The sight of 10,000 men alternately prostrating themselves and waving their arms as a white-robed figure screamed at them from a dais while great pens of women veiled down to just one corner of one eye waited like cattle, aroused in me something I thought I should never feel: affection for the FLN – the socialist governing party, and only bastion against these horrors. The police hung around awkwardly, nervous, like us. My mother asked a boy: 'Do women like being veiled?' The question perplexed him until he saw (he supposed) its meaning.

'Some have cheap veils and this is sad. But some – my brother's wife for instance – have very excellent veils: pure wool.'

Algeria is in a fix. French banknotes slip from hand to hand like pornographic postcards.

But the telex works. And so does the British consul. To be told on New Year's morning to cool my heels for a few days would have been as much as I deserved. To be told I could call in at 11 am, with two photographs, and leave on a midday flight was incredible. To be invited to our ambassador's New Year's Eve party was remarkably kind. And when Walid met us at the airport with news that *his* ambassador had arranged a party ... well, neither could be missed.

They were so different! The British ambassador, Patrick Eyers, commanding but relaxed, is now bound for East Berlin. This was his leaving party, and a jolly one. One moment I was dancing a conga through a most elegant residence, wondering why I ever left the diplomatic service, the next I was sitting on the floor of a quiet flat in intense discussion with men whose desert war was life and death ...

There was one sad moment. When Walid and I reached the imposing gates of the British residency, he tactfully turned back. It would have been better if we could have gone in together. Let us hope!

6.1.90

Oh Peru, Peru

OH PERU, Peru! What a mess ... Each time I come to Lima I see a nation on the brink of collapse. Yet each time Peru seems to stagger on to the next brink. This, surely, is the last.

'Only a few of us bother working,' said the airport taxi driver, 'now they have raised the price of petrol.'

'How much?' The usual taximan's rant.

'Thirty times.'

'Thirty times what?'

'Thirty times what it was last week.'

He shot across a red light. A bus called Heart of Jesus took routine avoiding action. Heart of Jesus was so tightly packed that the head of an Indian boy was jammed sideways against a window, immobilizing him. The whites of his eyes were showing and he appeared to be dead, but the glass against which his mouth pressed was steamed up, so maybe he was breathing.

Lima is full of tanks, jeeps, water cannon and soldiers. Between the airport and the Church of San Francisco we saw enough ammunition to sustain a small war.

'For security,' explained our driver. 'There have been bombs, hidden by Shining Path terrorists. Cars explode. Also donkeys, chickens, and children, with dynamite inside. Also there may be demonstrations and a general strike tomorrow.'

'Against?'

'Against inflation. Against *el choque* [the shock]. The president promised before the election that the economic crisis could be solved without a *choque*. Now it comes. People are angry. They may throw stones. Against inflation.'

It is true that the new president, the almost unknown Señor Fujimori, had aroused impossible expectations. Mrs Thatcher, the First Lady of Choque, would say he has only himself to blame.

By the Palace of the Inquisition, bewildered soldiers fingered self-loading rifles as a crowd of women demonstrated. 'Against prices,' said the taxi driver. 'The price of noodles has risen by 700 per cent.'

Ten dollars buys you a packet of notes in Peruvian intis, of which yesterday there were 310,000 to the dollar. The whole thing is a sort of Thatcher nightmare.

I peer out of the taxi window. Setting the seal on the nightmare, an old man – presumably mad – is walking purposefully down the carriageway, dodging rush-hour traffic. He is naked. Peruvians stare out of buses at him in mild alarm.

Lima is a purgatory. It sweats and shivers for half the year under a motionless grey bank of Pacific mist: a cracked colonial ruin in flaking baroque and blistered wood, surrounded by one of the largest shanty towns in the southern hemisphere: a sea of urine-soaked corrugated iron. To north and south is desert. Meanwhile the Pacific pounds the shore at the feet of crumbling cliffs behind which the city squats, tipping its refuse into the sea. This is a magnificently wrecked environment.

Beneath these cliffs we spent our first evening. Here, on a pier striding into the breakers, is the restaurant Rosa Nautica. Under glass pavilions, the Peruvian super-rich dine in tropical Art Deco splendour, amid palms, fans and tinkling pianos.

The gates of the pier were guarded by soldiers with automatic weapons. For 30 yards along the pier to the restaurant door, an Indian with a rickshaw offered my parents a ride. And there was a monkey in a frock. For a fee, the monkey would select a paper, telling your fortune, from her stack.

The soldier eyed the rickshaw man; the rickshaw man eyed the diners; the diners smiled at the monkey. The monkey eyed the soldier. Oh Peru, Peru!

25.8.90

Man eats glass tube

I HAVE just seen a man eating a fluorescent light tube. We were standing in the main square of Cuzco, in the Peruvian Andes. A small demonstration against President Fujimori's 'shock' economic policies ('Señor Fujichoque' they are calling him) had passed peacefully and the precautionary twentieth-century water-cannon was rumbling back to its stand-by position next to the sixteenth-century cathedral.

'This,' says my guidebook, 'was the great civic square of the Incas, flanked by their palaces. It was a place of solemn parades and great assemblies.' I bet they never ate fluorescent lights, though. As we watched, a small group of Indians – peasants and townspeople – began to form around a couple of street performers. Soon it was a crowd. We joined it. We were the only foreigners.

The performers' leader was of mixed blood, Hispanic and Indian. He had the patter. The other was quiet and looked a little nervous. He was a young Indian, about eighteen.

The warm-up act was performed by their accomplice, a boy who could not have been more than eight years old. He strutted around the ring, wisecracking with the hard-bitten, roguish familiarity of an Indian Artful Dodger. Childhood is very short in Peru.

'Now,' announced the half-caste, 'for the wonder of Cuzco. The fluorescent tube-eater . . .' Faces in the crowd registered perplexity. 'Yes, my friends, this man eats glass.'

The youth's brow furrowed. From the sack he drew an intact yard-long fluorescent tube. The crowd gasped. The youth gulped.

His senior comrade took the tube. 'The glass will be taken through the mouth' – he pointed – 'into the digestive system' – he patted – 'and finally depart.' He indicated whence. The crowd roared. 'After eating, a collection will be taken. All who doubt, get your money ready now.

'First, however, my friend will fracture the tube by breaking it over

189

his head. I present the marvel of the Andes, the electrician's nightmare, the tube-eater of Peru!'

For the first time, the young Indian spoke. His voice was soft. He lacked the pantomime bravado of his manager.

'I will break the tube on your count of ten,' he said. 'Every particle will be ingested. You will forgive me if I leave the metal elements.'

'He's stalling,' someone said.

'One,' shouted some cruel soul in the audience. 'Two,' the cry was taken up.

There was a pause after 'Ten,' then *smash*. Thin slivers of glass poured down over the Indian's head and his face was covered in fine white powdered chemical. A yelp of astonishment rose from the onlookers. In one hand, he held one half of the fluorescent tube, in the other, the remainder.

There was another pause. He opened his mouth. He had good teeth, strong and white. Silence had fallen on the crowd. The youth seemed to rally his confidence. Firmly he pushed about two inches of one jagged section, still raining white chemical, into his mouth, and bit. The crowd shuddered. He withdrew the tube, shorter now, and held it like a stick of lollypop. He munched. The crowd's curiosity had turned to horror, perhaps shame.

Gingerly, the youth swallowed, making two attempts. Then he opened his mouth for another bite, of the other half. At the fourth bite, I left. This morning, there were still slivers of glass around the spot where the boy had made his meal.

'The actual surface of the square,' says Peter Frost's excellent *Exploring Cuzco*, 'which is reported to have been of white sand from the coast, mingled with numerous tiny ritual objects, of gold, silver, coral, shells ...'

And glass.

1.9.90

Fred in Bolivia

FRED TURNS to me. His face is blue with cold and with the altitude, which is 15,500 feet. Snow covers him, and his hair gel has frozen stiff.

'Matthew,' he says.

'Yes, Fred?'

'I'm never, *ever* going on an expedition with you again.'

I had not anticipated the blizzard. I have lost the feelings in my hands and feet. Fred's trainers, and my Hush Puppies, are not ideal for an Inca trail over the Andes. I keep falling over, but a rucksackful of summer sleeping bags, schoolboy tent, ten bars of Sublime (Bolivia's approach to fruit-and-nut chocolate) and a half bottle of whisky cushion the impact. 'Cheer up, Fred. It's downhill all the way now, nine thousand feet downhill, actually. We'll be in jungle tomorrow. And look! You can just see the Inca paving under the snow. Magnifi . . .' I fall over.

Fred, who is not an Inca historian but a repairer and spray painter of shop-window mannequins, plods on, wordless.

Down and down winds our trail. The snow becomes rain, and Fred's hair gel runs. The sky clears. Suddenly a shaft of evening sun illuminates great folds of jungle below. We must camp now, before dark. An ideal patch is found; up goes the tent, down goes the sun; out comes the chocolate; and we decide to build a fire with wet wood and quarter of a candle.

While Fred is kindling the fire, I look up to encounter an astonishing sight. A procession of six middle-aged Germans, carrying ski sticks and umbrellas, followed by eight Indian porters and three donkeys fully laden, is winding its way on to our little campsite.

The Germans do not speak to us but confer in their unusual language, point to the ground in front of our tent, and bark orders to the Indians. The Indians unload from the donkeys and erect two vast tents for the Germans, *slap bang outside the front of our tent*. We are so close that the Germans cannot get in without kicking our guy-ropes.

The Indians look embarrassed and help with our fire. We end up sharing our whisky with them, and taking turns to blow the embers. The fire must succeed, because a German has laughed at it. We blow the ashes and drink the whisky until we're dizzy. Sparks fly, and we and the Indians giggle as strange guttural noises come from the battery-lit interiors of the zip-sealed German tents. Come back Nicholas Ridley: all is forgiven!

A frozen night, a sunny dawn, a day's march through forests, parrots, fuchsias and butterflies. Fred's hair gel totally melts. We sleep outside. In the dark, green fireflies dive-bomb and little black things bite our legs.

Dawn brings a final scramble down to the road. 'We can flag down a passing truck,' I say to Fred, 'to take us to Chulumani. Trucks are fun! Listen! Here comes one now ...'

'At a hell of a lick,' says Fred, as 20 tonnes of steel and wood drift round the blind bend, horn blaring, and anchors are jammed on.

It roars off again as we haul rucksacks up over the side and topple into the cargo bed. We are not alone. One Indian youth is giggling hysterically; others are hunched against the bulkhead, heads buried between their knees. We almost fly. Trees lash the sides of the cab while the wooden side strikes overhanging rock cuttings, partly smashing it. Dust covers everything. Fred's melted hair gel has turned to designer mud, and he crouches with the Indians. He looks up, only the whites of his eyes and the red of his nose – which is bleeding – visible.

'Matthew ...' he says.

'Yes, Fred. You told me already.'

15.9.90

Scowl on the Cheshire cat

SOUTHERN CHILE is like Massachusetts with volcanoes. On the way down from the northern desert we paused in central Chile, which is like Kent with bamboo: flat fields, hills and orchards and – an unusual sight – shantytowns of shacks and huts, inhabited by whites.

It is odd to see a white person coming out of a hut. One feels there must be some mistake. Is he perhaps a tourist who has gone into the hut to photograph the natives? No. He is in rags. He and many like him *are* the natives.

Chile is far busier and more prosperous than Peru, its immediate northern neighbour; but in contrast to Europe it is poor. Prices are low, the people welcoming and honest, facilities good and the natural setting spectacular – so why are there so few European tourists?

Perhaps we are not visiting yet because of General Pinochet. I am told that, incredible though I find it, there really are people who do not go to a country because they disagree with its government. If so, the problem with Chile will be that the General has not made a clean exit.

He is fading gradually. Like a malign Cheshire cat, soon all that will be visible will be the glint of medals and a disembodied scowl.

So who decides when it is acceptable for thinking people to start visiting again? Will someone fire a starting pistol? Will there be announcements in the *Guardian*?

CHILE: slight delay due to technical problems. SOUTH AFRICA: please wait for further announcements. SOUTH KOREA: indefinitely postponed. PARAGUAY: awaiting information. SPAIN: now boarding but avoid bullfights.

Our first port of call in the south was Puerto Montt, a town of wooden clapboard houses with painted tin roofs, looking out over a cold Pacific fringed with wooded bays and gorsy islands: a sort of downmarket Nantucket. It is cold and crisp and clear, and the smell of baking clams fills the air. The people there are so out of date that when you say you are from England, they ask you if you know Liverpool.

We visited Chiloé. This is a huge and lovely island, about the length of Wales, not far offshore. A gentle place, covered in flowering gorse, temperate woodland and little patchworks of fields, Chiloé (rather like Gibraltar) clung to its imperial mother after all the children had left home. Well into the last century the islanders refused to accept the independence of Chile and remained loyal to the Spanish crown. But Spain was unable to protect them; so in desperation their governor, with the support of the people, declared the island for Britain.

George Canning turned them down. What a shame! Canning was obviously a wimp.

The flight back to Britain was preceded by a day in Santiago de Chile, a graceless, smog-choked city of incredible bustle and life. On my last evening I walked past the Moneda Palace (bombed by Pinochet: Allende died there). Two armed soldiers in toytown uniforms stood guard at the portals.

As I watched, a car sped up. From it jumped a student, with two friends carrying cameras. The youth was semi-naked, plastered in soot and dressed as a devil, with horns and a tail. The car sped off.

He hesitated, walked nervously up to the sentries, and posed self-consciously between them. His friends glanced quickly round, half-expecting arrest, then took their pictures fast. The sentries, standing stiffly to attention, looked awkward but made no move. The students scampered off round the corner, giggling. The old General's scowl, now barely visible, hung faint in the smog, twitching angrily.

An odd parting image of South America: and not a dignified picture of the dawn of liberty. But poignant in its way.

24.9.90

8

But What If . . .?

1990: the year ahead

IN A shock January reshuffle, precipitated by the accidental salmonella poisoning of all the Anglican bishops at an ill-fated Synodal lunch, John Major will be made Archbishop of Canterbury.

'I see myself as very much in the learning-curve stage at present,' a delighted Major will tell journalists, poking at his battered Chancellor's dispatch box with his newly-acquired shepherd's crook and adjusting his mitre. 'I must say it was the last thing I expected.'

He will add that there is to be 'no change in policy – sorry – *doctrine*'. As for the rumoured merger with Rome (the so-called 'European Communion'), that would occur 'when the conditions are right': exchange controls and transubstantiation would have to be abolished before we could even consider *Urbi et Orbi* Stage II.

One of Major's last decisions before quitting the Exchequer will be an award of special pensions in response to growing public anger over the case of those who survive the London epidemic of listeria-poisoning which will follow the resort to drinking infected soda-pop when the Great Drought of 1990 cuts tap-water supplies and animal liberationists poison Perrier as a protest against McDonalds' introduction of the French horse-burger into their British restaurants.

The award to survivors will temporarily halt the slide in the Government's popularity. By mid-February, however, the slide will resume, prompting a flurry of interest in the re-named Social Liberal Party, which will be under the 'caretaker' leadership of Lord Grimond following the resignation of Paddy Ashdown in protest at a majority decision at the Young Liberals' conference at Cleethorpes that he should change his name to Gladstone Mandela.

In March, Mrs Thatcher will be the first Western leader to support the United States invasion of Mexico in self-defence after a disagreement over illegal immigration. To counter the wave of domestic unpopularity that this brings, the pensions of the remaining listeria survivors (more will by then have perished in the rioting on the London Underground triggered by the failure of its last functioning escalator) will again be doubled.

Nicholas Ridley will present his Budget. Its centrepiece will be a scheme extending tax-relief for employers on the wages of domestic servants, which he describes as 'a Budget for Service'.

In April, the Finnish economy will collapse, the wood-pulp industry having been killed off by a successful Green Party campaign which persuades the British population to switch to recycled toilet paper.

Lazard Brothers will win the contract to arrange the flotation for Mr Gorbachov's privatization of Lenin's Tomb. The issue will be massively oversubscribed, and many will complain that the country's heritage is being disposed of at give-away prices.

Poll tax demands start to drop through letterboxes in England and Wales. Due to a fault in the complex formulae devised to cushion the effect of this tax in high-spending Labour authorities, the amount of the tax-demand in each area turns out to vary in *inverse* proportion to the expenditure of the local council.

In the ensuing wave of outrage, the Government will triple the pensions of the listeria survivors after three who have managed to struggle up the non-functioning escalator at Holborn Underground station are gored to death by malfunctioning automatic ticket barriers.

In May, the Iranian religious leadership passes a death sentence on Barbara Cartland, after riots in Tehran protesting against her latest novel depicting the flight of a young heroine from an arranged marriage. Max Madden, the Bradford MP, attends a public book-burning of Miss Cartland's novels, explaining to journalists that 'while not necessarily condoning the death sentence as such, I feel it is helpful to be with my many Muslim constituents at this difficult and agonizing time.'

June will see Britain solve the Hong Kong problem. Changes within the Peking leadership bring to power a new forward-looking regime which offers the whole of the Kwang-Tung peninsula to Britain on a ninety-nine-year lease. Plans are made to resettle the Vietnamese boat people, along with the anticipated wave of Chinese refugees from Hong Kong's highrise broom cupboards.

To keep the peace, British troops are sent out in June 'as a strictly temporary measure'.

In September, the Labour leadership imposes on its party conference manifesto commitments to recriminalize homosexuality and to start building fifteen new nuclear power stations.

The Social Liberal delegates in Wigan are told by Lord Grimond to return to their constituencies and prepare for government.

October brings the United States invasion of Canada, in self-defence. Mrs Thatcher, speaking at her own party conference, is again the first Western leader to offer military help to Washington. The listeria survivors' pension is quintupled, and they are both reported to be very grateful.

Sir Anthony Meyer uses the anniversary of his challenge to Mrs Thatcher to announce his decision to stand for the leadership of each of the three major political parties in turn, explaining that 'while I shall succeed in none of these contests, my candidature may help create conditions in which more serious contenders will come forward'. He wins all three, displacing the existing leaderships and threatening a constitutional crisis.

This is only averted when, tragically, Sir Anthony is run over by the first of a fleet of Securicor vans bringing pension payments to the last listeria survivor. A service of remembrance in Westminister Abbey is attended by the Archbishop of Canterbury, the Prime Minister, the leader of the Labour Party and the Social Liberal leader: John Major. Leaving afterwards, he will tell waiting journalists, 'I am still very much in the learning-curve stage at present. I must say that when Her Majesty invited me for tea, this was the last thing I expected.

'It is a very great challenge to lead three separate political parties at once while running the government and remaining responsible for the spiritual well-being of the nation. Norma and I ask for your prayers. There will be no change of policy ...'

30.12.89

You and me vs the holographs

IT WAS in a bar in Peru that I first realized that most people do not exist. The barman, a young Englishman called Alex, had been away from home for some time. He knew nothing about me. 'Maybe,' he inquired, 'you know the bloke who used to live next door in England?'

'Poor Alex,' I thought.

'His name is Crispin Tickell.'

Tickell was a very senior colleague when I was in the Foreign Office. Before I could say so, a squeal of recognition came from the other end of the bar. Michelle, it turned out, our ambassador's nanny in Mexico City, knew Tickell.

This was a bar in the Andes. So can the British population really be 56 million? Then how is it that you encounter your friends by chance in motorway service areas? Why do people introduced at dinner already know half the people you know? It is as if, at key points in our lives, the faceless millions who make up the census figures, cause the traffic jams and constitute crowd scenes, stand aside so that just a few of us can keep bumping into each other.

As if? The truth is, they do.

Most of the people you think you see do not exist; they are holographs.

There really are only a few of us, and we are moving amid phantoms: millions of phantoms.

I discovered this by accident, after publishing a piece describing Mrs Thatcher (caringly) in terms of how some hyperactive people need ever larger slugs of stimulant just to maintain the same frenzied plateau of activity. My conclusion – 'They Shoot Horses, Don't They?' – was an obvious (I thought) reference to a movie about American dance marathons during the Great Depression. Everybody, 'everybody', saw and talked about this film when it was released in the 1970s. The theme music became a hit record.

Yet outraged readers wrote to me, believing I was urging people to shoot Mrs Thatcher. So where had the 'everybody' gone? I asked around, seeking reassurance. Nobody remembered the film. *Nobody*. Had I dreamed it?

No. The answer hit me: the film was real; *it was the 'everybody' of the '70s who had been dreams*. They were holographs projected into the era to give it substance and flavour. You and I were almost alone in the '70s.

Now the 'others' have been withdrawn, decommissioned, and we are surrounded by a new cast, the phantoms of the '80s: the 'majority' whose hair is cut in the latest style (is yours?) and who throw away all their clothes every month (do we?) so that the streets can be full of stylish people. These holographs do not remember the '70s for the simple reason that they were not there. We were, We persist, we bewildered few.

This explains why in the '50s almost everyone was called Rita or Avril, whereas now nobody is – yet you would expect the Ritas and Avrils from the '50s to be still around, simply thirty years older.

But they weren't there *then*.

How can we tell who is real and what is holograph? We cannot. These phenomena can walk and talk and crush you in railway carriages. Superficial relationships can be established with them and they can appear to return affection. But it will never come to anything: the holograph will disappear from your life and – call it chance, but it is not chance – never reappear. It has been switched off. Sympathy is wasted, for they are not sentient. They experience nothing, but only act as though they do. They could not, for instance, register the idea behind this essay. That you can, is proof that you are real. Welcome.

At first it is a lonely feeling, to know that there are only a few of us. But one is quickly overtaken by a sense of privilege. One day, perhaps soon, the holograph projector will be shut down without warning, and the few of us left (smiling at one another in recognition) will be called together for an explanation of why we have been put here and what this has all been about.

I'm really looking forward to finding out.

2.9.89

Tutus and wellies

THURSDAY'S QUESTIONS were to the Agriculture minister.

Ballet was not directly mentioned in the discussion that Mr Mac-Gregor led, but he can hardly be unaware that the two most subsidized groups in Britain are farmers and ballet-dancers. Government has recently announced a 31 per cent increase in the Arts Council Grant, much of it destined for ballet-dancers.

Now the problem with farmers, just like ballet-dancers, is that they cannot be privatized as they are already private. And farmers are accustomed to a standard of living whose maintenance requires them to grow more food than we can eat. To keep their income up the authorities used to buy and stockpile agricultural produce, but those rotting heaps caused hurtful articles to be written in the less thoughtful sections of the press; so the Government's new idea is 'set-aside'. The thought is to pay farmers for *not* growing things. The idea is that a Ministry official asks the farmer how much barley he was planning to grow. 'Thirty-five tonnes,' says the farmer.

'Well, I'll tell you what' says the Official, 'Don't bother. And the Government will give you £4,000.'

Disarmingly simple, the idea has application in almost every area of the economy. But today we shall look at ballet. Your sketchwriter knows less about this as he never represented a ballet-dancing constituency: but the subsidies are huge: and how many ballet-dancers do you know? Exactly. *Per dancer* the figure must be enormous.

To find out more, I went to a ballet recently, in the provinces. The auditorium was half-empty. In other words, supply of ballet exceeds the demand for it: we have a ballet surplus, along with the cheese mountain.

You will have anticipated our recommendation: a 'set-aside' scheme for the Arts Council, too. Ballet-dancers should be asked how many ballets they intend to perform. Then, they would be offered a generous sum *not* to perform them.

This way, Britain would still be cultured because we would still have ballet-dancers. We would still be rustic because we would still have farmers. But there would be no more dancing, or agriculture, than the public could bear.

Yet it is painful to think of the sheer boredom for farmers and dancers of having to stay at home, part of the dependency culture. So here's a final refinement: require the ballet-dancers to farm and the farmers to dance. This would *not* result in the resurgence of ballet or barley as neither would have the remotest ability in the other's field. Nothing would be produced.

And how to ensure that Farmer Giles dons his tights, and Nureyev mounts the muck-spreader? This is where Mr Douglas Hurd's marvellous electronic tagging comes in! Tune up your fiddles, farmers, to the Dance of the Sugar Beet Fairy.

2.12.88

Shuffle spouse with house

WE FEEL we almost know them – Norma, Sheila, Elspeth ... newspapers and TV have brought them right into our living rooms.

Sheila, the latest *Sunday Times* tells us, 'the sharp, ambitious wife of John Moore, has to adapt to the former Social Services Secretary's political demise'. Apparently she makes her husband drink camomile tea.

Norma is so different. Though John, her Foreign Secretary husband, may be out high-tailing it with Arab princes, Norma has always preferred 'to stay in the country, a credit to him in the local community. She is perfectly happy,' we are assured, 'to be a meals-on-wheels lady, Christmas card organizer for a local charity, and supremo of a jolly constituency version of *Mastermind*.'

They don't mention Elspeth. I'm not surprised. I've always been secretly a bit scared of Elspeth, haven't you? Elspeth is married to the *former* Foreign Secretary, Sir Geoffrey Howe. Her strong mind and firm opinions have been known to put even Margaret in her place.

Yet if we already know Norma, Elspeth and Sheila – and wish we knew Thérèse (Lawson) – are we not acquainted with their homes, too? Dorneywood (we can picture its leafy pleasures) has been much in our minds since Margaret took it away from Thérèse and had to give it to

Elspeth. Did Nigel ask Thérèse, do you suppose, before acceding to Geoffrey?

And then there's Chevening. One imagines something rather grand and flashy: and we are all worried, with the *Sunday Times*, whether it is the right thing for Norma. Sheila would love it.

As for Chequers – well, wouldn't it be one in the eye for Margaret if Elspeth got that? I suspect Norma might get to like Dorneywood, in time; and Thérèse could have Chevening; but, with Elspeth at Chequers; where would that leave Margaret? Does Elizabeth need *all* her palaces? Sandringham maybe . . .

Politicians have been shuffled since politicians began: but what a brilliant idea to shuffle their houses too. It adds to the fun.

There remains, however, one vital, final step which I hope Mrs Thatcher dares to contemplate. I do want to put this delicately. Let us be clear that no sort of sexual impropriety is proposed. The private side of ministers' marriages must remain inviolate. But if Norma and John are so happy together in their constituency home (and I hear they are) why *should* Norma quit her meals-on-wheels and trawl along in uncomfortable shoes to stupid international bashes at Chevening – when *Sheila* would actually enjoy it? And if Tony (taking over from Sheila's John as Social Services Secretary) wants a partner with whom to visit caring institutions and engage the elderly in conversation . . . well, wouldn't Norma be just ideal?

What we want to see on public occasions is the right wife with the right minister. But 'right' does not mean they have to sleep together, and if the wives go home to a different hearth with a different minister (or no minister at all) who cares? Mrs Thatcher has shown that the great houses of state can be shuffled, like their occupants. So why not the great wives of state too?

Nor need we be sexist. There are male consorts, too. Denis, clearly, should be the husband of *any* female prime minister: he was born for it. He could even be lent out abroad, whenever a lady Commonwealth PM finds the males of her own culture too bossy for the role. Frankly I don't think he would mind at all. He might not even notice.

And then there's Ray. One of the many sadnesses of Edwina's departure was the loss of Ray. This rugby-playing, pint-down-the-local accountant is the ideal consort to a thrusting lady junior minister. Lynda (Clive's wife) is now doing well at Overseas Development, but *Clive* has an unhealthy interest in politics. It could hold Lynda back. Ray would be marvellous.

So, in those ghastly exchanges of letters that are published after ministerial sackings, let us hope to read, next:

'*... and of course we shall all miss Thelma, at your side, who has been such a wonderful support. Thelma will be glad to hear, therefore ...*'

Tell them when they get back from their summer hols.

5.8.89

Out to grass

FIVE YEARS ago *The Times* published a letter in which I proposed an important extension to the Common Agricultural Policy. Under my 'common industrial policy' the EEC was to buy thousands of unsold Morris Marinas at a guaranteed price, pile them up on the Isle of Dogs and offer them at half-price to the Russians. My proposal was ignored or, worse still, treated as facetious.

Four years later I remarked in these columns that the ornamental concrete cows one can see from the railway near Milton Keynes could be the key to solving Europe's milk surplus problems. Again, only giggles were heard in response.

For a radical visionary, it is disheartening to be treated in this way. So what follows is my last word on agriculture: a most modest proposal, refining – but in no way altering – principles which already underlie our agricultural policy.

Farming quotas are a way of curbing production without the vulgar uncertainties of a fluctuating price. Each farmer is guaranteed a fair and stable price for his produce. In return he guarantees to keep production to an agreed limit. So far, this quota system has been applied mainly to milk.

Quotas caught British dairy farmers unprepared. Some went under. We Tory backbenchers had a rare old time being yelled at by National Farmers' Union members at meetings in our constituencies. For a few weeks we all called on Michael Jopling to resign as Agriculture minister; Welsh farmers threw eggs at him. But he gritted his teeth, sat it out, and was eventually rewarded. The murmur at NFU meetings now is that quotas aren't so awful after all. 'Stability', 'security', 'Well, I'm still here, Jack: got to keep the other fellows out! Haul up the ladders ...' etc.

Thus is land nationalized by stealth. Farmers still 'own' the land, of course, but it is no longer worth owning without a quota. In time, quotas create among farmers a constituency of support for quotas – after all, anyone who hasn't got one isn't a farmer!

After imposing quotas, the ministry needed the means to redistribute or reduce still further. So it introduced the 'outgoers' scheme, offering farmers a once-for-all payment to stop producing milk altogether. The problem here is that they switch to producing something else, thus contributing to a new surplus.

Happily, quotas and the outgoers' scheme can be replaced with a unified approach which achieves the ends of both.

The government should supply concrete cows, tastefully painted in cow-like colours with gloss enamel paint. In exchange for these, farmers would be invited to surrender an equal number of real dairy cows. Each concrete cow thus acquired would attract an annual stipend payable by the ministry to the farmer: in this they would be rather like the wooden 'hotels' you can buy in Monopoly to place on your property in Park Lane or Mayfair – but with one crucial difference: each 'cow' must be sited in a paddock with as much real land as the ministry deems requisite to a real cow. No other beast may graze there or crop be grown, thus 'sterilizing' the land against food production of any sort.

The concrete cows would trade among farmers on the open market or they could be returned to the ministry on payment of a fee for the release back into production of the sterilized paddock.

Simply by varying the rent payable on concrete cows (fixed annually in the Budget) or adjusting the fee for redeeming sterilized land, the minister would have in his hands a sensitive lever to control milk production. Farmers, for their part, would generally want to keep a mixed portfolio of real and concrete cattle: movements in the ratio would reflect their expectation of the future supply of or demand for milk, and the minister's likely response. There would be no need for production quotas.

This flexible scheme offers farmers a fair mix of stability with risk, and it would leave the countryside looking as the Ramblers' Association would like it. There is only one drawback. It would become necessary to ensure that real cows were not secretly reintroduced beside their concrete sisters.

That requires surveillance. How?

I favour hot-air balloons. The EEC needs to brighten its image and there is something festive about balloons. The enormous quantities of nylon needed would help ICI in the switch away from agricultural fertilizers. Soon, the technology could be with us to produce plastic cornfields – by the square metre, like carpet-tiles – on which the balloons could also check, eliminating the need for cereal quotas, too.

Farmers would stay indoors, listening to opera or learning Portuguese. Outside, the Barley Barons Balloon Patrol would hover above, its gas-flares roaring, its nylon flanks caught in the harvest gold of an autumn sunset ... and from the cowsheds, only silence.

19.11.85

Just a dab of treacle

A FRIEND who lays tarmac on people's drives, took an afternoon off this summer to visit the Bakewell Show. He was standing innocently by the prize goats' enclosure when a woman sidled up and suddenly threw her arms violently round him.

'Ooh!' she said, adding: 'Don't worry – it's not you. I just *love* the smell of hot tar!'

So do I. At any time since infancy I could more blithely have buried my head in a bosom smelling of carbolic soap than in one smelling of rose petals. Are the marketing people not closing their noses to a whole world of potential allure?

There are more perfumes in heaven and earth, I think, than are dreamed of in their philosophies.

Gear oil, for instance – EP-90 or EP-140, it matters not, though EP-140 is less likely to run in warm weather or moments of passion: a spot of that behind the ears and who could resist? It has a wonderful, slightly acrid smell: powerful and clean. I have an old boiler suit which was once completely drenched in it. Washed often since, the tang still clings. Sometimes I get the urge to rip the garment out of the drawer, bury my whole face in it, and just breathe deeply in.

Or the mowings of freshly-cut grass. Why can't they make a personal deodorant that smells of that? There's something faintly disgusting about armpits smelling of hyacinths; but if it were freshly mown grass, who wouldn't crave a snuffle?

Perfumiers cultivate the myth that the flowery scents they peddle are subtle, mysterious, complicated. Rubbish! Lilies, roses – these are the easy, obvious pongs, the primary colours, the reds, whites, and blues of the olfactory world, designed to catch the attention of wandering bees.

It takes a more subtle creature to thrill to the smell of Mary Poppins: 'toast and starchy aprons'. Or to know exactly what the woman meant who, faced with Wilfred Pickles's famous question, 'What's your favourite smell?' replied, 'Hot water.' Or to run down into grandma's cellar – as I did when a boy – just to get a lungful of that heady mixture of moss, mildew, damp and coal dust. Though I have never touched a cigarette, I prefer to kiss people who smoke.

Or drink. Isn't gin a delicious perfume? I am tempted to splash it on as an aftershave.

The whole world of food and drink, in fact, is shamefully ignored by the purveyors of scent. Roast beef and Yorkshire pudding is surely a perfume which would commend the older type of woman to the hungrier type of bachelor. Why can't they spray *that* on? Or – for the evenings perhaps, with long dresses – mint sauce? A case of mutton dressed as lamb?

A girl I know is wild about baked apples and says that the boy who wore a clove in his left ear instead of an earring would have a head start on all the others. And one of the advantages of so many of these scents is that they can be found in the home, without the intervention of Elizabeth Arden. Cloves are cheap. Mint sauce could come straight from the jar, though one would need to wipe the superfluous green specks from behind the ears. Gear oil is only a few pounds a gallon and gin is cheaper than Chanel No. 5.

Even when an essence did have to be scientifically extracted and sold across the counter, marketing would be much simplified. Gone would be those baffling magazine ads with pumas and moonlight. Instead there could be a picture of a sizzling joint of beef with the caption beneath: 'Smell like this!'

Gone would be the images of garlanded maidens, swaying palms and waves crashing on an exotic shore. Instead, there would be a picture of steaming treacle pudding smothered in gallons of custard. 'TREACLE TABOO, by Nina Ricci,' it would read, 'Yum!'

Crikey, this train of thought is distracting! I swear that if a woman were to walk into the room now, smelling not of lily-of-the-valley but of hot baked bread, then – even after all these years – I could be turned.

11.11.89

Lager-and-lime all round

BUSINESS QUESTIONS are when members ask John Wakeham (Leader of the House) why the world continues to ignore the topics that pre-occupy them, and he replies that it is none of his business. 'None of My Business Questions' would be more accurate.

Yesterday Mr Wakeham heard Labour's Peter Pike introduce what was to prove the afternoon's sub-theme: the student demo against loans, going on outside.

Interruptions and points of order on the students' behalf (some of which had a genuine and worrying ring) disturbed what was otherwise an intelligently combative speech from John Moore, announcing new payments to the elderly.

Apparently you will be able to get extra benefits once you reach the age of seventy-five, and you hit the jackpot yet again if you get to eighty. The logic is irresistible. On people's ninetieth birthdays they'll need Securicor vans to deliver the weekly pension ...

Such thoughts were distracting and I began to daydream about Mr Nicholas Ridley's latest idea, that the *nouveaux riches* should take over the stately homes of England, and the aristocracy – whom he regards as a load of titled dossers – should stop whingeing for subsidies for their central heating.

But why do we not take Ridleyism forward, and abolish the fusty old order altogether? Are titles devised in our dim pre-capitalist past appropriate, at all, in the thrusting new entrepreneurial world that Mrs Thatcher has ushered in? Let Mr Ridley take this bull by the horns and devise an *alternative* aristocracy: and let him start from first principles.

There are two great goals in our brave new Britain: Money and Fame – forget honour, valour, beneficence and every cobwebbed virtue that would pass no muster in a business-sponsored City Technology College.

Well, then, there should be two new titles, one relating to Money, the other to Fame. So the first order is easy to propose: the Order of Fame. Those upon whom it is conferred would choose (as now) a place-name as anchor to the title, being referred to as 'The Fame of (wherever)'. Examples from our dynamic era spring easily to mind.

Cilla Black, who presents *Blind Date* (on which scores of new variations will be needed after the Broadcasting Act becomes law) would become the Fame of Scouse and be referred to as 'Your Celebrity'. Terry Wogan, the Fame of Limerick, would take Devonshire's seat and be the man who put the Chat into Chatsworth House.

The Wealth title presents difficulties, as Mrs Thatcher prefers to emphasize the benefits that personal wealth spreads to *others* and Tories are slightly sensitive about the agreeable nature of the conditions for the wealthy themselves.

So I propose the title of 'Wealth Creator'. Thus, Tiny Rowland might become the Wealth Creator of Zimbabwe, addressed as 'Your Richness'.

The subsidiary honours (to replace MBEs and the like) would be Lagers. One would be awarded a Lager (and referred to as Your Round) for minor services.

Rather higher up the scale would be Lager-and-Lime ('LL' after the name), and top would be a Pineapple-and-Malibu. One can just picture Ian Botham (when he has walked enough for charity) as 'Ian Botham, L, LL, P & M, FDW & AP of C' – that is: 'Lager, Lager and Lime, Pineapple and Malibu, Four Double Whiskies and a Packet of Crisps, please.' Any flavour.

25.11.88

The Gulag in a rosy glow

A VODKA advertisement caught my eye on the Underground the other day. 'Stolichnaya', it said, above some lines of Russian script, 'made in the USSR'. What intrigued me was the picture. It shows a ghastly concrete building with silos – late Fifties style, probably of reinforced concrete.

But then a second sentiment overtook me, and I swear it was nostalgia. This was a Russia which is disappearing forever. These days it's all *glasnost* and Raisa and Mr Gorbachov feeding squirrels in the park.

And my mind went back to those images of Cold War boyhood. The 'revolutionary art' – harsh posters in primary colours – big black Zil cars and a style of architecture – perhaps one might call it Totalitarian Brutalism – of which this vodka factory was an example.

I'm going to miss it. For of all the world's people, are we British not the biggest suckers for becoming affectionate about eras, styles and forms, simply because they are threatened, dying or dead?

What other race would be 'listing' hideous concrete buildings from the Fifties? I can just remember the Fifties. They were awful the *first* time around – and now there's a fashion for recreating the style. Dreadful suits, tasteless jackets, advertisements in pastel shades with triangles coloured in *eau-de-Nil* with arrows and dotted lines. In the Fifties, I recall, we thought the Thirties were crass. I still do. But Thirties style is modish now as well. As for the Edwardian and Victorian eras, they lacked all grace. Without restraint there can be no elegance or poise. Yet we actually celebrate monstrosities like Big Ben, which in their time were rightly reviled.

Today there can be no railway of which the proposed closure would not elicit a dozen tearful protest meetings. They would be attended by exactly the same type as those who opposed its construction – the Victorian counterparts of those now so outraged by BR's plans to carve a new line through Kent.

And we are the same about religion. It would (I trust) never be seriously argued that Jesus would tolerate thirty seconds of the goings-on that characterize the Established Church. So far as I can understand, they are just the sort of approach He came to destroy.

These things plainly have no association with the gospels, but they aren't supposed to. Their association is with a more recent epoch – the Middle Ages. By clinging to medieval forms we can forget the demands of the awkward faith they clothed. It is probably a precondition of celebrating a style that the substance which once accompanied it is safely dead. That is why we can all be enthusiastic about the monarchy.

And that is why Marxist-Leninist nostalgia may be imminent. But we should start gently. It is probably a little early to become misty-eyed about genocide, forced population migration, or lunatic asylums for dissidents. In time no doubt we shall, but it will certainly take time.

Nor are we quite ready yet to enthuse about environmental wreckage, huge sulphur-dioxide emissions, or salt mines – although their hour too will come.

For the moment, though, aren't we beginning to miss Wartburg cars, Homburg hats, tea with added woodchips, queues outside GUM for skis in July, and suits that don't fit? Where, soon, will be those enormous, anonymous, shapeless party officials' wives, dressed in black, with stockings ending at the knee? Where will be the annual failure of the Agriculture Plan?

Where will be the ballet defectors, the brave Berlin Wall hoppers, and the Aeroflot plane crashes? Where will be the dodgy Cambridge dons? Indeed, where the whole *raison d'être* of the British Intelligence establishment? And where the Red Square military parades? I read on Thursday that the East German army is to abolish the goose-step. Has it come to this?

25.11.89

Not down, but sideways

Ex-Prime Minister Edward Heath had just returned from a mission to free hostages in Baghdad.

WHAT DOES a government minister do once his political career is over? Shocked by the enormous City salaries being commanded by retired ministers, this question has recently engaged our interest.

But nobody asks what a retired *prime* minister is to do.

Jim Callaghan has his farm and Harold Wilson his memoirs: but Mrs Thatcher has never cared for travel, for gardening or for literature, and has no hobbies at all. And I worry about her.

What, after all, does leading a country best equip you for? It equips you, she would contend, for leading a country some more.

It was when I was in Albania, the week before last, that the answer came to me. What she needs is another country.

For what is there about the job of being a national supremo which, almost uniquely, should demand that the profession be exercised among one nation only? Why cannot that wealth of talent and experience be shared with other peoples? Why should we be so selfish? Here is a career skill that could be internationally saleable; and there is no reason why leaders should not be headhunted by employment agencies, just as dustmen and brain surgeons are.

Here, then, are a few proposals of my own, starting with Albania. A surprisingly gentle and friendly country, Albania faces two major problems. Sooner or later it will have to move towards a market economy. Albanians have no experience at all of such a system. But further – and this is the second problem – after forty years of rigidly authoritarian rule, they are unaccustomed to personal freedom. They are used to being told what to do and would be confused by too much liberty. In short, what Albania needs is a leader who offers a halfway house between Stalinism and the capitalist system.

That is where Mrs Thatcher could help. She would make an immediate and businesslike start on privatizing the olive groves, but there would be absolutely no nonsense about pornography, late-night parties, or not going to work. Some world leaders might find Tirana lacking in charm, luxury and cultural facilities; but that would not bother Mrs Thatcher at all, and I think she would settle in fast. For their part, the Albanians – accustomed as they are to the cult of personalities of the severest sort – would find her (by comparison with King Zog or Enver Hoxha) very much a fun-person. Plans should be made without delay.

But this would only be the start. Next, Mr Gorbachov should go to the White House. George Bush lacks the charisma of his Soviet counterpart. Gorbachov is much better at handling the American media and dealing with rebellious legislatures. Mr Bush might try his hand at keeping the Soviet Union together. He wouldn't understand the ethnic problems, which is the best way to start, with ethnic problems.

Helmut Kohl should be moved urgently to Luxembourg before he absorbs any more countries. The obvious danger that within months the unification of Benelux will be celebrated on the streets of Brussels and Amsterdam is countered by the second element in my plan. President Mobutu of Zaire is to be installed as prime minister in Brussels. That will serve the Belgians right – if anything can – for what they did to their African colonies. Their existing prime minister, who I believe is called Mr Martens – will take over in Dublin, to bore the Irish into submission. Charles Haughey then becomes mayor of New York.

I realize that the installation of Saddam Hussein as ruler of Monaco will be controversial. But he has been missing out on so much of the gaiety of life, and needs a holiday. And he may bring a welcome sense of rigour and national purpose to a nation of croupiers and party-goers.

That, of course, leaves Iraq without a boss. I did say that *return* tickets to Baghdad are expensive.

13.10.90

Tales untold

'THE HALF,' said the eighth-century Greek poet Hesiod, 'is more than the whole.' I now know what he meant, for I have read the *classified* section of the local freesheet, *The Peak Advertiser*.

Here, in flat schoolboy prose, are a hundred tales half told. Here are the clues – casually dropped – to affairs of the human heart on a scale of tragedy and triumph so wild as to make a Brontë blush.

● *Spong mincing set, unused, £5. Two ladies nightdresses, size 40–42 £2.50 each. Tel: Matlock 73* ... No, on second thoughts I shall omit the telephone number.

● *Austrian blind, 5' across 6' drop, with matching lampshades £25. Ladies two-piece suit, jacket short sleeves, tailored skirt size 14, never worn* ... Ah! with what unspoken sorrow was that phrase penned –

and with what suppressed anger the postscript: *No offers.*

Was it the lady who had no offers? The phone number betrays a Hope Valley exchange. Was she out of place, there, where sheep graze on the high moorlands? Were the sleeves too short, the skirt too tailored for the rainswept informality of rural Derbyshire life?

No, I picture a different story.

There *was* no lady. She existed only in the mind of a deluded Austrian professor, conscripted into Hitler's air force, shot down and given forced wartime labour repairing dry-stone walls near Hope. He stayed, believing that his young Viennese fiancée would surely join him.

That was 1946.

They broke it to him gently, of course. They told him of the Italian captain who had swept her off her feet. But four long winters – biting wind and bleeding hands (hands more used to classical translations than heaving gritstone blocks), through which the will to survive came only from the certainty that, one day, dear delicate Erminstrudel would fly to his arms – four years of purgatory would not allow him to doubt that heaven would soon be his.

He never returned to his studies. At the local pub they used to smile at the ragged fellow in the corner, silent, solitary, painfully polite, staring into the single glass of peach schnapps over which he whiled away each evening. The landlord kept a bottle, just for him.

'Jilted,' they whispered – as if he couldn't hear! He would turn away in pain. 'D'you know he was once some kind of professor. Repairs walls, now. Lives in a caravan. Partitioned off one half of the van and set it up – furnished like – for the girl who jilted him. He meets the train, every week.

'Austrian blinds – in a caravan, for God's sake! – and matching lampshades, of all things! A wardrobe with clothes he had bought for her – fancy suit from Vienna, they say. Poor old boy ...'

No offers. Oh, editor of the classified section, what pain do those two words hide!

And what is this? *Snooker table, with balls, £50. ¼ size Violin with case; red swivel vinyl chair* ... This seller should meet the chap, one column on, flogging the *electric fire, one bar* and *ladies showerproof coat.* They could invite the vendor of a *grey polyester country and western jacket, £10* together with *Skoda car manual ('72–'85)* and have a party. Frankly, the bloke offering a *storage pouffe, pink dralon, new,* and a *Belling electric fire, flame effect* would be out of place – happier, maybe, with the family selling *electric organ and a concrete half ton coal bunker.*

But something stops me in my tracks: *Epilady leg shaver, never been* used, £20 o.n.o. Motorcycle jacket, leather £20 ... Come, come, Mrs Thatcher. Surely it is too early, yet, to throw in the towel?

19.11.90

Howe relegates transvestite

TWENTY THOUSAND feet above Dundee, en route from Aberdeen to London, I reached the other day for my copy of *The Times*. 'Sir Geoffrey, who is 63', said the front page. I decided to study this important matter later, and paged on.

Page 13 was an overseas page. I glanced at one of these 'other news' columns of assorted mini-stories, a broken-biscuit box of items that may yield up an engaging bus plunge in Colombia, genocide in Burundi, bloodbaths in Liberia or some other such tittle-tattle – the small change of news reporting after you have spent your front-page fiver catching up with the latest news from the boardroom at Polly Peck.

Something caught my eye. A tiny, one-paragraph story ...

São Paulo. A Brazilian transvestite sprayed gas into the cockpit of a Varig jet carrying 348 passengers, forcing the captain to land his plane in the Canary Islands. Passengers said that the plane lost altitude after a male passenger dressed as a woman used the spray can. The airline said the man had been deported from Portugal because he had no money. (Reuter)

Wow! Now that's what I call news! Why was this wonderful story buried on page 13? By what eccentric editorial logic could the resignation of Sir Geoffrey Howe be page one?

Has Sir Geoffrey ever brought an airliner down? No. The very thought of him wielding an aerosol spray is ridiculous; he wouldn't know where to press. Nothing in his long career justifies the slightest hope that Sir Geoffrey might be a transvestite, otherwise I should be organizing his campaign for the leadership right now: for spice is what this splendid man lacks. The merest glimpse of a high heel peeking from beneath the turn-ups of Sir Geoffrey's grey flannel trousers and the man would be unstoppable.

Now if *I* were Editor of *The Times* ...

BRAZIL NUT DOWNS
JUMBO ON CANARIES
Mystery airspray saga

What a front-page headline! It would be in modest-size type – nothing vulgar, for this is a quality paper – right across the top. The story, 'From our correspondent in Tenerife', would start: 'Hundreds of shocked passengers staggered, reeling, from a Rio-bound jetliner forced into a mid-Atlantic emergency landing, here on the tiny island of Tenerife this morning. As embarrassed airline officials began piecing together evidence from eyewitness accounts, a bizarre story emerged.'

And so it would continue, packed with news, views, comment and background 'colour'. Who was this transvestite? What spray did he use? Why? What was he wearing? How common is it to deport transvestites from Portugal to Brazil? Do they deport them the other way, too? What is the cross-Atlantic balance in cross-dressers between Lisbon and Rio? Which city is more convivial for a transvestite . . .? Oh, the possibilities are endless.

At the end of the article, which would fill most of the front page, and be illustrated with a map of the Atlantic indicating the Canary Islands and the flight path of the aircraft, would be an onward reference to '*Leading Article, page 15*' – where, in calm and measured prose, readers would find a judicious review of the many implications raised by this disturbing affair.

Oh – and in the bottom corner of the front page, among the snippets of news 'within' would be a single sentence: '*Deputy prime minister resigns – other news, page 13.*'

17.11.90

9
I Wonder...

Smug warning

After Iraq ...

NEVER MIND the smog warning: before the next war, could they issue a smug warning? I wonder whether we are altogether the most sanctimonious nation on earth, or only finalists for some sort of World Cup in the piety league? I wonder whether there is anything at all – any small endeavour, however trivial – over which we do not feel bound to moralize? I wonder whether it is possible for an Englishman to clean his teeth without constructing it into an act of virtue?

I wonder whether this is some kind of intoxication? Do we, perhaps, become smug-drunk? And can you suffer from a smug-hangover? Will we, months on from this wretched war, wake up with pounding head and blink: 'Oh cripes! Was I very smug, or just slightly? Did I make an idiot of myself – or were the others all smug too?'

And a comforting voice will say: 'Don't worry, dear. You *were* just a bit on your moral high horse, but we all were. It does no harm, once in a while ...' And we will try to piece together the events of the weeks past – the newspaper editorials, the saloon-bar sermons, parliamentary questions and letters to the editor – and remember what we said, in case there are apologies to be made.

'This is rum!' I hear friends mutter. 'He seems to oppose this war – an ex-Tory MP!' Not so. Not for so much as an instant did even a flicker of doubt as to its point or its prospects cross my mind. Plainly, Saddam had to be stopped. So I can steel myself against the guns, the bombs, the killing, the blood; it's the moralizing I can't stand.

Take all this guff about the United Nations. It is perfectly clear that nobody is interested in the UN except when the organization can be bounced into backing up our own opinions. By a rather remarkable coincidence, that occurred this time. This happy circumstance, which will almost certainly never be repeated, arose because the Soviet Union was too punch-drunk to conduct its habitual spoiling operation. Once you've got a Security Council resolution in place it is hard to dislodge. The war therefore proceeded under the UN's notional auspices, although it was really an American enterprise with backing from America's friends, and Arabs who are more afraid of Saddam than of President Bush.

The United Nations consensus stands no chance of surviving 'the peace', and so you already see Western governments cooling their UN rhetoric, fast. Quite right, too. This bizarre organization should no more stop us following our own judgements than it stopped Tony Benn when he disagreed with it. Soon we shall revert to the familiar position in which Benn is in favour of the UN and everyone else is against. It may reduce the level of hypocrisy in the air. I wish they had a bunkum-count instead of a pollen-count with the weather forecast each morning, so that I would know whether it was safe to go out.

In Chekhov's *The Cherry Orchard*, Gayev (a sententious old bore) gives an impromptu homily on the one-hundredth birthday of a bookcase. Next morning he turns ruefully to his sister Ranyevskaya. 'Think of it,' he groans, 'I made a speech to a bookcase.'

There are bookcases in the House of Commons full of Hansard reports of parliamentary proceedings. It would not surprise me if, these past few weeks, MPs had been addressing homilies to the shelves. They should read what's on them. They will find a little sentimentality, a good deal of self-interest, and not much else.

4.3.91

Splashes that dry up

PLEASE, WHAT has happened to salmonella? Has the threat receded? Have the Ministry's new measures eliminated it?

I made some inquiries. No, came the answer: the threat is still the same, but the camera has moved: people had looked at one picture for long enough and wanted another.

It set me thinking. Does the news, in fact, follow a moving picture, or is the picture still while the cameraman moves? I decided to follow up another recent 'story': injuries and deaths caused by car crashes in high-speed police chases.

You may remember that there was a rash of such stories this spring. It led one to suppose that we were witnessing a sharp deterioration in policemen's driving, or an increase in hot pursuits, or both.

We were witnessing neither. Available figures suggest that these accidents are occurring all the time, and have been for years. At any hour you care to mention, a police car, somewhere, is chasing a wanted driver, and they are continually crashing – as often as, but no more than, before. What happened was that a particularly horrific crash qualified for the headlines earlier this year. By chance, and before this had faded from the public mind, there was another newsworthy crash.

The second story could now be garnished with 'commentary' reminding us that this was not the first crash of its kind, and asking whether there was too much of this sort of thing going on.

There was a point – it came about six weeks ago – when the saga could have gone either way. One more grisly crash and there would have been no stopping the story. A village bobby would only have had to fall off his bike to hit the headlines. The issue would have emerged into the sunlight as does the dragonfly from the chrysalis, to flit around us all summer.

These are not isolated examples. Child abuse, for instance, faltered badly earlier this year once the Cleveland inquiry was over, then found a second wind and is now a dragonfly that we shall see all summer. Rottweilers are bidding fair for stardom and have knocked Alsatians for six, but probably need one more good bite to secure an extended run.

Bus plunges, on the other hand, are having a bad year, as, curiously, is rape. Headlice made an intriguing start last week, but faltered after early promise. Possibly they peaked too early.

Readers, cast your mind over that list: phenomena whose occurrence is as regular as clockwork, as enduring as the rising and setting of the sun. Yet if you were to plot upon a graph the intrusion of these stories into the news media, you would have the impression that such ills were visited upon us as were the plagues upon the pharaohs: nothing at all, then all at once, then all gone.

For the newsman's job is rather like those clever TV documentaries which bring to life and explain a celebrated oil painting. The music swells, the camera darts from detail to detail, lingering here, panning back for an overview there, then zooming in for a dramatic close-up before returning for a second look at a key detail. All is movement.

But the picture is still.

3.6.89

Patent nonsense

DON'T TELL me, I know. One makes light of others' afflictions at one's peril. To question the scale of the horror which is 'gum disease' will be to learn from tomorrow's post that thousands of *Times* readers are under the doctor with their gums; dozens, at death's door, are outraged at my insolence; and even now a lynch-mob of angry dentists and dribbling, toothless desperadoes is combing the Derbyshire hills, seeking my hideout.

But what *is* gum disease? I have just bought my tube of toothpaste. I do so annually; and this year I knew the time had come when I chipped a tooth biting the end of the tube to get the last squidge out. This panic measure was all that was left once I had exhausted (throughout May) the spoils extractable by inserting the bristles on the end of the tooth-brush inside the nozzle and scouring round for the occasional smear.

Down to Matlock for toothpaste. This year I chose Macleans because it was on special offer. For me, buying toothpaste is a big event, and to help arrive at the final decision I read the claims made on each of the rival boxes. Sensodyne fascinated me.

'Sensodyne,' said the label, 'relieves the pain of sensitive teeth.' Gosh! Do I have sensitive teeth? It isn't something I have ever considered. How sensitive should they be? One would not wish to be spoken of as having *in*sensitive teeth. How will toothpaste help, anyway? The label didn't explain, so I opted for Macleans.

'Fights plaque,' said the box, 'the cause of gum disease.' A moment's perplexity was followed by the heady thought that here was a threat I could ignore, for it touched neither my own life nor that of loved ones. But then I thought: 'For how much longer shall we be spared? Better leave nothing to chance ...', and I carried the Macleans to the checkout counter.

Since then I have questioned many friends about gum disease. All said they had heard of it, but nobody seems to have had it. Is it something you admit? Is it like sensitive teeth?

Or chapped hands? Those hot-air dryers encountered in public lava-tories always boast: 'Protects against chapped hands.' I shall probably carry on drying my hands on my trousers.

Or problem hair? I cannot decide whether I have 'greasy', 'dry', 'flyaway', 'out-of-control', 'difficult' or 'unmanageable' hair. Each sep-arate affliction, apparently, needs a separate shampoo. As the purpose of shampoo is to strip your hair of oil, I don't know why people with 'greasy' hair don't try Vim, or petrol. But what is 'brittle' hair? Perhaps it's what you get chapped hands from running your fingers through.

My sister-in-law has made a foray into a Body Shop. She reports that you can buy 'Sebutape' there. Applied to the body this tape tells you whether you have 'oily', 'dry' or – oh no, my friends, not 'normal' skin, for normality does not call for treatment – 'combination' skin. This, apparently, helps you deal with the 'oily T-panel' which runs across your forehead and down your nose. I must act fast.

While I am about it, I must treat my eyes, too. Apparently, untreated eyes are 'dull'.

But I draw the line at 'foam toe-separators'. Even the Body Shop which sells them offers no explanation.

Home, now, with the Macleans. I place it next to the Frish. 'Frish kills germs, even under the lavatory rim,' says the container. Another problem I didn't know I had! What mischief are these 'germs' doing? A few yards down the plumbing, in the septic tank, bacterial action is vital.

But what about a few yards back *up* the system: my digestive system? 'Directable!' says my green plastic bottle. Crikey! Surely not?

18.6.90

Tappers, toppers and other rituals

AT SCHOOL we were always taught that 'goodbye' really means 'God be with you'. Or once did. Now we have abbreviated the sentence and extinguished the sentiment. We have turned what once had meaning into a swift commonplace. The expression passed from full-length to a shorthand version, and finally to a usage which has forgotten even what the shorthand once stood for. It must be one of a score of such words.

Or actions. 'Around the maypole frolics Miss Prism,/Little knowing its symbolism.' In Catalonia my nieces and nephews get their Christmas presents only after their grandparents have tapped on a log of wood – a perfunctory twentieth-century reminder of some obscure pagan ceremony perhaps? No doubt historians will, likewise, know why Dame Jill Knight (or any other MP) has to put on a top hat in the Chamber before making a point of order during a division.

My father always used to tap the end of his cigarette on the cigarette box, before lighting up – though the days when you needed to compact the tobacco were long gone. Genteel hostesses serving tea offer the milk in a milk jug, though it must be the better part of a century since the alternative was a churn.

The ritualizing of things, though as old as man, surely continues. What can we spot, passing stealthily from the real – today – to tomorrow's ritual?

A friend tells me that most Catholic churches now have sound amplification systems for the priest. The sight of Father O'Flaherty walking up to his microphone before the service and tapping it twice to check that it's still working is as much part of the form of worship as the bells and incense. A friend speculates that one hundred years from now (when microphones are obsolete and sound amplification automatic) an obligatory part of every priest's kit – along with chalice, napkin and other accoutrements – will be a small black bulbous object on a stick, which he will solemnly place before him, and tap, twice, before beginning Mass.

And should you, after Mass, take the family to a restaurant for lunch, future generations will see a strange ritual when, the meal over, it is time to go. In those days, of course, no bill, money or plastic will change hands; each potato will have been charged electronically to the customer's account as it is served. Nevertheless, Dad will signal departure by raising his left palm, open, in the air, pinching together the thumb and index finger of his right, and (holding the right six inches from the left) moving the pinched hand across the palm, left to right, in a squiggling motion.

The aircraft emergency routine, demonstrated in the aisle by cabin crew before the plane takes off, is surely another budding ritual. Hardly anyone watches any more, unless the air hostess is glamorous. You never get this routine on buses, which also have emergency exits and which are far more dangerous as a way of travelling; but doubtless the insistence on this procedure was framed when accidents were more common. Now they are rare, but if your 747 does fly into the Atlantic, you are frankly a goner, and most unlikely to find yourself sliding down those colourful plastic chutes.

Often, now, the instructions accompanying the demonstration are a tape recording; and the cabin crew go through the motions in weary, zombie-like fashion. As a performance, it approaches a dance routine, and sometimes reminds me of a jaded stripper.

So why not formalize the dance, and make it more entertaining? Why not bring on the air hostess wearing a little slip of a dress in the airline's livery, or the steward in silk boxer shorts, and let them do a dance *based* on the plane-crash instructions? The choreography I envisage is somewhat in the Egyptian style, with arms waved expressively, fingers stabbing in the direction of the emergency exits and exaggerated head movements.

Everybody could applaud, and anyone who really wanted to know about the life raft could read the instructions.

3.3.90

It doesn't work

AS WE all know, some things just don't work. The Advanced Passenger Train didn't; the Sinclair C5 didn't, really; and there are as many cures for baldness as there are disappointed dupes. But these failures rapidly become history. People get wise, and the product is withdrawn.

More intriguing are the failures we carry on with.

Supermarket trolleys with minds of their own, which drag you, panic-stricken and wrestling with the controls, on a collision course with the pile of Israeli melons on special offer ...

Modern shoelaces, no longer made of cotton, which no longer stay tied up ... how many small curses rise heavenward daily from people trying to retie that knot from a squatting posture on a busy pavement?

Canteen-issue plastic tea-stirring wands which don't stir, UHT milk which squirts up your shirt as you puncture the foil top of the plastic mini-tub, cream-cracker packs wrapped in mega-strength cellophane which cannot be opened without reducing the biscuits to rubble ... Aaargh!

And why do crayons always break? Millions grow up with feelings of personal inadequacy, unaware that other kids couldn't handle these things either. Why do the devices provided to hold up the toilet seat as the train sways always drop the seat at the awful moment? Why do BR's revolting rubber foot-operated basin-tap switches cause the flow to dry to a trickle just as you've soaped your hands? Why do those time-delayed hand-push taps force you to soap your left hand individually, while your right hand holds the thing down? In desperation, your soaped hand strays to the handle and the handle then pollutes your rinsed hand. Then the hot-air hand-dryer doesn't work, and you wipe your unrinsed hand on your trousers and run screaming from the loo.

If a sum total were to be made of all the human misery arising from all the failed, arm-wrenched, finger-mashed attempts to start portable engines with pull-cords, I believe it would exceed the misery caused by the Spanish Inquisition. Let's face it: the two-stroke internal combustion was a good idea; but it doesn't really work.

And, in this mood of engineering humility, could we have an amnesty on moving travclators? They usually don't. And electric shavers? They sort of do, but only sort of. And pop-up toasters? Down through the age of the pop-up toaster, what is the ratio of toast satisfactorily toasted to toast charred beyond recognition? And is there anyone at all who has actually succeeded in getting a bar of chocolate from a station platform chocolate dispenser?

Isn't it time, too, that somebody admitted that in-flight music headphones don't really work unless you cup your hands to your ears and apply constant pressure? Is it too late to come to terms with the failure of perforations on sheets of stamps to tear with an acceptable fatality rate? Who has not ripped a cheque from a chequebook with a flourish, only to have our bravado backfire?

It is time to march. The ranks of those permanently disabled from an encounter with a mouse-trap-sprung letterbox, swelled by millions who have tangled their last with coiled cables attaching handsets to telephones, and joined, now, by every wretched soul who has snaggled the bathplug chain, abandoned hope of getting the curtains open with the pulley-operated curtain-pull, and finally spilled the milk all down his trousers while trying to pour from a Tetra-pack carton opened in rage by Caesarean section ... All join me in one despairing cry: 'It doesn't really work!'

18.8.90

I didn't like to ask

'DRAUGHT GUINNESS, now available in cans,' says the voice from my clock-radio which rouses me each morning. Sometimes I wake up and wonder whether the dream world from which I have just come is more real than the one I now re-enter. Will a little lady pop out of the Guinness tin and pull you a pint on the spot?

I sit on the number 15 bus, longing to ask the other passengers for their own reaction to this and other questions. Am I blind to the explanations which are obvious to everyone else? Or does each of us travel wrapped in a cocoon of private mystification which he dare not share?

Take, for example, the common aspirin. How can it work? It is supposed to make pain go away. Yet try swallowing one, then pinching yourself. It still hurts, doesn't it? And you can feel your toes. So how does the aspirin know which, of all the nerves, selectively to mug?

Or aeroplanes. Why don't the wings drop off? The whole of aerodynamics perplexes. Why does a bird's flapping its wings cause it to fly? And how do birds mate? On the wing or on the perch? How I yearn to ask the lady on the seat beside me. And fish – what do fish do? And why do you never see cats making love? And ... but, no, we enter a realm in which it would be indelicate to tread.

Sex – treated as a branch of engineering rather than literature – surely prompts technical inquiries to which millions long to know the answers. I wonder whether, if we all wrote these questions down on secret ballot papers and experts collated the results, it might be found that most people share the same perplexities? This exercise should replace the council elections in May; the results would be more interesting.

Then there is hair. Why are short-haired dogs short-haired? Does each strand of a boxer's fur know when it has reached the length appropriate for a boxer, and stop? Or does it drop out at half an inch, while a collie's knows to drop out at five? Why are there not short-furred and long-furred humans?

And how does frizzy hair know how to frizz, and where? Why aren't there people whose hair frizzes in patches and grows straight in others?

Epidemics worry me too, as our bus passes a hospital and somebody coughs. Surely the more a communicable disease spreads, the faster becomes its rate of spread – so why didn't everyone finally die of the Black Death, and why haven't I had Hong Kong flu?

And those 'Now wash your hands' signs in lavatories: what is the point? You have to touch the tap to turn it off after you have washed them, don't you? Ten seconds ago you grasped that tap with unwashed hands. So wash them again! And what *are* the 'chapped hands' against which those hot-air dryers that don't work protect? Do you know anyone with chapped hands?

The whole realm of hygiene is, surely, more ritual than real. If the slightest touch were really red-hot with communicable perils, then the precautions we take against their communication would be hopelessly inadequate. In the end, almost everything has indirectly touched almost everything else. Yet we survive.

Then there are chimney-sweeps. The last time I employed one in Derbyshire he drove six miles from Matlock with his van and ladder and spent half the morning making a very thorough job. All for £5. How does this man live?

And how do you know people are looking at you? One can spot and return a glance across fifty yards, yet the eye-deflection that marks the glance and defines its target is tiny: can you in fact see the pupil of another person's eye, at all, at that distance?

Bursting with curiosity, I alight at the Strand. My bus pulls away, taking with it fifty fellow-citizens I may never meet again. I wonder if they knew any of the answers.

2.4.90

Fast-forward

'I WAS sixty-seven and I just went into the kitchen to fix myself a coffee,' an old lady is said to have remarked. 'I come out and I'm eighty-two. Where did it all go?'

Someone has pressed the Divine 'fast-forward' button. Somewhere above, an invisible hand is winding events on, faster and faster until, to the cackle of demonic laughter, we shall all fall flat on our faces.

As the Commons reached its short Spring Recess, gasping, on Thursday, MPs and journalists reeled across New Palace Yard towards the gates. Through our minds span the parliamentary circuses of the last few days: the Badgers Bill, Ravenscraig, the Agriculture minister's daughter's hamburger, the Labour Party's new policy document, Edwina Currie's return from Bucharest ... it is all happening at once. The sublime, the ridiculous – jumbled, shuffled and speeded up.

Already, there is too much. Romania, Czechoslovakia – hey, what happened to Yugoslavia? – Estonia, Latvia ... What's that you say – Pakistan back in the Commonwealth? When? I missed that. Somebody keeps moving the furniture around and I can't remember where I put my drink.

Reactor rods emit radioactivity in a field around them with a force which dwindles over time. We measure 'half-life': the time it takes before their potency is half its initial level. Do not events, too, exert a forcefield? At first their influence is strong, their reputation flares. Gradually it fades.

But time is not the only factor. Rival events dull each other's shine, too. The next big story drags attention away from the last. The faster things happen, the less time we allow each on centre stage.

There seemed to be an era when big shocks were helpfully spaced out. When they did occur they retained potency. Suez, Hungary, the Berlin blockade ... these things cast strong shadows far out over the Cold War years. The Vietnam war, the Algerian wars, Mau-Mau and Eoka in Cyprus – they seemed permanent. Shockwaves from the Soviet invasion of Afghanistan reverberated for years. Each of these events (it seemed) had a half-life which was very substantial. They continued 'making' history long after they were over.

Politicians, they say, now stagger from crisis to crisis. But the crises have lost their power to bite. Their half-life has shrunk. I lose count of the things that were going to be the last nail in Mrs Thatcher's coffin: the Libyan bombing, her go-it-alone on Europe, 'top people's pay awards', bus deregulation, Mark Thatcher and Cementation, the privatization of water ... Where are they now? I cannot even remember the order in which they came.

If we placed news stories, like pop records, on a weekly hit-parade of topicality – the charts from the 1950s to the 1970s were slow-moving. 'Evergreens' lasted for years, and even the stories of the moment stayed in the charts for months. But now nothing tops the parade longer than a week.

Abroad, it started with glasnost; the overthrow of Ceausescu; the breaching of the Berlin Wall; Poland; Germany ... and there you go again, spinning faster and faster ... What's that you say? Namibia? Remind me, what *is* Namibia? And Listeria – where was that again? Remind me, too, what *did* happen to the story about Lithuania in chickens?

As New Wave hit music, so, in domestic 'news', punk rules. The greenhouse heats us, prisoners lynch sex offenders, mad cows totter, and crack spreads. Journalists everywhere are rapping and vogueing like things possessed. It is the news equivalent of sensory overload.

And I weary. Play me, please, just one more time, the golden oldies I once knew by heart: Harry Truman and his orchestra – they had tunes you could remember; Nikita K. and the KGB boys – that was a rhythm you could hold on to; Jack Kennedy and the Cuban missile strings – it rhymed, the words made sense; or the big band sound of Yalta. Now there was something you could whistle.

26.5.90

But mum . . .

THEY FOB you off with things when you are a kid, but you notice. You notice that you are asked to take the side of the Three Little Pigs against the Wolf, and then your mother gives you roast pork for dinner. You notice that no tears are shed for Grandma, who is summarily eaten, but we are all supposed to get agitated about the safety of silly Little Red Riding Hood.

You notice the way Good and Wicked Fairies are hauled in, *deus ex machina*, when the storyteller is too lazy to invent more credible ways of advancing the plot. You notice that powers to cast spells are accorded only when this suits the action. Why the Good Fairy does not simply come on and banish the naughty people and put things permanently right at the very beginning is a question to which your mum – and, later, your Scripture teacher – never gives you a satisfactory answer.

These and many other things you notice, and resolve that when you grow up you will bring them to the attention of the authorities.

Then you do grow up. And you find that you are the authorities, and the pressure is on you to defend the status quo, and anyway you need a job, and a mortgage, and a girlfriend, and your acne's playing up, and life closes in, and you're done for. Well, my acne's gone, I've paid my mortgage, I don't want a girlfriend, and I am *not* done for. I am going back to basics. I want to know why Cinderella's parents were so horrid to her.

It is never explained. Her father obviously loves her, so why doesn't he stand up to the Ugly Sisters? What a wimp! And where does his wife stand? Surely she, not her two nasty daughters, is the real villain?

Then there's Buttons. Now, no beating about the bush: is he or isn't he? Is it 'like a brother' that he loves her, or is he physically interested? If he is, then surely *Cinderella* is a tragedy. Buttons, who really loves her, is upstaged when his girl's head is turned by a yuppie – a toff, who could have had any girl he wanted. What sort of compensation do you think all that rubbish about becoming a manservant to the royal couple would be? Salt into the wound! Or is a *ménage à trois* being hinted at: a touch of the rough for Cinders, and perhaps Prince Charming too?

The pumpkin I can believe, but how does Buttons rustle up the white mice, the rats *and* the lizard at a moment's notice in winter? And why midnight? Anyone who can do this sort of thing with rats can surely extend Cinders' bedtime. If the Fairy Godmother can turn a pumpkin into a coach, why didn't she turn the Ugly Sisters into toads years ago, saving a great deal of unnecessary pain?

Then there's the slipper. Why glass? And why was Cinders' the only foot it fitted?

Like other practical inconsistencies this is not explained. Yet my strongest objection to this tale is not practical, but moral: almost theological. Is virtue its own reward, and is that reason enough? The Church, and our whole moral culture, hedges a most critical issue.

Why should girls who are put upon bear their fate cheerfully? Because it is right? Or because it increases the chance that their prince will come? If in hope of reward, is that really virtue, or only prudence? There could hardly be a more important ethical question: can we, should we, count on being rewarded, now or later, for the virtuous life? *If not, why did they mention future reward so often?*

Cinderella, and, indeed, the Gospels, fudge this question, in my view disgracefully.

4.2.91

Latter-day sins

SITTING ON what the Southern Railway used to call a 'fast and frequent electric train' from Waterloo, I was immersed in solitude. My mind turned – naturally – to St Anthony of Egypt, said to be the man who first identified the seven deadly sins. 'As fish die,' he once remarked, 'when taken from the water, so does a monk wither away if he forsake his solitude.'

Poor St Anthony. I expect they're tiresomely companionable in the Egyptian desert, yet here in my crowded carriage he would have found solitude enough. And I wondered whether, peering through time from his mountain-top hermitage, the saint could see as far as Clapham Junction. What new sins, especially besetting our age, would strike him?

I was drafting a mental list for St Anthony as I called into Richmond & Co. to compare prices of waste fittings in their plumbing department. I needed a shower tray – the shallow pan you stand in. They had a 'slightly damaged' one for £5. It was plastic – light enough to carry. But with my other shopping I could only manage it resting upturned over my head. This would have blocked vision – except that I could see through the plughole. I navigated thus up the Northcote Road. People looked mildly surprised.

The plughole was divided by spokes into six segments and punctuated by a round central hole. It gave the world outside a seven-sectioned Gothic appearance – as viewed through the rose window of a cathedral. It helped me to see Clapham Junction as St Anthony might. It kept him with me. We went sightseeing together.

Litter scudded around our ankles. A blank-faced queue patiently awaited the non-arrival of those hated new conductor-less biscuit-tin double-deckers which don't work. They had been waiting – we don't know how long, because the clock above the post office doesn't work either. It hasn't for years. Nobody complains. People accept it – like the stamp machine, also broken. The only way to get stamps is to join the static queue of pensioners – silent, patient, resigned.

And the first deadly sin of our age screamed at St Anthony and me, from all seven sections of my segmented vision: *patience.* Putting up with things. We tolerate; we forbear; we have let things go slack.

I do mean slack. For modern Britain falls depressingly short of total collapse. That sort of excitement is for other nations. We opt, resignedly, for a passive mediocrity. On passing faces I can see boredom, indifference, but seldom the impatience and despair that rouse to action. There is neither the time nor – quite – the provocation to kick in the post office window before tea. Overturning and setting fire to a new-style bus would be thought intemperate. 'Patience is a virtue,' one was taught. I disagree.

For our kind of patience, far from bringing with it a Zen-like tranquillity, is accompanied by perpetual moaning. Dolly from up the road mutters into focus through the top section of plughole, shopping trolley in tow. She's complaining about the litter in front of her council flat. 'Mind you,' she says, 'I'm not one to sit on my backside and moan. Oh no' – a proud and independent snort – 'I've written to the council about it. Three times. It isn't fair.'

In Dolly and her countrymen's world, very little is fair – and it is always somebody else's fault. The air around us is filled with the whistle of accusation, the shuffle of responsibility, and the bouncing thud of bucks being passed. 'Look at this filth,' says the newsagent to me, waving towards the shelves of pornography with which his shop is stacked. 'I blame the Government.'

Ah, the Government. Of course. Not him, or his customers, but the Government. Or any other big, faceless punch-bag that comes to mind; so long as it's clear that it isn't *his* fault. Blur the focus, collectivize the guilt: 'It's all so unfair.' A ritual chant; not a call for personal effort, but a substitute for it, an excuse for not trying oneself. *Fairness* is the second sin.

But we must move on. Our newsagent is blaming Asian newsagents for causing unemployment – by working too hard, it seems: 'It isn't fair trade.' St Anthony and I have had enough of this.

The shower tray is getting heavier. At the kerb's edge, though, the ramps the council are constructing keep me from tripping. But something odd is coming into focus, painted on to the road in front of these ramps. A symbol – of a person in a wheelchair.

Let us pass over the question of who, in a wheelchair, having got so far, would need a picture to tell them what a ramp is for, and ask only this: why picture a wheelchair? Why not a pushchair? Or a wheelbarrow, or a shopping trolley? Why advertise the benefit only to the disabled? Are they more numerous? No. Are they more stupid? No. Are they more ... but my eye lights on some political flyposting: 'Help us to carry on caring.' Ah! Now we have it. The disabled symbol isn't really *for* disabled people. It's for the people who painted it, and what it really says is, 'This is a caring community. Be it known that we, the carers, shall inherit the earth – or, at least, the council.' All the political parties are at it, each in their different way, but all aiming to reassure us that somebody else is feeling sorry for disabled people on our behalf. The intention is not to prompt any action on our part, for never has there been an age when old ladies were less likely to be helped over the street. Caring, in the modern and wholly corrupt sense, has become anything but an individual's disposition to act kindly towards other individuals. It means moralizing (usually in an accusatory way) about what other people (usually an institution) ought to do, or boasting (as though one had done it oneself) about what has been done. It is a morbid and passive preoccupation with affliction which patronizes the disabled and calls sometimes for private charity and sometimes for public funds, but almost never for the sacrifice by any individual of his time or his convenience.

Caring, then, is the third sin. Another ritual word, intoned sanctimoniously, leached of all meaning. Another hollow substitute. St Anthony, who hates ritual, has fallen silent.

To cheer him up, I had planned to let him keep sloth for our fourth sin. It came to mind as a leisure arcade bobbed past the plughole. The bingo and fruit-machines promised anything but leisure: something much closer to sloth than to recreation; and the council's own 'leisure' centre (more bingo) seemed hardly better.

But one must be rigorous. Not all sloth is bad. Stretched-out, mind-clearing relaxation, if sinful at all, is a refreshing sin. Leisure – in Britain that means playing games of pure chance oneself, or watching other people play snooker – is not a refreshing but a stultifying sin. So *leisure* it is – the fourth sin: that multitude of lazy, easy, shallow passivities which dull the mind and numb the spirit. Soap operas, horoscopes and talking about sex are favourites with the working class. Food, cricket and talking about AIDS are middle-class equivalents. Peeping, chattering, everything except doing – it's all the same at root: a substitute for action, leeching off the real experiences of real people (or actors, playing them). No real risk. No real fun.

The whole of St Anthony's marvellous old sin of lust collapses, with us, into a sub-section of leisure: peeping. 'Spanking MP in new sex row,' screams the newspaper placard. What a clucking, prurient, sniggering people we have become. Giggling, slavering and tut-tutting over what somebody else says somebody else is doing. Mary Whitehouse and Cynthia Payne each make their special contribution – for being outraged is all part of the fun – to this extraordinary, collective, English insanity.

It's not new, of course. More novel, and deeply disturbing, is the intrusion into our national life of a fifth sin – one to which we were once defiantly resistant – *style*. It seems to be breaking out everywhere. Take fashion: clearly one does not want to attract attention by being unusually dirty, smelly or ragged. But, beyond that, attention given to personal appearance is plainly a sign of weakness of character. Surely mature people have better things to think about than the shape of their lapels, or whether their trousers fit; and better things to do than put jelly in their hair to make it stand on end?

Wilfred Thesiger, in *The Life of my Choice* describes a Sudanese tribe who wear nothing at all. When prevailed upon to don shorts, their chief, finding shorts uncomfortable, left the buttons open, hanging everything outside the garment. This shows a wonderful unselfconsciousness, wholly absent in Britain.

Children, who used to take pride in disarray, save up for designer-labelled sweaters. No sooner does a sort of greeny-blue become popular than *everyone* is wearing it. What have they done with their previous clothes? Thrown them away? St Anthony and I are nonplussed.

And have you noticed how an ugly new style of lettering, reminiscent of the 1950s, is now being slavishly followed? Wide gaps are left between letters, often punctuated with silly marks. It offers, I suppose, the reassurance of modishness to empty minds.

Indeed, some motorists boast about how *new* their cars are. Yet I remember selling a Land-Rover in Dar es Salaam by boasting of its age and recounting the trials it had survived! Those days are gone. *Style* is the fifth sin.

And the sixth is *health*. St Anthony and I agree upon this when a pasty, overweight yuppie in a jade-and-turquoise satin jogging suit lunges towards our plughole, panting.

Supermarket shelves are stacked, these days, with products low on 'additives'. Of course all ingredients are additives, but the term is taken to mean any substance for which no homely word happens to be available. Thus baking power, vinegar and salt have had a lucky escape – but no one has found a folksy way of saying 'monosodium glutamate', so that is out. Most Englishmen suspect, deep down, that somebody is trying to poison or gas them. And upon this incipient mental illness an entire industry is being based – by hard-faced men who have done well out of bran.

It is true that I am a long-distance runner. I enjoy racing buses and beating people. But I have never supposed that it was good for my health. It is plainly bad – or it wouldn't make me feel so sick. I am *just* prepared to accept that doctors can patch up or sew back on bits of the body that break or drop off. But to imagine that they have the slightest idea of what makes the machine tick is inherently unlikely. After all, every previous age has been wrong in its medical wisdom. It is blasphemy to imagine ours is different. St Anthony nods approvingly.

Unaware of the thoughts he has triggered, the perspiring jogger has receded until he is no more than a speck in the little round hole at the centre of my plug vision. Evening is drawing in, and we are not far from home. We've passed the garden centre and the third of four new building society branch offices. The busy hammering from the seventh new estate agency, soon to open, reminds me – tunnel- (or drain-) visioned as I am – that the next turning is mine. I take it.

What's this? A new skip? Great Scott – the people at the top of the road are redecorating again. Do people in Britain do anything else? Are we mad? Abroad, people hardly seem to bother: they just rent. But for us, house-and-garden is a god, a sun, a fixed point around which career, income, marriage, family – the ephemeral parts of life – revolve like subsidiary moons. There must be some terrible inner insecurity to which we are all prey, that purchasing and repapering our little shelters, and imposing upon their pocket-handkerchief gardens a crazy-paved geometry and herbaceous borders, should be the rock upon which our national life is founded. St Anthony recalls his goatskin tent and concurs: *home improvement* is the seventh sin – a sort of harmless, collective mental illness.

At last! The front gate. Damn! The dustmen have tipped rubbish over the pavement again. Maybe I should complain, but one must forbear. A cup of tea, perhaps? Reach for the low-fat milk substitute. Stare lovingly at the shower tray. Tinfoil-effect shower curtains, very stylish, would be nice. Decide later. First, the evening paper: what *was* that about Elton John? Good heavens! And there's Joan Collins again, splashing money about. Think of all the poverty there is – it just isn't fair, when pensioners are dying of starvation. Doesn't anybody care? Of course, I blame the Government.

St Anthony slips silently away.

21.6.87

Cross words, pointless ritual

I AM almost sure I am not from this planet.

It would be no surprise now if a great hand were to come down from the sky and scoop me up from where I stand and a great voice were to say, 'Okay, Matthew, your testing time is over. You were right. They *are* all mad. But you are not one of them. You never were. Come and have a cup of tea, and we'll explain the whole thing.' And I would be led away.

I have been expecting this since I was a toddler. And the first thing I would want to ask about is crosswords.

In the pages opposite there has been a portracted correspondence going on, again, about these stupid things. I have never done a crossword in my life and I hope to die in the same condition. Why in heaven's name one man should want to spend his time guessing which letters 'go' in little boxes devised by another man beats me. Have they nothing else to do? If they have so much spare time and need an intellectual challenge, why don't they learn how escalators work, then tell London Regional Transport?

People like this will sit for hours watching TV crime serials – or reading whodunnits – as though it matters who did it. If they really want to know, why not turn straight to the last page of the book, or fast-forward the video?

As a child, three things bored me rigid: riddles, games and rituals. Riddles came in those awful books of *Things To Do On A Rainy Day*. Question: *I am three parts animal and one part vegetable. What am I? Answer. A boiled egg in a wooden egg cup.* Well, sod that for a game of soldiers. The best thing to do on a rainy day was to go out and block the gutters to see what happened. But some kids didn't want to get wet. These are the ones who now do crosswords.

The prevalence of this type of person is almost certainly a harbinger of the collapse of an effete and doomed culture.

When I was six I couldn't for the life of me see why my little companions wanted to construct silly 'rules' and then rush around, tripping each other up, shrieking and being horses or lions, as they evidently *weren't* horses or lions. Now I am forty and see them (or their sons) on the rugby – 'pitch' is it? or 'field'? Who cares? The people are the same – they are still tripping each other up and blowing whistles, the rules have got even sillier, and I still can't for the life of me see the point of it all.

Some people put money into a machine, knowing it to be a machine constructed to take more than it gives, and pull a lever *in case* it gives them some. Why don't they get their own machine so they can at least get their money back?

Then there is ritual. Do you remember those infernal 'children's' stories? '... and then the *big* bear said "Who's been eating my porridge?", and the *medium*-sized bear said ...' Oh for Pete's sake, mum, get on with it. Cut the crap, will you. What happened?

The only thing that kept me going was the thought that one day I would grow up and there would be an end to this rubbish. And I began to grow up. And there was marching around in uniform in the Boys' Brigade. And I grew up more. And it was black gowns and Latin graces at Cambridge – *oculi omnium in te sperant, Domine* ...

And I grew up completely. And there was '... and the Epistle ended, the Priest shall say "here endeth the Epistle"'; and there was 'I refer my right honourable and learned friend to the answer I gave some moments ago ...' And the ritual got longer and longer and stupider and stupider and still there is no respite. If anyone tries to say rhymes over my grave I swear I'll rise up and clock them.

Riddles, games and rituals. The *Times* crossword is really a classy amalgam of all three. The intellectual equivalent of a posh caged hamster's exercise wheel.

But, my friends, the cage door is open!

10.2.90

10

Not Many People Know This

It's all wrong, say 99%

As so often, a small clue started me on the trail. '*Walk alongside the Thames*,' my note had instructed a friend, '*downstream. Pass the National Film Theatre, turn right ...*' and the rest is immaterial. The instructions proved useless. My friend, a Londoner, did not know which way the Thames flowed. 'Well it flows both ways,' he protested, 'depending whether the tide's going out or in.'

'Precisely. But which *way* is "out" and which way "in"?' Baffled silence. 'Okay. Which way is Southend?'

'On the A13. Or go to Fenchurch Street station.'

This was a graduate; but the notion that a place he couldn't walk to or see had a spatial direction relative to London was a conceptual struggle. 'Point,' I suggested. He pointed upriver.

If the tabloids were to report that the Indian government had suspended gravity and everyone on the subcontinent had gone spinning into space, pursued by the Taj Mahal, most readers, I think, would murmur 'Oh dear!' and send blankets to Oxfam. The rest would start hoarding rice.

Is this a defect of our age only, or of all ages? The generality seems neither knowledgeable nor even curious about the mainsprings on which life proceeds. It has learned to navigate with great skill across the complicated surface of modern living, but it is quite heedless *why* things are as they are.

'That's an unreasonable price for Ovaltine,' said one of my relations, recently. 'There should be laws against overcharging.'

During the ensuing argument I realized that this person – you could describe her as a professional woman – had not the faintest grasp of the theory of market economics. She thought a 'fair' price for goods could be established by means other than the operation of supply and demand. She thought you could price things by contemplation.

It was as if Adam Smith had never written. Yet this woman was no Marxist: she had never voted for anyone, she said, 'but Margaret Thatcher'.

I told her she should stop doing so immediately – the same advice I once gave a soldier who had told me he was a socialist but voted Tory because the armed forces had to support the government of the day.

'Certainly not,' she protested. 'Maggie's far better than all those political parties.' I put it to her that Mrs Thatcher led one of 'those political parties'.

'Not really. She has to fly the flag of one party, of course: but she's above all the stupid argument that goes on in Parliament.'

I put it to my relation that she had not grasped the essentially adversarial nature of our constitution, which relies on vigorous conflict between parties.

'Does it? Well I don't agree with it, then. MPs should make sensible decisions for the good of the country. If they stopped squabbling and looked at things *factually*, then everybody would reach the same conclusions.'

'So you think that in a court, instead of having one lawyer to prosecute, and another to make the best possible defence ...'

She interrupted: 'That's another thing I don't agree with. How dare lawyers defend people who have committed horrible crimes, when they're sure they're guilty? It's all wrong. What's more, you'd find 99 per cent of the population agreed with me.'

I did not ask about gravity in case 99 per cent disagreed with that, too. For had she not already rejected the cornerstone of our economic, political and judicial systems: the idea that if opposing forces are given free play, things will find their natural level? It may be that with gravity, too, the conservative mind rejects *laissez-faire* and would prefer matters to be settled by abstract justice: which way – and where – *ought* the Thames to flow?

They say our ancient democracy is based upon 'consent', but they never say to what. What was the question? When did they ask? And if they haven't yet, would they please call off further inquiries? I'm worried – and, I'm sure 99 per cent of the country agrees with me.

26.8.89

Insurance as Neo-Marxism

PETER BOTTOMLEY, the Roads minister, recently gave his blessing to a controversial new idea from the insurance world. Pearl Assurance has said it will not compensate future policy-holders for accidents caused by their own drunkenness.

Well, you may say, Pearl is free to attach what conditions it pleases to new policies; and the public are free to look elsewhere for an insurer if they wish.

But are they? Mr Bottomley's intervention is significant, for it signals to other insurers, too, that this is the way forward. Mr Bottomley, it seems – not just Pearl Assurance – wants to stop us from insuring ourselves against one particular risk: the risk of getting hurt when drunk.

We remain free to get hurt when stupid. You may still drive like a maniac because you *are* a maniac, or because you are exhausted, angry, late or just plain incompetent, and Pearl Assurance and Mr Bottomley will allow you to recover costs. Be as reckless as you please – throw judgement to the winds – but don't have a sherry beforehand. That is the message.

And that is where the Bottomley ruling, in all its austere splendour, falls down. It does not go far enough. The minister's logic is impeccable, but it is also unstoppable. His argument is that to allow an individual to insure himself against his own stupid behaviour is contrary to the public good, for two reasons. Firstly, it encourages him in that stupid behaviour, by protecting him from its consequences. And, secondly, it unjustly redistributes wealth from the prudent (who pay the premiums, but seldom claim) to the foolish (who hit the jackpot every time they come a cropper).

These two propositions are (a) inescapably true, and (b) an argument against *all* forms of insurance. I have long believed that the availability of insurance against personal risk rots the national character and undermines individual responsibility. Bottomley's bold stand encourages me to say why.

Insuring yourself is a form of gambling: a negative version of the pools. For a small, regular payment (which the odds are you will forfeit completely) you purchase a statistically tiny chance of a large payout.

As with Littlewoods, so with Pearl Assurance, the organizers have made the shrewd actuarial calculation that the generality will pay more than the generality gets back. Subtract the latter from the former and the balance equals the directors' BMWs.

It is always irrational to insure unless (1) you are a bigger risk than the premium reflects, or (2) you are emotionally incapable of keeping your fear of catastrophe in proportion to your chances of catastrophe.

Both insurance and the pools provide pleasure – one by supplying the hope of gain, the other by reducing the fear of loss. But, once the punter has filled in his pools coupon there is nothing he can do to improve his chances, so gambling does not affect his behaviour. But a flutter with an insurance company does. It reduces his incentive to guard *himself* against the loss for which he is covered.

Insurable risk can be reduced. Sickness, injury, burglary, fire or accident happen to the careful, but happen more often to the careless. Insurance must tempt some into acts or omissions they would not otherwise chance. Surveys prove that people unconsciously drive faster with seat belts on. Insurance is no different.

And it is the more careful policy-holders who pay. The whole insurance idea displays all the most objectionable features of socialism. The insured, as a class, inhabit a sort of privatized mini-welfare-state whose citizens are the fellow-insured and whose taxes are their premiums. Let me say again, lest anybody think I am joking: spreading risk reduces individual exposure to peril. Exposure to peril is a mainspring of a free society.

Insurance is anti-Thatcher. Insurance must go.

24.6.89

Flashing in Shadwell

EVERYONE HAS ideals: I had two. I would never own a flat in Docklands; and never buy lampshades in Peter Jones. Buying a lampshade in Peter Jones for the Docklands flat the other day, I asked myself whether anything survives of the principles of my youth.

Yes. It's not Wapping and it hasn't got a view of the river. It's Shadwell and has a view of the Southend to Fenchurch Street line and the Docklands Light Railway.

Have you ever wanted to flash? I never thought I did. But in a bedroom twenty yards from the Light Railway, with carriages full of po-faced journalists gliding by to write editorials about Christian values for the *Daily Telegraph* on the Isle of Dogs, the temptation is almost overwhelming. They'd be whisked away before they knew what had hit them.

Wapping is over the road and I've only been there twice. Wapping is coachloads of Japanese tourists at the Prospect of Whitby and arty-farty boutiques at Tobacco Dock.

Writing for *The Times*, you might think it helped to live near the office but, in fact, there's no need to turn up in person: it's all done with computer linkups. If only fatherhood could be arranged like that.

So I live in Derbyshire and roost midweek – when Parliament's sitting – in Shadwell.

And I'm not knocking it. Shadwell clearly used to be a place. It is a Tube station on the East London line, with frequent trains to New Cross Gate (hooray!); and a platform on the Docklands Light Railway.

You can go one stop to Tower Hill, or commute to Mudchute.

Cable Street was famous once: a string of brothels, where only a fool walked alone. Communists and Fascists rioted there in the Thirties. But the old street was bulldozed and, today, it's probably safer than ever before in its history. A pity, for its spirit has been broken.

You can't drive it any more, as the carriageway has been segmented into one-way sections in alternate directions. Enterprising local residents reverse their cars up the wrong-way sections and then point forward again for the right-way bits. As there's a fire station here too, whose engines ignore the road rules: so you may see a high-speed procession of fire-engines going forwards and old Cortinas going backwards.

Avoiding the stupid railings erected for pedestrian safety, everyone walks in the road, clambering over the mini-roundabout of which the summit is possibly Shadwell's highest point.

Standing there last week, I could see past the railings to the white towers of St George's in the East, a beautiful Hawksmoor church which is actually only an historic shell with Sixties trash inside it – rather like the Church of England itself.

Behind me the red-brick council blocks breathed a more militant culture: curry and Islam. This is what the smarter parts of Dacca must be like; but, outside their enclosed world, the huge Bengali community scarcely ventures.

Not so the Catholics. The Vaughan Club, a friendly-looking centre just off Cable Street, boasts a bar and snooker tables; but the big attraction is tap-dancing. Lively sessions occur on the first floor and the ripples spread outwards. Our flat looks across to the backs of a terrace where, on one minuscule balcony, a woman has tap-danced all through the summer to the music of *You Make Me Feel So Young*.

The dancing has to be virtually on the spot, as she has a baby, and there is just room on the balcony for its inflatable paddling-pool which she fills with water from a plastic bucket, placing the baby in the pool and *You Make Me Feel So Young* in the cassette-player.

Then she dances, until something calls her into the house. While she is away the baby gets out of the pool and tips it sideways against the railings, cascading the water down on to the neighbours. Mother returns, swears at baby, refills the pool – and dances on.

I suppose that's what they mean by 'community'. There's precious little else. My friend Claudia – an optimistic soul – says there are 'some marvellous local characters'. She is referring to some notorious local alcoholics.

As for East End charm, if a few drunk old women sitting around in pubs singing 'We'll Meet Again' is what they mean then I think we've been conned.

Not that Shadwell lacks street life. It was my fortieth birthday last week. Bringing the rubbish down next morning, I witnessed a dispute between two neighbours.

'Just shut your f—ing mouth or my son'll shut it for you.'

'Your son, eh? Don't you know your wife's a f—ing prostitute?' They were interrupted by a van driving up the street. A man got out with a huge bouquet of flowers. They were for me.

So why do I live in Shadwell? Funny, that's what the flower-man asked. Well it's better than f—ing Belgravia, innit?

16.8.89

I really mean *it*

'AND ONCE again our thanks go out *to* the emergency services for their skill and courage ...' I shifted irritably in the press gallery of the House of Commons. Why had the minister put the emphasis on the word '*to*'?

Try saying it yourself. There are a couple of possible emphases: a minor one on 'thanks' and a major one on the '-erge-' of 'emergency'. So why do our thanks go out *to* the emergency services? Had someone suggested that thanks went out *from* the emergency services?

This happened last year. I started watching out for misplaced emphasis wherever I heard it. And I heard it everywhere. As the evidence piled up, an explanation began to shine through. It is offered here tentatively, for in a light-hearted essay we should not attempt an academic dissertation.

But somebody should: and I hand the torch on to any professor of communications who may care to take it up. First, the evidence. Misplaced emphasis is to be heard wherever men and women speak, but there are three groups of flagrant offenders: politicians; television and radio reporters; and British Rail platform announcers.

'We regret to announce the late running *of* the 07.56 "Master Cutler" service from Sheffield. This is due to engineering works *at* Chesterfield.' Or: 'A selection of sweets, drinks and light refreshments is available *from* the buffet car which is situated at the rear *of* the train.'

But if BR irritate, television and radio reporters infuriate – probably because their subject matter is not inherently trivial and is delivered in tones of false urgency whose insincerity sets the teeth on edge.

You can almost hear the producer-director by the reporter's shoulder, out of shot ('Once more, love, and could you hit *dead* and *dying* a bit harder?') as the reporter stares significantly into what the viewer thinks is his sitting room, but is actually a large piece of card with the words written on it, held above the cameraman.

'At dawn, as this small community counts its dead and tends its dying, there is just one thought in the minds *of . . .' ARRGH!*

Examples multiply: but you've got the point. More interesting is to ask why. I am now certain. Misdirected emphasis is a protest by the ego against the super-ego. To put it in everyday language, it is an unconscious rebellion by the inner man against the lies he has to tell.

I reached this truth from two observations. Firstly, misdirected emphasis is not random, but perverse. It regularly falls upon the word which is *most* unsuitable to bear it. The inner man is saying 'sod off!' to the meaning of the sentence.

Secondly, the two most often-observed single occurrences are on the prepositions following the words 'apologize' and 'grateful' and in circumstances where we suspect that the individual himself doesn't care a fig.

He is forcing himself to pretend. And the underlying honesty of the unconscious man – or woman – is protesting in the way that every child knows: by doing what it is told, according to the letter, but contrary to the spirit.

It is probably the reason why people who can read fluently simply *cannot* 'say their lines' in poetry or recitation except in a flat and unnatural way, yet they are perfectly capable of using the same phrases normally as part of their everyday lives.

So next time you hear the Prime Minister intone: 'And can I say how grateful I am *to* the Basingstoke Townswomen's Guild for including me *in* this splendid occasion . . .' don't hear, in that, the sound of the political glad-hander.

Listen, instead, to the voice of a little girl called Margaret Roberts from North Parade, Grantham, who didn't want to go to the party. But the Prime Minister *would* insist.

23.9.89

Columnist bites reporter

HERE IS a message for all dogs who like the occasional nip and want their names in print. Firstly: poodles, Labradors, family-style dogs. To get into the provincial daily press (The *Barchester Evening Chronicle*) you must bite. Hard. Preferably kids. And draw blood. It's got to support words like 'maul' or 'savage attack' in the headline.

To get into tabloids like the *Sun* or *Daily Express*, a good bite alone won't do. So pull out all stops. Bare your teeth, think 'demented', 'devil-dog' and 'intensive care', and you're in with a chance. And to hit the Fleet Street qualities? Don't bother. The *FT* doesn't photograph retrievers.

Rottweilers. Much easier for you. The provincial press will take nearly anything with 'Rottweiler' in it – just a little graze, an abrasion, a whimpering toddler ... you can even make it by biting another dog! For the national tabloids, though, it has to be a jolly good bite. And the quality papers? Yes, worth a try, but you really must go for it.

How do I know this? Easy. Two research assistants, a mobile phone, the *Willings Press Guide* list of daily papers, a notepad, and two little lies:

Lie 1. 'Hello? News desk? I'm a stringer [freelance journalist] temporarily in your area. Look, I've got a Rottweiler-biting for you ... yes, local ... No, only the outline so far, but there's a phone number ... Yes I could sell it to you; but they're friends, so I'd better check first. Do you want me to follow it up?'

Lie 2. 'Hello?' News desk ... Got a dog bite story ... What's that? No – not a Rottweiler. Just a biggish, mongrelish Labrador-style pooch. Shall I follow it up? What kind of thing are you likely to use?'

We got through fifty papers. With the nationals (which were unlikely to notice the coincidence) we tried both stories. The outcome was startling.

Reaction was remarkably uniform across papers of similar types. Papers of every type would report our Rottweiler bite if it was sufficiently serious. How serious depended on the circulation – and the pretensions – of the paper: the smaller the circulation, the smaller the bite. Most provincials were interested in anything with 'Rottweiler' in it. 'Oh yes! Rottweilers are all the go at the moment!' exclaimed a Northwestern daily. Its East Midlands sister was '*certainly* interested! For the first edition please.' 'We'd love it,' said a South Coast daily.

Fleet Street demanded more from the delinquent Rottweiler. The broadsheets insisted on grave injuries, while the tabloids wanted what one called 'a good mauling'. 'If the wounds are more than superficial,' said another. 'Any chance of a hospital bed?'

And what if the dog was only a 'Labrador-style pooch'? Fleet Street, both tabloids and broadsheets, treated our inquiries with contempt. They were not interested in the severity of the wounds. 'I don't think so somehow' summed it up. 'Thanks but no thanks,' said another. And about half the provincials took the same attitude. As one Northeastern daily put it: 'Now if it had been a Rottweiler ...'

Of the remainder, some were noncommittal ('Not desperately. Get back to me when I'm not so busy'); some were interested, and most were typified by a Mersey daily: 'Ah, we get lots of that sort. It would have to be a fairly decent bite to arouse our interest'; or (from Lancashire): 'We *would* want something dramatic.'

Britain is a big country. At any time, canine teeth of every breed are sinking into human flesh of every texture; walls are falling on pedestrians and children are being sexually abused. It is not to diminish the seriousness of these things to observe that it is not necessary for an epidemic to occur for honest reporting to give the impression that it has.

Art holds not a mirror, but a filter, up to nature. Selectivity, not dishonesty, is the greatest liar.

My thanks to researchers Jason Mitchell and Matthew Nicholls and, for advice, to Sam Fay of the *Matlock Mercury*.

10.3.90

The news we can afford

THE FRONT page of my newspaper the other day had something about the poll tax.

But a one-paragraph insert caught my eye. Entitled 'Lithuanian crackdown', it suggested that the Kremlin had put one of its own republics in a virtual state of siege. Apparently troops were being mobilized. Readers who wanted to learn more were directed to page eight.

Is it just because Eastern Europe has lost its novelty that such stories are now less likely to hit the news? I have a theory that it is not. There is also the question of cost. Did you realize that news programmes have budgets? And that they run out – just like yours and mine?

When budgets are low and a story has proved too expensive to cover well, there is a key difference between its treatment by the press and by television. A newspaper (with acres of space where pictures are secondary and words cheap) will include it, but relegate it to an inside page. Television (to which time is gold and pictures are paramount) will often drop it altogether.

When I worked on LWT's *Weekend World* programme, we were given a certain allocation every year, within which we calculated how many foreign trips we could afford. One year, I remember, a faction within our team thought a 'show' (as we called it) on problems in Sri Lanka would be timely; another was rooting for Poland, while everyone agreed that it would be eccentric to ignore the US Democratic party primaries.

South Africa looked interesting, and one of our researchers was deputed to Japan to see whether there was a show in that. He returned to report that there wasn't. I put in a late bid for Spitzbergen, but got nowhere.

I think this was the period when we ended up doing lots of shows on Aids. These are very cheap to make, requiring only a trip to a London hospital, some animated coloured drawings of viruses, me interviewing Kenneth Clarke (clipboard memo on my knee: *Whatever he answers, just say 'Why aren't you doing more?' angrily*). And a short video of me standing in front of an Aids poster on the Cromwell Road, saying 'It's posters like these ... (etc)'. We did a show on the greenhouse effect, too, with a world map and aerosol cans. It's scripts like these that can save a series from bankruptcy.

I certainly do not wish to question the gravity of Aids, and I probably do not wish to question the importance of five demonstrators shouting rude words about the poll tax outside Hackney town hall, when I put it to you that the prominence an issue gets may depend on how much a programme has left in the kitty at that point in the calendar.

Take the present moment. Last year gave us riots in Israel (manageable); the usual carry-on in Nicaragua (predictable) and the ups and downs of international tension (for which any financial controller can budget). Then came Tiananmen Square (costly: it's not cheap to send a camera crew to Peking). That probably came out of the reserves.

Then Gorbachov went crackers and Moscow was news (pricey: reserves running low). Poland and the Berlin Wall came next (rush off application for emergency budget), closely followed by Romania, Czechoslovakia (finance director in despair), Hungary, Yugoslavia (scrub Yugoslavia: no funds) and then – oh crikey! – they're letting Nelson Mandela out. Whack a team off to Soweto ... Ethiopia, did you say? Millions about to starve? Sorry, can't afford Ethiopia. Any demos in Camden this week?

Dear viewers, in the final months before everything falls apart and the realization hits us that cuddly old Mr Brezhnev and charming Mr Botha were the last bastions of liberal values against the advancing tide of bloodcurdling nationalism, tribalism, anti-Semitic pogroms and the lunacies of Islam, spare a thought for the accountants at LWT.

And if you don't see something on television, don't assume it isn't happening.

24.3.90

The tram mentality

A WEEK at Blackpool has reintroduced me to a fine old British mode of transport. Trams. In all my life I have never seen a more stupid way of getting around.

'They should never have taken them away you know they don't cause any pollution,' says the voice of the man behind me in my tramcar, droning on to his wife without pause for breath. 'They're realizing that now mind you you used to be able to get a tram anywhere in Sheffield and now there are buses of course but they aren't the same.'

Of course they aren't the same, you moron. They're buses. Buses are better. Does this fellow think the bus superseded the tram overnight, by oversight?

About thirty seconds' thought makes it perfectly clear why, once buses got going in earnest, the writing was on the wall for trams. After five days studying Blackpool's tramway system, here are my conclusions – nine things you didn't know about trams:

● One short-circuit and the whole fleet fails.

● Trams are slow. They have no acceleration and take ages to stop; so you dare not drive them at more than a trundle. Metal on metal gives no adhesion.

● Trams are highly dangerous. Apart from bad braking they cannot swerve to avoid hazards. They seem safe because they are so lethal that everyone gives them a wide berth.

● Trams are much noisier than buses.

● A tram system is uglier than a bus service. The steel posts and overhead wires are a permanent, hideous blot.

● Trams cannot make detours. If the road is up, so is the whole service. You cannot divert a spare tram on a day trip to Windermere.

● If one tram breaks down, the whole service is jammed. If the first tram is full the next four pile up, empty, behind.

● Bad braking means succeeding trams must keep their distance and cannot mingle with other traffic. So the service really needs its own private highway, as wide as a two-lane road yet unable to carry the same density of traffic.

● It is true that trams do not pollute Blackpool. They pollute Sweden, where the acid rain from our power stations falls.

The case is proved. Steel on steel was a good idea, before rubber was invented. With rubber, inflated wheels in concrete tracks gave better, quieter adhesion, as the French demonstrated; but even that became obsolete once the idea of independent steering dawned. All that was needed was an individual power source and hey presto! The bus was born.

So why do we go all gooey-eyed about trams? The Labour conference in Blackpool this week gives a clue. Consider the concept of the tram. Two parallel steel rails, fixed and undeviating, along which must pass conveyances for the collective transport of citizens, at a standard price, as and when the management decides, and in a fashion that prohibits any one citizen from overtaking (or falling behind) another. Or from travelling anywhere the authorities have not ordained.

Do we not have, here, the essence of socialism? Is it not the socialist in each of us that loves the tramcar? Consider the role of the tram driver. He is in charge: the skipper at his craft. He has limited powers of acceleration and certain powers of braking. He can stop. He can even reverse. And he has the right to discipline his passengers and exclude would-be boarders.

But he cannot steer. The route has been laid down in advance according to a theory of the public interest. He holds and exercises authority, but does so *by* authority. I wonder whether, when he was a boy, Neil Kinnock ever wanted to be a tram driver?

A notice on my tram said: *Conveyance of Children: Children must not occupy seats while adult passengers are standing. By Order of the Company*. 'Isn't it nice,' says the man behind me, 'to have it laid down and spelt out like that?'

6.10.90

A cornflake too far

FOR THE *purists. Pour into bowl, add cool, fresh milk and give your taste buds the perfect start to the day ...*

I've never thought of myself as a purist. Yet that is how those of us who eat our cornflakes with milk and sugar are described by Kellogg's. This is clear from the instructions on my cereal packet: *Great Ways to Enjoy Crunchy Nut Cornflakes.*

The purists' way is outlined first. It is tactful of the manufacturers to call us purists as I think what they really mean is 'unimaginative stick-in-the-muds'. Already I feel ashamed. All my life I have been an Oliver Cromwell of the cereal world. Now a horizon of sinful, mind-broadening experiment opens before me. I will broaden my breakfast experience, so narrow until now, by reading on.

● *At lunchtime try the rather special combination of slightly softened ice-cream with a generous topping of flakes – smooth and crunchy.*

Wow! Recently I was lunching with Lord King. The tactful peer can have refrained from ordering cornflakes himself only to avoid showing me up.

● *Invite some friends round, put on that video you've all been dying to see, and serve bowlfuls in the intermission.*

Good gracious. Which video? The one *I've* been dying to see? They might not like it.

● *Be a little adventurous and sprinkle cornflakes into natural, unsweet-ened yoghurt for an unusual and delicious taste sensation.*

With yoghurt? Are you sure?

● *Cut the lawn, mend the door handle, pay the bills, do the washing, paint the ceiling, walk the dog ...*

So soon after the yoghurt-and-cornflakes?

... and then sit down with your favourite music playing, and savour every wonderful spoonful.

I don't think I'm feeling too well. The Wagner is making the milk curdle.

● *Brighten up that old favourite dessert, banana custard, with a layer of flakes freshly sprinkled on each serving.*

With *what?* May I take a raincheck on the banana custard?

● *Don't invite those friends around. Put on the video YOU'VE been dying to see ...*

Ho ho! You mindreader, Mr Kellogg ...
... *curl up in the armchair* ...
Oh no! I can feel it coming!
... *and crunch to your heart's content ... through all the quiet bits.*

This is too much.

I place the video on Hold, flinging the cornflake packet over the television, narrowly missing the uneaten banana-custard layered with cornflakes, knocking the discarded spoonful of cornflakes by the record player onto the newly-walked dog, bouncing off the newly-painted ceiling and scattering cornflakes over the newly-laundered washing.

The stamped, addressed envelopes containing bills and the cheques I have just written to pay them, sitting ready for posting, have fallen into the bowl of milk with cornflakes set aside, earlier, for that unsuspected purist in me.

I make for the door. Luckily the handle has been mended. The friends I invited round to watch the video I didn't want to see have long gone, leaving behind the unfinished yoghurt with cornflakes. My gaze lights on the ice-cream topped with cornflakes.

I thrust it from me and rush outside, collapsing on the newly-mown lawn. I am overwhelmed by a longing for Rice Krispies.

1.10.90

11

True Stories –
and Wilder Claims

Nor iron bars a hero cage

I REALLY had only three heroes, and two have just fallen. Mr Macmillan has taken a peerage and Elton John has taken a wife. Now I have lost the third. I write this on the train back from his cremation.

Mr Fred Hill died last week. He was serving his thirty-second, and, as it turned out, his last sentence in Pentonville Prison. He was seventy-four.

I met him only twice. Once when he came to the House of Commons to address a little meeting of rather embarrassed MPs; once when I spotted him standing anonymously at the back of St Margaret's Church, at a colleague's memorial service. The Prime Minister was there too but I fancy that, among all that distinguished congregation, Ronnie Bell (whose passing we were there to mark) would have been happiest to see Fred.

Fred (everyone called him that) refused to wear a crash helmet. He believed that he was a safer motorcyclist without one. More importantly he held that, right or wrong, the decision was his to take and his alone.

He was bitter that the freedom to take it was extended to Sikhs without being extended to him – a convinced atheist. Many Sikhs agreed with him.

So Fred used to venture out, helmetless, on his old motorbike – perhaps the last man in Britain wilfully and persistently to do so. The police knew him and turned a blind eye when they could. Often enough, though, they had no choice but to prosecute, and the magistrates before whom he would appear had no choice but to send him to prison because he refused to pay fines.

Thirty days was the usual sentence but this time – responding perhaps to the splendid new mood of deterrent justice – they gave the old man two months. Some way through the sentence Fred suffered a heart attack and died.

Heroic? He did not, when I met him, seem cast in the mould of a Thomas More or a Joan of Arc. He neither suffered nor was persecuted in the heroic manner. He was courteous, mild, sane and utterly unself-righteous: a somewhat unlikely figure ... bemused almost.

A victim? No one meant to be unkind to him and many, including policemen and prison warders, tried to rescue him 'from himself'. I doubt whether he was made very miserable by the treatment he received. He felt he had a mission in life, took his jail sentences stoically, and used to help other prisoners write letters. He was happier than many pensioners I meet.

257

Ludicrous, then? I never thought so. Some people would have sneered at the huge wreath in the shape of a motorbike, sent to the cremation by the Motor-Cycle Action Group: I found it rather moving, for I knew that there would have been a rally of thousands there, if the family had wanted it. Rhodes Boyson (under whose headmastership Fred had once taught) did not think so either. He once wrote of him that he was 'one of the finest teachers I have ever met'. Both his MPs (one a Social Democrat and the next a Conservative) admired him.

Yet, though his father (a steelworker and trade-unionist) and his mother (a suffragette and millworker) were convinced socialists, Fred is unlikely to receive the Nelson Mandela treatment. No 'Fred Hill Crescent, NW1', no 'Fred Hill Gardens' on the South Bank, for him! Not wearing a crash-helmet is unlikely to become one of the great socialist causes.

Nor do the Tories have much time for Fred's kind. All his career he refused to teach in the more 'privileged' state schools. He had no time for the socially advantaged. A bit of an embarrassment, really, in his unsmart clothes and eccentric opinions. Individual freedom, to the Conservative Party, may be indivisible, but we tend to get more worked up about the freedoms of having and holding, of possessing and augmenting and passing it on. Freedom to be an embarrassment to the relations, freedom to be silly, is not quite what the Prime Minister has in mind.

Were you silly, then, Fred? Well, yes, maybe ... 'Got it all a bit out of proportion,' I think my colleagues would say.

Keep it out of proportion, Fred! Ignore the angels and archangels: take no notice of the cherubim and seraphim: you just keep plugging on about crash-helmets! Cherished freedoms be damned – nobody who wants to be re-elected will touch the cherished freedoms: it's the uncherished ones we've got to watch: freedoms to do things the public consider silly, harmful, immoral or unnecessary.

You hurt nobody by riding bareheaded – nobody but yourself – but you inspired me and all who really knew you.

Your courage and resolution were finer even than the PM's because they never did you any good and you never thought they would. You didn't even expect recognition in the next world. You didn't believe in Heaven.

I hope you are wrong. I hope there are helmet laws there too, because you'll know just what to do, Fred!

14.3.84

Going Nowhere

I GAVE a lift to three yobs the other morning – the kind who have brought this country to its knees, shamed us abroad, etc. Two boys and a girl, they were hitch-hiking from London to Liverpool. I was driving from Westminister to Derby. Their plan was to look for a bit of trouble in Merseyside. I was to address a meeting of the Duffield Conservative Association. It is hard to imagine which of us was expecting the most fun. I drive a battered old car, never washed; but they had been waiting (they said), an hour before I stopped so they accepted the lift, looking apprehensive. They still looked apprehensive when I dropped them an hour later, but by then I had realized that neither the car, nor I, was responsible for their insecurity.

I seldom tell people that I'm an MP. People are either impressed, intimidated or contemptuous, and one does not care to excite any of these emotions. Half clam up and the other half unleash a speech containing all the things they have been meaning to tell Mrs Thatcher, if they ever meet her. I told my passengers I was a food inspector.

They asked if that was anything to do with the government. 'Not really,' I said. 'The police?' (nervously) – 'No, no connection.' They relaxed visibly. One of them told me about a rotten meat pie he had bought in Bow and I undertook to report it.

The two boys were about seventeen and something between punks and skinheads: pinched faces, thin arms and legs, scruffily and scrappily dressed, but without the style to be full punks or the muscle to be real skinheads. Whatever trouble they were looking for would obviously not involve any sort of courage. The ginger-haired boy had sunken cheeks, a pasty face, and many studs in his nose and ears. He looked as though he wouldn't get up if you knocked him down. The blond boy, a Tin-Tin with nervous eyes and a face lined beyond his age, looked as though he would have run away before you had time to hit him.

The girl was about sixteen and tougher. She told me where she had been at school and I recognized the name as that of a special school for maladjusted girls. In my experience, there aren't many maladjusted girls, but those that are, are *very* maladjusted.

None had been to Liverpool before and none had hitch-hiked before. Only one had been on a motorway. They didn't understand about service areas, or where you could hitch and where you couldn't, and I had to help them spell 'Liverpool' on to the piece of cardboard that I explained they would need to display when I dropped them. One of them wore a heavy old coat because his mother had said it would be icy cold in Liverpool. They had a friend there and hoped to stay with him but he wasn't expecting them and didn't have a telephone and they only knew the name of the street where they thought he lived.

Ginger's mother worked; his father had 'gone'. Tin-Tin's mother didn't work because his father hadn't completely 'gone' and sent money, sometimes. Chris, the girl, didn't know or care what had happened to her parents. I suspected that she might have run away from somewhere. None of them worked or had any ideas about a job. When we get unemployment down from three million to one million, they will be part of the one million.

I asked about football hooliganism. Ginger said it was disgusting – no doubt to please me, because Chris giggled. Ginger had a badly scarred wrist and forearm. Chris said it was Them Italians what started it and even if it wasn't she didn't think the trouble-makers had meant to cause *such* a lot of trouble. She didn't say *she* was looking for trouble but if they were going to Liverpool to spend money they would have had to steal it first; and if free entertainment was what they were looking for I suspect that the public libraries were not what they had in mind.

When we passed a police Range-Rover standing off the hard shoulder, I could feel the tension mount among the three. The two in the back shifted uneasily and Tin-Tin all but ducked. 'What's the use of that?' Chris said, the danger past. 'You can see them too easy. In Battersea they jump out when you ain't expecting it!'

I left them, blinking in the sunlight (at the service area, holding their new 'Liverpool' sign), with a heavy heart: I to Duffield and they to their bit of bother. A huge and inappropriate and undirected feeling of sympathy for them came over me. Silly, really, because it is the old ladies whose bags they might snatch for whom one should feel sympathy.

Sympathy, in any case, is useless. These people are as irredeemable by social scientists from Essex University as by Tory MPs from Cambridge. The gap is unbridgeable – except perhaps by the infectious certainties of a Wesley or Booth, or Mosley or Benn.

My three passengers were not very bad people, nor were they at all good – nor 'misunderstood', nor 'interesting' nor 'worthwhile underneath'. They were shallow and underdeveloped and, most of all, they were weak. Yet they were capable of all kinds of harm: of setting a football stadium alight; of firing a couple of blank rounds; of inflicting a nasty wound with a Stanley knife on a dark night; capable of theft – but the kind who always get caught, paraded before magistrates and sentenced, only to offend again. The gross cost to the state of each of their lives will be staggering: but it will be paid and they will be contained, that is the happy – or sad? – truth of it.

These people will never wreck society. They are damage-limitable. They have nothing to give, nothing to withhold, and a potential only to irritate, spoil, and wound: not to overturn, defeat, or seriously challenge. They are not the stuff of which armies, or rebels, are made.

What a strange irony that our welfare state, beloved of the left, has proved so potent to castrate the human beings from whom the socialist revolution was to come. What a paradox that the right, who hate the nanny-state, should be protected by the very system of bread-and-circuses-and-special-needs-payments whose financing they so begrudge.

Ginger, Tin-Tin and Chris may be the signs of dissolution, but they will not be the instruments of it. One day, perhaps, a redeeming fire will destroy them and many like them, making of those who learn to survive the men and women of whom revolution *is* born. But not yet, and not these. I was able to carry reassurance to Duffield.

18.7.85

I don't think I know you . . .

How ODD that, queueing for taxis, we almost never sort ourselves into groups with shared destinations. This too would require an unsolicited approach to strangers. I tried it once, but people avoided my eyes and shuffled away. They would rather freeze. So I shuffle slowly forward and am conveyed, alone, to St Pancras Station.

There is a queue for tickets. Over a mini-tannoy, through the cosh- and germ-proof screen, an Asian clerk tries to explain to a deaf lady that the special *return* ticket is cheaper than the single. 'BUT MY SISTER IS BRINGING ME BACK' she keeps shouting. The queue pretends not to hear her – nor the student hawking (at half price) the unused portion of his Sheffield-London-Sheffield ticket. It's a bargain, for someone. But nobody dares. We don't know him. We would rather miss our train.

I do just catch mine, to Derby, but too late to get a seat. Why does one never see passengers wanting seats buying them from passengers who would rather take the money and stand? After all, reserving your seat through BR displaces another passenger without compensating him. Deal direct, and *he* gets the cash instead of BR. But no, we must be seated *through* the company, buy our ticket *through* the clerk, arrange our taxi *through* the cabbie, sell our home *through* the agency. Heaven defend us from direct and uninvited contact with unknown persons who have no uniform, status, or agreed role.

Platform 2B at Derby station is one of the coldest places in the world. The waiting room, thoughtfully decorated in battleship grey, is just as cold, because the heater's broken. But the tannoy works: a woman's voice carrying a hint of Correction and Discipline (third floor) advises: 'British Rail regret to announce the delayed departure of the 1700 hours service to Matlock.' (Expectant pause.) 'This train is at present receiving fitter's attention ...' (disapproving pause) '... in the sidings.'

Attention received, the train arrives. And we, the small, still-silent band from the waiting room, who have yet to speak to each other, board and sit back, but not for long. For it seems the fitter was insufficiently attentive. The brakes bind. The engine labours. The train shudders to a halt. Silence, for ten minutes. Then, another tannoy, the guard: (confidently) 'We regret to announce ...' (less confidently) '... that this train is ... has ... *stopped*' (stammering noises). 'This is due to ... *unit failure*.'

Suddenly all the passengers are laughing. We giggle, groan, expostulate. We *talk* to each other. An emergency! A shared crisis! A joke? Only minor, you may say – but enough to suspend the rules about strangers, which are cheerfully, almost excitedly, brushed aside. Whatever shall we do? Perhaps another train will run into us! What a jam we must be causing on the main line! Look at it snowing! Will there be a bus? Shall we share taxis? A passenger knows where there are minicabs; a boy starts chatting up the girl across the carriage ...

But then the tannoy again: '... and we shall be returning up the down line to Derby, where a fresh train awaits.' And it is fresh and it does await, and on we get and off we go. Soon, the last tannoy: 'We regret the delayed departure of this train, which was due to ... the failure of the previous train.' Laughter – but this time from the tannoy, as driver ribs guard into breaking officialese to: 'Which was due to ... the brakes, which ...' (very long pause) '... was tuggin' at the wheels.'

Now, though, there is no reaction from the passengers. The emergency's over; we have no further business talking to each other. Rather like that game where the lights go out, and everyone can move, and then come on again, and everyone must freeze, it is in the brief, unscripted interludes that we unlock to show what we could be – no, are. But they are so brief: glimpses, only.

Just for a moment, our little group in the train could have been friends, could have been a team, could have been an army – and could have been individuals, too. Just for a moment, we could have moved mountains, changed signals, and derailed trains. And I would have pitted us against any team, from any carriage, anywhere else in the world outside Britain.

Where is the philosophy, the ideology, the party – where the leader – able to speak to that spirit in us, able to encourage it? One side bleats of comradeship, but in a way which makes you think of grey waiting rooms and railway clerks. The other barks of liberty, but in a way which makes you think of estate agents and Volkswagen Golf GTI's.

When we reached Matlock, the last bus had left. I guessed that the woman next to me might be driving my way . . . but I didn't like to ask.

15.1.87

After Maurice Oldfield's funeral

ONE OF the more endearing methods of the Spanish Inquisition proceeded thus: unbelievers were invited to declare their conversion to Catholicism. Then they were executed, for lying.

This, I think, was the reasoning commended in the *Times* leading article on Friday, about Sir Maurice Oldfield. By contrast the *Sun* was splendidly candid, under the headline: 'PM SAYS HEAD OF MI6 A POOF.'

The poof in question came from the small and lovely village of Over Hadden in Derbyshire: for which I was Member of Parliament. I cannot remember that people there talked like that about him, although his homosexuality was quite widely guessed at and came as less than a shock.

His funeral filled the little church to overflowing.

I never met him, and have no window into the details of his private life, nor desire to pursue them. The thoughts that follow are directed not so much to the man, as to the press and political reaction to the simple truth about him.

It is time that somebody who can command respect and authority said – and said plainly – that it is possible to be of some service to the State, and to be homosexual.

It is time that this was said uncompromisingly; not hedged about with ifs and buts and limitations as to how and where: and when and

263

when not. It is time that the intimation of some unspecified link between homosexuality and treason – an intimation never quite voiced, denied when challenged, but never quite withdrawn – was firmly and finally repudiated.

The argument for the 'security risk' forms (like many of the worst arguments) a perfect and convincing circle. It proceeds in a series of logical steps which conclude by justifying the position from where it starts:

1. Homosexuals are a security risk.
2. Key jobs in government must therefore require a disavowal of homosexuality.
3. So, only by lying can homosexuals get such jobs.
4. Liars are blackmailable.
5. Therefore homosexuals are a security risk.

This chain of argument is capable of perpetually renewing itself, generating events which prove its adherents right. Such self-reinforcing prejudice must be tackled head-on: it is not cured by time or agnosticism, but feeds upon itself, finding new energy.

The Oldfield story which, heaven knows, should *undermine* the myth, already bids fair to reinforce it. The small voice which whispers, 'Gosh! The head of our intelligence for all those years was a homosexual, and did a splendid job!' is scarcely heard beneath the calls for more vetting, stricter tests, clear guidelines.

Why? 'He could have been blackmailed,' people say. Well, there's a simple way of ensuring that he could *not* have been blackmailed, and it lies within the hands of the superiors who fear he might have been. They could have told him that homosexuality was no disqualification from office.

This assurance is not available whatever may be pretended. Yet to offer it would remove the *apparent* security risk, and address (what I shall suggest) is the real and more important risk.

The apparent danger is that someone who loves his country could easily be turned to sustained treason out of the simple fear of blackmail. This seems to me not impossible, but inherently unlikely.

I am no expert on spying, but would wager that the most dangerous and effective traitor is not the would-be patriot whose arm is twisted by blackmail or bribery, but the man who has come to hate his own country and his own people: who *wants* to betray them, and has found some twisted moral reason for doing so.

And it is here where the real danger lies. A sense of persecution; a feeling that one has oneself been disappointed or abused; that devotion offered to the State has been spurned; the experience of contempt or rejection by one's own countrymen ... these are the engines of personal alienation.

And personal alienation is the greatest security risk. We have all felt it, in some small, momentary way. An over-mighty tax inspector, a bullying traffic policeman, some little incident that triggers resentment that one's obedient and patriotic endeavours seem to be getting no answering respect from King and Country – these things well up and are soon gone.

But someone who is homosexual can be made to feel almost continuously aware of them. He or she is likely, on the whole, to be quite law-abiding. Despite the caricature that gay activists have popularized, he tends to be on the cautious, conservative side.

He is working as hard as and paying more tax than his married countryman. He does not regard himself as an evil, corrupt or dangerous person. When his career is blocked, or threatened, or (more likely) he is worried that it may be, when his pub is raided by police wearing surgical gloves, when newspapers sneer or snigger, and when politicians seem to look the other way ... well, it is perhaps surprising, not that occasional embittered security risks result, but that so few do. Maurice Oldfield never deviated, it seems, from his devotion to his country. If, now, he can hear what it is saying about him, will he feel that it was his country's trust that was misplaced. Or his?

26.4.87

Not to be consumed before ...

I WAS first turned on to foods that have passed their sell-by date purely by accident. I found a tub of Spanish fruit-flavoured yoghurt at the back of the fridge. The eat-by date was 20 April, and the date I found it, early June 1987. There was nothing else to eat, and it seemed worth risking.

It was delicious – distinguished by a slight fizziness, champagne-like. Only upon idly re-examining the tin foil top to the empty tub did I realize that there was a year on the date stamp too: 1985.

The incident occurred not long after washing my hair with a shampoo whose label had torn and floated off in the bath. The bit still stuck to the bottle retained the 'mpoo' of shampoo and said '*work up a good lather* ...' but the rest was printed in the floated-off bit, but still legible.

I started to decipher it during the pause after I had worked up 'a good lather'.

'... *over the entire body*' said the fragment: '*eliminates fleas and ticks!*' Dog-hairs snaggled in the plug chain confirmed my fears. '*Not for human use*' concluded the label.

Occurring together, these episodes at first shook confidence in my ability to sort out instructions but, hours after eating the vintage yoghurt, I still felt splendid – ready for the next. And my hair had a lustrous sheen.

Tentatively at first, I began to experiment with foods that had passed their shelf life; a trial run with three very elderly Scotch eggs produced no ill effects. Indeed, I possibly escaped the 'spongey brain' virus in more recent Scotch eggs. Then came the discovery that you can toast bread which is mouldy. Blue spots go dark grey.

I started to confide in close friends. My comrade John immediately confessed to having done the same for years, whenever his wife was away. We celebrated by eating a tinned sponge pudding four years past its sell-by date, garnished with Fowler's Black Treacle which John provisionally dated *circa* 1968 as he remembered moving house with it.

We moved on to a cook-chill chicken and mushroom pie which had spent the fortnight since John's wife had tried to throw it away *outside* the fridge. This caused a twinge with both of us, but it soon passed, and we finished with a three-year-old jelly which had an original nutty texture.

The sense of shared deviance somehow strengthened the bonds of our friendship. We learned too, that a good way to discover whether food is off is to smell it, or offer it to the cat.

But the strength to be found through eating expired foods goes beyond wisdom. I spent six weeks in Peru last year with three English companions. Peruvians are not very big on sell-by markings. One of us collapsed with food poisoning at the airport and had to be taken to hospital. The other two suffered continuous and debilitating diarrhoea which, after five weeks, began to sap their morale.

In the sixth week my own continuing robust health and good humour became a source of such annoyance to my comrades that for a night I pretended to have an upset stomach, rushing behind trees and groaning realistically, just to cheer them up.

10.6.89

Running for Parliament

THEY CALL it a race but it's more like nuclear war. There are no winners, only survivors; no losers, only casualties.

They say it's friendly. 'All in it together,' they say. Together? Can there ever have been an occasion when so many thousands gather to do the same thing, in the same place, at the same time, yet each entirely alone, each in his or her own world, each with so different an idea of why he is there?

No winners, just survivors, an assembly of loners – like politics, really: and I've tried both. As Member of Parliament for West Derbyshire, I entered the '81, '82, '83, '84 and '85 London Marathons, and finished them all.

It is, for anyone, a nervy feeling, pacing Blackheath too early on a cold Sunday morning, seeing the crowds and yet blind to them, hearing the loudspeakers and yet somehow miles away, wondering why you ever entered and – worse – why you ever *told* everyone you were entering. And, for an MP, the 'everyone' you told includes 69,000 constituents, 649 critical fellow-MPs, twenty-five newspapers, four TV channels and the Prime Minister.

Adjusting your off-the-shoulder black plastic binliner in case a constituent should spot you on television, and shaking your head in sheer disbelief at your own folly, you eye the starting paddocks.

The faster you predict your time the further forward you place yourself. So everybody cheats. But what if they check? The ignominy! It might be raised in the Chamber, and the Liberals are sure to put out a leaflet in the constituency.

Then the cannon – and you're off. Wave at the cameras, just in case. It's human traffic-jam. Why didn't I cheat *more*? Then the road clears and – hey – this is okay! What's wrong? Why am I going so fast? Surely I can't keep this up? Ooh look – somebody's recognized me – they're all waving and cheering ... a frenzy of applause – surely I can't be *that* famous. Correct. I'm not. It's Jimmy Savile in a gold lamé tracksuit, in front.

Tower Bridge and it still feels fine. I can't *train* this fast, so how am I running this fast? It can't last ...

It doesn't. A sudden stitch. Grit your teeth and keep going – but this must be the beginning of the end; only half way and already I'm in trouble. Disaster looms. Will I even finish? The shame of it – to be beaten by Colin Moynihan!

How did I even think I could carry this off? Obviously I'm too old. At 36 I should have bowed out with dignity last year ... all that training wasted ... eighty miles a week for four months ... those 2 am sessions down the Wandsworth Road after a late sitting in Parliament – the policeman who thought I was a midnight smash-and-grab raider until I showed him my MP's pass. I chuckle and wave to some of the many people who don't know me in E14.

They cheer back ... And that stitch – where was it? Gone. Disappeared while my mind was off it. Speed up a bit. Ask the time. Great. If I could only keep this up – no, don't think about it. Just run.

I catch a snatch of news on a bystander's transistor: 'The Olympic cox and MP Colin Moynihan, who has had trouble with his knees during training, left the race at Tower Bridge. Apparently he had another engagement ...'

Trouble with his knees, eh? Shaking with fear I expect. 'Another engagement.' Huh? With the pavement, no doubt. Wimp. My pace quickens. People in front of me are collapsing, wobbling into the arms of spectators. Good. Let them.

The miles around the Isle of Dogs melt, and I'm feeling fine. The carbohydrate-loading diet really did work then. All that stuff about 'hitting the wall' at 18 miles was just old wives' tales ... and I power past the nineteen-mile marker; seven to go. Nothing can stop me now surely – why, I'm virtually there. 'Keep it up Matt,' yells a fellow Herne Hill Harrier, 'Dave Glassborow's only two miles ahead of you.' Suddenly, the wall hits me.

God, this is awful. More people around me are dropping out – poor devils. I know how they feel. Seven miles – why that's damn near a third of the race left. I'll be lucky to finish. Slacken a bit and grind on.

I pass under Tower Bridge. Isn't that Gary Waller, MP for Keighley, crossing it only now? No mistaking that silhouette – like an amiable bumble-bee. Brave sod. He never quits but he's got three hours still to run. Unworthy thought, but wouldn't it be nice to finish in exactly half Waller's time? I feel better, quicken my pace again, and run alongside a woman entrant, savouring the roars of the crowd. Roaring for *her*. She's doing well – for a woman. Well, damn it, *I'm* doing well – for me.

Big Ben at last. That final mile is agony. A House of Commons policeman, on duty as I run past, calls 'Nearly there, Mr Parris!' and I am literally too tired to raise my eyes from the road to acknowledge him. 'Tomorrow,' I think, 'you'll remember this and you won't understand how it was possible to be too tired to look. But you understand now.'

'2:32:55, 2:32:56 ...' And I come in at 2:32:57: fastest MP ever, in this race. I stride into the Hercules, where Herne Hill gather for the post-race drink. 'Okay Matt? You finished then? Did you hear Dave Glassborow's time? Club record. We're celebrating.'

I buy Dave a drink.

So no, not this year, and never again. I hold the parliamentary record and it's all I'll ever hold.

'I won't cling,' said Mrs Thatcher this week. 'I'll know when the time has come to go.' I did, anyway.

21.4.89

I'm sorry, Miss Pinder

As a student, I once gave a lift to a man who had scurvy. One of his teeth dropped out onto the uncarpeted steel floor of my old Morris Oxford. He picked it up, put it in his pocket, and told me that a clinic had diagnosed scurvy and advised him to eat lemons. Did I perhaps have a lemon? No? Could I, then, at least park my car where he could sleep in it? No? Well, could I just leave him with the price of a lemon at Victoria Station where it would be warm?

Though ill-dressed, unkempt and smelly, his pride was very much hurt by his tooth falling out, and his explanations were fulsome. I thought of him last Sunday, when one of my front teeth dropped on to somebody's kitchen floor.

It was a London Weekend Television tooth. They had begged me to get my teeth fixed from the day I started presenting *Weekend World*. Miss Pinder, my dentist, took a look and advised that having one tooth stick out was 'Nature's way' (I treasure that phrase) – 'Nature's way' of fitting four big teeth into the space of three. I could choose between four smaller ones, or (and she did not recommend it) the replacement of just the two front teeth by one central, cyclopic tooth.

Miss Pinder engaged a technician. They told me he had done Ted Heath's and Colonel Gadaffi's teeth, and this bothered me. There should be limits to how far we make Western knowhow available to Mrs Thatcher's enemies. But the technician made a perfect job.

And now I am punished for my vanity. I cannot stop using my teeth to strip the insulation from copper wire; and it causes one tooth to keep coming loose. Miss Pinder keeps having to stick it back and is advising me to insure them, in case of major mishap.

Now don't you agree that LWT should pay for this? True, they no longer employ me, but it was they who set me up with a lifetime's commitment to maintaining these elaborate teeth. What use is it bequeathing a man Versailles unless you have bequeathed also the means to keep the place up? The question pressed heavily last Sunday, as I scrabbled on the floor for my priceless peg.

This was in Derbyshire, my hostess a physiotherapist. 'What glue do you have?' I asked.

A search turned up only wood-glue, so we tried that, immersing the copper pin and the base of the tooth in lashings of it, as well as poking some up into the little shaft drilled in the gum to receive the pin. I kept my mouth open for a quarter of an hour, until everything was tacky, and – hey presto! – it worked.

Not for long. Driving home, the tooth fell out when the car went over a bump.

I was alone, now, thrown upon my own resources. These included an old tube of Airfix. This worked better. Not until late that night, when I accidentally hit the tooth with a glass of blue Curaçao in a gay bar in Derby, did misfortune strike again.

People were very kind and we found the tooth among sweepings of dry roasted peanuts. I departed to the lavatory, clutching the Airfix I had prudently brought. Luckily there was a mirror. But I could not – or would not – stand with my mouth open in a public convenience for a quarter of an hour. The jury would never have believed it. One of the reasons one does not buy the *Daily Telegraph* is to avoid reading court reports about that sort of case.

So I swivelled the nozzle of the hand-drying hot-air blower upwards, bending down to place my mouth directly over it, and pressed the button. It worked marvellously. Once, a man walked in, glanced in horror and rushed straight out. But it worked.

There is only one problem. All week I have been subjected to a sort of drip-release solvent abuse. Intermittently, the warm taste of model-aeroplane glue trickles down the back of my throat and I have been feeling strangely light-headed.

I see Miss Pinder on Tuesday. I want her to know, to repair and, if possible, to forgive.

1.7.89

On Thursday night it rained

ON THURSDAY night it rained. It seemed like months since the last storm. In our part of Derbyshire there were lambs in the fields which had never seen rain. Whole generations of nettles were unaware of the phenomenon. Moths looked skyward, and marvelled.

And I was asleep, sleeping the sleep of one who had forgotten what it is like to live in a wet climate.

The wind slammed the window shut. I awoke and looked at the digital alarm by my bed. It was 3.39 in the morning. Rain lashed the side of the house. 'Good,' I thought, 'this may revive the roses.'

Then I thought: 'Hell! The kitchen window!' I staggered downstairs naked, having abandoned pyjamas when the hot weather came, and lost them.

The word-processor left by the open kitchen window was drenched. I dried it with a tea-towel. 'Better try it out, now,' I thought, illogically, and slotted in its damp diskettes.

'*Disk-boot error in drive B*,' its screen protested, mutely, '*Abort? Retry? Ignore?*' I groaned. How could I dry this machine out? It needs gentle heat till morning. I wedged it behind the back of the fridge, above the warm heat-dispersing grilles. Rain beat the window.

'Hell!' I thought, 'my sun roof!' It wasn't just the sun roof, it was the boot too – left open as though it wouldn't ever rain in England. I closed both, grabbed a bowl of sugar – now reduced to slurry – from the garden table, and stood in the dark, suddenly aware – like Adam – of my nakedness. Rain on my back. An *arriviste* sheep stared at me from the rose bushes. 'Hell!' I thought, 'I've a guest, staying. If Michael looks out of his window he'll think I'm crackers. Especially with the sheep, and the bowl of sugar . . .' The sheep shot a wary glance in my direction, and hustled its two lambs away towards the fields. 'What about Michael's car?' I thought, and darted through the rain towards it. Squelch. Mud between the toes. Rather nice. Took me back to boyhood.

I wound up his windows, too. 'Hell!' I thought, 'the barn!'

The barn door was flapping in the wind and, upstairs, I remembered that the skylight was open. Where was the light switch? No, better not. What if Michael looks out of his window and sees me cavorting in the barn with no clothes on? So I stumbled up the stairs in darkness and secured the skylight.

Back to the kitchen. Squelch. How to get the mud off my feet? Of course! So *that's* what bidets are for! The little, upwards waterjet sprinkled teasingly between my toes.

How about the word-processor – one more try? Hooray! Thank you, Olivetti.

Good. Everything shipshape now. Back to bed, then? I scampered up the stairs. Hope Michael doesn't choose this moment to come out of his room. 'Hell!' I thought, 'Michael's bedroom window!' I could hear it banging. The curtains would be getting soaked.

I called softly: 'Michael?' No answer. Asleep, luckily, for I had again forgotten I had nothing on. I snatched a towel from the airing cupboard. 'Michael!' Still no reply. I knocked. No answer.

What do you do? Do you enter a guest's bedroom in the night, uninvited? This guest was a Member of Parliament. He might think I was a terrorist. I chuckled, remembering the time Michael used the return half of my 'non-transferable' charter air-ticket from Barcelona. 'But your name is not Parris,' they told him at the check-in desk.

'Of course it isn't,' snapped Michael. 'I'm an MP. I never travel under my own name. An obvious target for terrorists.' The check-in official apologized profusely ...

His window banged again, harder. Holding the towel round me with one hand, I flitted in, shut the window, and flitted out.

Back in my room, chilly for the first time in weeks, I snuggled contentedly beneath the bedclothes. The digital alarm said 4.17 and as I drifted off, it was still pouring outside. Down in the field I dimly heard Tracey's horse, whinnying.

Can you leave horses out in the rain? I can't remember. It's so long since it rained in Derbyshire.

12.8.89

My brother can speak

THE STORY is told of an Oxford undergraduate who spent his first term in college without discovering where the lavatory was. On day one he was too shy to inquire. By day two it would have been embarrassing, as people knew this was his second day. So still he did not ask. He carried on as he had started – walking half a mile to another college whose ablutions he had, mercifully, discovered.

A general once told me he had concealed a small ignorance for his entire military career. Only upon retiring and after much brandy did he ask male friends which way other men shave – with, or against, the lie of the stubble. 'People would think it is something a general would know,' he told me. 'But in fact we shave alone.'

Women of my acquaintance report that girls face a similar problem with shaving their legs. They don't like to ask other girls with smoother legs about the relativities of Immac, wax or razor, for fear of discovering that other girls don't have to: so they wear tights at school, and make secret visits to London, to study the advertisements on the Underground.

These are trivial examples of a serious problem. Nature abhors a vacuum. But *human* nature builds walls to protect its vacuums from exposure; and time only strengthens them.

I spent seven years as an MP without having the least idea about parliamentary procedure. Why was Dame Jill Knight putting on a top hat to raise Points of Order? What was an Attorney General, and how distinguished from a Solicitor General? Nobody ever explained. I failed to ask at the beginning, and never found out. There was no 'Teach Yourself To Be A Member of Parliament' book in the racks at W.H. Smith, no anonymous help line for shy, desperate parliamentarians.

And, if these are the gaps in knowledge one dares confess in a newspaper, what (you may ask) are the gaps too awful for a political journalist to reveal? Dare I say it? Oh, go on!

I'm not ... *quite* sure exactly *which* one Clement Attlee was. People talk about 'Clem' as if we all knew. Bevin, Bevan ... Crossman, Crosland ...

Mine is a proud family, I realize that. My brother, Roger, commuted for three weeks in a train where a fellow-commuter talked to him in sign language, which my brother does not know.

Neither of them, in fact, was deaf-mute; but it seems the man had tried to strike up a conversation with Roger, who finds it hard to talk to strangers and kept his mouth tight shut, nodding mutely. The man thought Roger might be deaf, dumb or both and, instead of asking, tried sign language. Roger was so embarrassed that he just smiled goofily, and nodded some more.

The situation had gone beyond retrieval. Day after day, Roger encountered the same man, who was determined to bring some joy into a disabled person's life and gesticulated energetically at him continuously, like those little people in the bottom left-hand corner of television screens, during party conferences. Roger just kept nodding.

Eventually my brother was forced to find another way of going to work. One would like to report that he had the good grace to find out the sign language for 'goodbye, you have brought me much happiness during the last few weeks', but instead, he just waved.

16.9.89

Letters that tick

YOU, AND I, appear anonymously in hundreds of snapshots. For it is impossible to walk in London without blundering across the viewfinders of a dozen tourists at the instant their cameras click.

And what about the Yorkshire Ripper? This man, too, must lurk unrecognized in scores of family albums. Such documents constitute a set, scattered beyond collation, yet logically intact.

This week I was reminded of another mysterious set: the 100,000 (or so) written replies to members of the public which went out between 1977 and 1979 from the Office of the Leader of the Opposition, Mrs Thatcher. They went in the name of her correspondence secretary – me.

On Thursday the House discussed the ambulance dispute. Busy with my parliamentary sketch, I wandered from the Press Gallery, nodding at a knot of lobby correspondents. 'Probably waiting for Bernard Ingham,' I thought, brushing past.

'Ah, Mr Parris,' said one of the great ones, in tones of mock gravity. 'May we have a quote from you?' I smiled. A little joke, obviously.

'Seriously: what's your comment on *this*?' They thrust a letter at me. It was dated 22 August 1978. '*Dear Gentlemen*,' it started, '*... on Mrs Thatcher's behalf ...*' The penny dropped. It was a reply (apparently) to an inquiry from a group of ambulancemen. It stated that when Mrs Thatcher advocated linking pay to inflation in the 'emergency services', she meant ambulance as well as fire personnel.

'This is dynamite,' one of the journalists said. 'Where did the policy in this letter come from?'

Of course I haven't the faintest recollection. But how many more of these replies might there be, tucked, forgotten, into unused drawers, ticking quietly away? You see, this is not the first.

Back in 1979 I wrote 'on Mrs Thatcher's behalf' to an angry lady. Her letter complained about immigrants, noisy Down's Syndrome children, and the thin walls of her council house. Her letter lacked charm but I do see now, that it was unwise to reply on Mrs Thatcher's headed notepaper that people in council houses should be grateful to have a roof over their heads provided at the taxpayers' expense.

Weeks later, as the 1979 election loomed, the *Daily Mirror* printed my letter as a 'front-page exclusive'. Next, the Labour party printed three million copies of the letter, in leaflet form, to be distributed nationally to council tenants. 'The Letter that let the Tory Cat out of the Bag', it was called. By a twist of fate, the lorryload of leaflets was delivered to Conservative Central Office because the driver had seen Mrs Thatcher's letterhead on the leaflets, and assumed they must be for the Tories. CCO took a look then sent them over to Transport House.

Have you ever been called into Mrs Thatcher's office for a ticking off? No? For me the experience still burns in the memory.

She has never been anything but kind to me and she comes out of this pretty well. It's just that I could tell she thought me completely mad. Probably still does. She looked at me, head slightly on one side, with an expression that said: 'There's something not quite right about that boy.' Her tone confirmed it. 'Nanny is not,' it implied, 'going to shout. Nanny is not even going to raise her voice. Nanny is *not* cross. Nanny is just very, *very* sad.'

'Why, Matthew?' she said. '*Why?*'

Her private secretary, Richard Ryder, gave me a stiff brandy afterwards. Yesterday I had to make do with a cup of tea provided by the *Guardian* sketchwriter. 'Are there more of these letters?' he asked, gingerly.

Who knows? Is there perhaps a night on a moonless March equinox when all the unrecognized snapshots of the Yorkshire Ripper, and all the latently lethal letters we ever wrote, turn pale luminous green, slide noiselessly from forgotten cupboards and fly towards some nameless Welsh mountaintop, to dance?

13.1.90

No, you could never blackmail me

Allegations that Scottish judges had frequented gay bars were in the news.

OH DEAR. 'Lord Denning speaks out' – and a *Times* leading article about sex.

I'm sure they're both right, of course. As to Lord Denning, his shock at events in Scotland is natural. The mere thought of entering the gay discotheques of Whitchurch, Hurstbourne Priors and Wooton St Lawrence, and finding Lord Denning attempting the lambada, outrages as much by its improbability as its impropriety. Any sneaking reflection that in such fantastic circumstances one might want to give the old boy an encouraging squeeze on the arm, rather than an admonitory slap in the face, must be banished almost before it is entertained.

As to *The Times*, it would be impertinent to tease. Those leading articles are guiding stars not just to the political but also to the personal side of one's life; and I found great comfort in the final paragraphs of yesterday's leader, which assured me that it was not wrong to be tempted, only to succumb.

I confess, though, that the earlier part of the article worried me. Apparently, I am in danger of being blackmailed. This is perplexing. Since the day when I decided it was best to be honest about my sexual preferences a few impediments have been put in my way, but the likelihood of blackmail seemed (to my untutored judgement) to have diminished.

Of course the Sunday Shockers are skilled at turning common knowledge into an exclusive revelation. 'WE REVEAL,' one might have read, 'the House of Commons speech on the Sexual Offences (Northern Ireland) Order, that Parris thought only he and Mr Speaker knew about. (*See p17 for more stunning extracts from* Hansard.)'

I suppose there was a time when I really was (theoretically) blackmailable. That was after I joined the Foreign Office but before it struck me that you only live once. Of course I should never have joined. After Cambridge, MI6 had already offered me a job as a spy and 'positively vetted' me, and if that didn't suggest I was a security risk, then what would?

I should have reflected on the fact that, were my private life more public, I might be sacked and decided there and then to forsake my choice of career. Oddly enough I decided to stick to my career choice, and keep quiet about my private life. Few would react like this.

In the event only one attempt was (arguably) made to subvert me. A very good-looking Bulgarian diplomat approached me at a north London party given by a mutual friend in the Foreign Office, and asked me if I would give him a lift in my car to the Cromwell Road. I agreed.

He sat rather too close. That is how I knew he had terrible breath. His assignment failed! There is a lesson, here, for the Bulgarian Intelligence authorities. Some months later he sent me a friendly postcard from Bulgaria. I handed it immediately to the Foreign Office security people.

But I could not have been blackmailed because I believe in justice, and in a country which accepts me; and which I love. The only times when I feel subvertible are when something causes me to doubt that acceptance, or justice.

So, dear reader, next time you see a Scottish judge in a gay bar, then, so long as he's not doing anyone any harm or breaking the law, take my advice. Shake his hand!

20.1.90

An impressionable age

YESTERDAY MR David Martin, a young Conservative MP for Portsmouth, lost the sailors' vote.

'Any proposal to reduce the age of consent for hohmoh-sex-ewells,' he told the Prime Minister, 'would be unacceptable and ...' – here Mr Martin, who looks a clean-living and serious-minded fellow, paused, searching for words which adequately reflected the depth of his horror – 'and ... *utterly* ... *crackers*!'

Across the floor, Tony Banks (Newham NE) peered cheekily up from his notes. 'Give us a kiss!' he shouted.

Mrs Thatcher agreed – with Mr Martin, not Mr Banks. This, she felt, would give 'totally the wrong signals' to young people.

Surely the Prime Minister is right! The purpose of an 'age of consent' is to make sure people are old enough to know what they are doing. Were there, for instance, an age (or height) below which you were not permitted to be a Sports minister, our young Colin Moynihan could not have been corrupted, by a much older woman, into unspeakable aberrations involving plastic cards and steel turnstiles. Little Colin may never recover from this horrific interlude – though to her, of course, it was just another 'affair', one of many, easily forgotten.

Young people can very easily become 'fixed' in a pattern of behaviour, if thrust upon them too early and before personality is fully formed. I have some evidence of a personal nature to submit.

In the late Sixties when I was nineteen and at Cambridge University, the Government changed the law. There was opposition to this reform from many Conservatives, but it attracted better support from Labour and was carried.

So one morning – quite unexpectedly – I found I was entitled to vote.

But was I ready for decisions like this? Who knows? All I know is that a much older boy, a stranger, wearing a blue rosette, came round and talked me into being a Conservative. He explained that I always had been really, underneath. His name was Keith Raffan, he was chairman of

'Pressure for Economic and Social Toryism'. He has since become MP for Delyn.

Later that term I sneaked out and *voted* Conservative. After that I found myself looking for more opportunities to do so. I found it hard to raise interest in any other party. I voted Conservative again and again. I even voted for Mr Heath! Three times!

I have often wondered whether, had I been sheltered from Mr Raffan and allowed to develop politically at my own pace, my life would have gone the way it subsequently has. I will never know.

16.2.90

A little white lie

WHAT A smashing place Torquay is!

'And Torquay's *changed*,' the lady taxi-driver confided. 'I shouldn't say this, but I will: you couldn't get green peppers here five years ago.'

The Imperial was splendid. The National Caravan Council, which I had come to address, could not have fitted into a caravan, anyway.

Green peppers are not the only novelty to have hit the town. Mounting the rostrum, glancing nervously at the massed ranks of the cream of the caravanning world, I caught sight of a green wedge of slanted glass mounted on the lectern, palely luminous in the darkened hall.

Aaargh! AutoCue. I hate AutoCue. I knew it wasn't for my speech, yet the very sight of the thing was chilling to the core. And all because of a very elderly lady called Mona who lived in an old people's home in Hampstead.

My friend Carl, on the death of his grandmother, took to visiting the home once a fortnight to talk to some of the residents who had few surviving relatives, and therefore few visitors. Mona was his favourite.

And when she discovered that he was a friend of mine, Carl became her favourite, too: for she loved the programme I was then presenting on television, *Weekend World*. She watched it religiously every Sunday and was my greatest (perhaps my only) fan. She was, apparently, wild about me personally. Very old ladies often are.

'Carl,' she said. 'I want you to settle an argument for me. You know that Mr Parris gives long explanations on television of all what his programme's about and such like, and why – with graphs and diagrams and sometimes just him looking at us ...

'Well, he knows it all, doesn't he? There are lots of stupid old women in this home and they all think he's *reading* it, off some kind of a machine, invisible to us viewers. They all believe that, except me. I know it's really him that's saying it because he *knows* it. But the others won't have it. They say I'm ignorant and nobody on TV these days would do it without a machine, and they're all really just reading. Tell them they're wrong about Mr Parris.'

Tactfully, Carl just said he didn't know, but would ask. He reported this to me. 'Tell her she's right,' I said. 'What can a little lie matter?'

Two weeks later, my AutoCue went haywire. It was in the middle of a complicated passage I was reading, to camera, about the characteristics of the Aids virus. I couldn't understand a word of it myself, but adopted the presenter's 'grave-sincere' pose, and ploughed on.

'Funny,' I thought, 'this passage about white blood corpuscles sounds familiar. Could it be a case of *déjà vu*?'

It was. The Autocue had got into some kind of a loop. I had gone back to near the beginning of the programme and was starting all over again. I felt the blood drain from my face. What to do? 'Stop!' came the instruction over my earpiece.

I stopped. 'Sorry,' I said, 'but I'm sure I've read that before.' I fumbled for the script on my knee – and began reading it in the wrong place.

'*Stop!*' came the voice. Someone rushed in with a new script and pointed to the right place. And on we went.

Recovering (while a recorded talking head explained more about viruses), an awful thought struck. Mona would be watching. Her hero's answer to her question would be proved a lie, in front of the others. She would be the laughing stock of the home.

A day or so later I learnt that Mona had died, twenty minutes before the programme. I went to her cremation, with Carl. We got there too late. If anyone else had attended, they had gone. Dear Mona. I hope she would have forgiven me. I didn't want to disappoint her – that was all. Honestly.

Anyway, that was years ago, in the days when you couldn't get green peppers in Torquay.

26.3.90

279

Needs must ...

CIVILIZATION CONTINUES in Nairobi, though its end has been 'imminent' since independence. In the suburbs the flowering trees continue to flower, the lawn-sprinklers sprinkle and the herbaceous borders are intact.

'Jim,' called my hostess to the bare-footed black gardener, 'do get Hague out of those nasturtiums.' Jim extracted a snowy-white Scottie dog from a sea of orange, and led him away.

'And tell Lorna to bring the sandwiches. Ham and cucumber, please, on white bread. And *thinly* sliced, Jim.'

She turned to me: 'The girl will put the ham *with* the cucumber, I daresay. One has to spell things out to them. Friends of ours went to church the other day leaving the cook with instructions to put the bird in the oven. Result: one charred budgie for lunch. They were inconsolable. More tea?'

She was an English lady, quite elderly now, but still with grace, humour and a very determined gentility – unshaken by the inconveniences that three decades of independence had brought. Her husband had been a senior officer in the colonial police force, but they had stayed after independence. He had gone into a local business and prospered.

'Milk, Yes? Sugar? I was telling you about the Mau Mau: you know, far more of them were murdered – by each other – than us. That was never reported in the English newspapers. But we saw it at first hand, Richard and I.

'It was his first post, after we came out from England. He was in charge of a station in a remote area where a lot of the fighting was going on. Hardly any other Europeans at all. We were just married so you can imagine it was quite a shock.

'Especially as part of our job was to keep police records of casualties. I say *our* job because you couldn't just sit at home and leave it to your husband. It was before the boys were born, so I soon found myself mucking in ...'

'*Jim!*' she shouted. 'Go in, would you, and tell Lorna to hurry up with those sandwiches.'

'What was I saying? Ah yes – identifying the bodies. A ghastly business. After any "incident" – as we used to call them – Richard was expected to take the Land Rover out to the scene and make as complete a record as possible.

'Well, of course, the cause of death was seldom much of a mystery, and when it was our people who had been killed one seldom had much difficulty in establishing identity.

'But as for the Africans – well, one didn't have the least idea who they were and their relatives were hardly going to identify them. But Richard simply had to have *something* for his records. So we brought the bodies back and if we couldn't find any other means of identification, we took thumb prints. The right hand. Grisly business. *Lorna! Sandwiches, Lorna!*

'This didn't last long. It was dangerous. There was only us and the Land Rover and simply no time to shuttle backwards and forwards humping corpses around. So we tried carting our fingerprinting equipment out and getting the prints "in the field" so to speak.

'Richard wanted me to wait in the truck but where was the point of that? So I helped, applying the ink. All those thumbs! You've no idea! And as life got more dangerous, so did hopping around in the mud with ink and sheafs of paper ...'

From the blossom in the tree above us came an English song, rather like a blackbird.

'... aren't those birds delightful? Hague! *Out of those nasturtiums!*

'So we hit on another idea. We took a good sharp bush knife, tore off to the scene of each incident, leapt out, cut off the hands – off the dead Africans that is – piled them into the back of the truck, and drove hell-for-leather back to the station. One could then put the kettle on. Do you know, I can't *remember* what we did with the hands afterwards ... Ah, Lorna, at *last!'*

The sandwiches had arrived: ham, and cucumber, quite separately. 'Oh *Lorna*,' said my hostess, affectionately, 'They're just like doorsteps. Slice, Lorna, *slice*. Don't chop. *Slice*, delicately.'

15.10.89

My Uncle Don

'TOO MANY painters today base their work on a love of art rather than a love of life ...' *Donald Young (1924–90).*

My Uncle Don was not one of life's obvious high-livers. A lonely working-class boyhood behind him, he turned away from one class and never sought entrance to another. He stammered, and didn't like parties. Anyway, he had Joyce, and a few good friends, and chess.

He wouldn't sell his paintings and found promoting them unendurable. He just painted: from the day he left art school in 1947 he was painting, or fretting that he wasn't. The house in Beckenham was stacked, floor to ceiling, front room and back rooms, walls, stairs and corridors ... four decades of Don's work. When he died there was a painting on the easel. It was all he cared for. He was not listening for the clink of the champagne glass or the braying of modish approval. Nobody cultivated him, few believed in him. Except my Auntie Joyce.

It cannot have been easy for a butcher's daughter to bring home a shy youth, a lighterman's son who had won a scholarship to Chelsea School of Art but whose work was hardly what my grandparents considered 'art'. Angular daubings with funny noses, whimsical things yet painfully intense.

I remember the whispers: '*Joyce* can draw. Her birds really look like birds. But she doesn't draw much now.' My aunt, a schoolteacher, became the breadwinner.

They never had children. It was just Joyce and Don, the goldfish, Snowball the cat – the late Snowball – and, each year, more paintings. Now Don has gone: leaving Joyce, a house full of paintings and a new cat. The cat was indifferent to the paintings. The fish is no more. I mentioned the fish to Joyce. 'It would have been his birthday this month,' she said. The new cat died last week.

Joyce is seventy. She has started a complete cataloguing of Don's work. As she points out, when a future age discovers Don, it will matter. Meanwhile she is spreading the word. She rang me to say she had arranged an exhibition at the Fairfield Halls in Croydon that I must see before it closes next Friday.

I went. Nobody in the foyer knew about it. 'There's art upstairs,' someone said, 'but I don't recall the name Young.' I went upstairs. The paintings (of the painstaking school), including one of the old Croydon airport control tower, were not by Don. I turned to go, glancing down an un-signposted corridor.

And spotted Snowball – my favourite painting, where he is a blizzardy blur, tangling a ball of wool that Grandma and Joyce are trying to wind: a wonderful picture, to me.

Joyce had arranged the whole show. Things Don had written had been typed, and posted with the pictures. Wall cards told you about Don's career. Each painting was titled, and some of his best were there: the chess game '*when Joyce won despite non-adherence to elementary principles*'. And two powerful self-portraits. After an hour with them, Don's presence seemed to grow.

Sometimes people passed the corridor and, for Don's sake, I willed somebody – anybody – to stop and admire. Nobody even glanced. Snowball, still tangled in his wool, winked across at humorous figures sketched in oils in Don's teasing way.

Through glass doors two elderly men discussed Croydon airport control tower, of which they approved. 'Yes,' said one in a bowls-club blazer, 'a lot of work has gone into that. You can see each stone.' He peered towards Don's territory. 'What's over there?'

I heard Don's stammer, behind my shoulder: 'Don't bother!' – almost pleading – 'you honestly won't like it.'

'Don't bother,' said the bowling gent's friend, 'Picasso sort of stuff.' They turned and left. Snowball resumed his game.

Don smiled with relief. He did not need these people. He only needed Joyce . . . and Snowball, who was concentrating on the wool and unconcerned with art. Don hated art.

22.10.90

I sell my first book

IT HAPPENED last Saturday lunchtime, at the lounge bar of the Midland Hotel, Derby.

The Midland has now been restored to its early-Victorian elegance and become a pleasant oasis amid the railway sidings. Nearly a century and a half has intervened since Victoria herself dined there, famously, on '*Les cotelettes de mouton*' and the menu is still proudly displayed. In the carpeted hush, it is easy to forget the basis of such wealth, which is illustrated by a sign not a hundred yards from the hotel foyer: 'British Rail Engineering Ltd, *Bogie Manufacturers to the World*.'

The carpeted hush was interrupted by me, my interviewer and his tape-recorder.

We made an engaging pair, Geoffrey Hammersley, of The *Derby Evening Telegraph*, and I. Geoff had lost his voice, and was rasping in a manner that suggested a bit part on a pornographic phone-line. I, having almost forgotten our rendezvous, was wearing a scruffy T-shirt and jeans that have torn knees; not because George Michael's jeans do, but because I cannot sew. I had left my cashcard in London, and had with me £4.36 for the weekend.

Geoff was to interview me on the eve of publication of my first book. He bought drinks. I calculated that if I bought the next, that would leave £2.57. At first I tried whispering, too, to reassure him. The barmaid eyed us suspiciously. As I in my torn trousers and Geoff, clutching his tape-recorder and copy of *Inca-Kola*, tramped into the lounge, she seemed to contemplate summoning help, then decided we were harmless.

The interview went well. The book is a light-hearted account of my escapades in Peru, and formality evaporated as I recounted more adventures. I babbled away, Hammersley croaked and the tape-recorder whirred. We were alone.

Or almost. Across the room were three diners. I now know them to have been Mr and Mrs Powrie-Smith, and a chap I take to have been their son.

It is easy in a noisy room to ignore extraneous conversation; but in this silence, broken only by my account of prostitution along the gold-rush tributaries of the Amazon, and Geoff's stage whisper, it was impossible. Poor Mr and Mrs Powrie-Smith's quiet snack was wrecked. I went over to apologize.

'Oh no!' said Mr Powrie-Smith, 'we were fascinated.' Mrs Powrie-Smith nodded. Their son smiled politely.

'In fact,' said Mr Powrie-Smith, 'we were wondering if we could buy a copy of your book. Perhaps we could ask you to sign one for us?'

They meant it! I did have one copy, but it was my only one.

'Not really,' I said, 'But you could always write to Weidenfeld and Nicolson ...' I began to give the address, then faltered. I reached into my bag.

'Here,' I said, 'I do have just this one ...'

But what about the money? The generous thing, surely, was to refuse payment? On the other hand, there was my little problem of the £2.57 ... Mr Powrie-Smith solved it.

'Take this,' he said, holding out a £20 note. I found I had grabbed it before even considering how a writer is supposed to behave in this situation.

'I owe you a fiver,' I said.

'Keep the change,' he said, 'towards your second book.' Mrs Powrie-Smith nodded approvingly, glancing at the holes in my jeans. Their son smiled. I signed my book, thanked them, and left.

One of my brothers says that when he told Dad that he wanted to be a pilot, Dad said: 'Good. You'll be the only one with a proper job.'

Stepping, now, from the portico of the Midland Hotel, I fingered the £22.57 in my pocket, thought 'What was that, again, Dad?', broke into a run, and leapt, unexpectedly, into the air.

27.10.90

Through a glass, darkly

1972 SEEMS just a few days ago, somehow. I had dropped in on Simon Mabey's rooms on M Staircase to see whether he would stand as a 'moderate' for our students' union. He had a pleasant, youthful gravitas and seemed a marketable candidate, but I did not realize he was going to be Lord Mayor of Westminster.

And Tuesday seems just a few days ago, too. I shook Simon's hand and thanked him for including me in a splendid mayoral dinner. I had left the keys to my flat on my desk at the Commons, so I walked over to collect them. It was rather before midnight, but the Sitting was staggering into the small hours. The lofty Central Lobby echoed. Stragglers clip-clopped in gothic gloom across the tiled floor. And there I encountered two more figures from my past.

Like me, Sir Nicholas Lyell was in black tie. 'Good evening, Solicitor General,' I bantered. 'You seem to be much in the thick of things lately.'

He and I first met as new boys in the 1979 Parliament. We were backbenchers together but then Nicholas became a QC, a knight and the Solicitor General. Even in 1979 you could not mistake his intelligence, though you might have overlooked his ambition, for he is a quiet and unusually courteous man.

'Can't complain,' he replied, 'but, yes, it *has* been hectic. There's the legislation, of course, and now, this week, the Guildford Four. It never stops.' We said goodnight and Sir Nicholas walked off, passing Mr Andrews on a bench by the wall.

I went over to Mr Andrews. He was smartly dressed in a suit (as he always is at Westminster) but his collar (like mine) is beginning to fray. And one of the lenses of his spectacles had been replaced by darkened glass. He never tugs sleeves but waits until you have time to talk. He anticipated my question: 'Yes,' he said, 'I've been in the wars a bit, recently.'

I first encountered Mr Andrews as one of Mrs Thatcher's regular correspondents, back in the late Seventies. He had an analysis of the geopolitical situation to put to her, and proposals for a realignment of world military forces. It was not possible for her to discuss these with him personally, and I used to explain to him that her time was limited. Unlike others, Mr Andrews accepted this good-naturedly. Politely, though, he would come to the Central Lobby after work, in hopes of meeting Mrs Thatcher or one of the other senior politicians with whom he corresponds. He has been doing so for years. MPs stop for a chat, for he is a familiar figure and the doormen and police know and like him. I remember once asking him why he looked so tired that day: he replied that he had been up all night learning by heart a chapter of the book he was writing, in case Mrs Thatcher should cross-question him on it.

'I was hit,' Mr Andrews said to me now, 'on my head by accident, by a workman's plank in a hotel lobby. It's a trying time for me as I still haven't sorted out the question of the BBC's broadcasting from my home. And now this. The hospital can't seem to get the sight back properly in my left eye. But the right eye is fine.'

He smiled wearily. 'And I battle on. So much to do, so much to explain to people.' I wished him well, and said goodnight.

One of the pleasures of the Lord Mayor's Dinner had been to be seated between the two daughters of the late T.E. ('Peter') Utley. I met their father, one of the greatest Conservative political columnists, when (years ago) I debated with him in a hall above a pub in north London. Mr Utley was blind.

Oblivious of what an awful, dingy place the hall was, and how thinly attended, Mr Utley was confident. I was young, had achieved little, seemed to be going nowhere, and could see the hall. I was miserable.

If I had been able to see where I was going, or if Mr Utley had been able to see where he was, if Nick Lyell, Simon Mabey, could only have seen ... or if Mr Andrews could see through more than a glass, darkly ...

I hope his eye gets better.

28.10.89

Lawrence Newcombe

THE SMOKE clears from King's Cross, but the public inquiry ploughs on through the tangled evidence. Cast your mind back, though, to the confused stories of heroism which raced into print at the time. To me, two stand out. Both describe men running back into the smoke to rescue others, and dying in the attempt. One story can hardly be unfamiliar: that of Colin Townsley, the brave fireman who became a national hero.

The other name may mean little – unless you saw the *Daily Mail's* front page: BLAZE HEROES IN AIDS SCARE: 'Fire-fighting heroes face Aids test after it was revealed last night that a victim carried the deadly virus ...' or the *Colchester Evening Gazette*: 'WE KNEW HE HAD AIDS': Blaze Hero's Family Tell of Secret Heartache.'

Both these headlines were strictly untrue. The *Mail's* amounted to perhaps the most ignominious send-off that it would be possible to contrive for someone who (on reading the smaller print) emerges as the real hero of the story: a young nurse called Lawrence Newcombe, about whom I have now discovered much that did not find its way into those headlines. First, though, let us look at what did.

'WE KNEW HE HAD AIDS'. Lawrence did not have Aids but, being HIV-positive, he faced the prospect of one day developing the disease. The distinction is important both to those promoting public understanding and those carrying the virus, who may have many healthy years ahead.

Every headline like this makes it harder for tens of thousands to keep their grip on that truth. 'AIDS SECRET', shouted the *Express*. 'Aids Punk', *Today* called him.

How about 'BLAZE HEROES IN AIDS SCARE'? 'Blaze heroes'? Hold on – *Lawrence* was the hero! He ran back. Indeed, the reporters go on (in smaller print) to acknowledge his own courageous energy – as they must if they are to stand by their insinuation that many were at risk. Inconvenient that Lawrence did not go round biting people, rather than trying to rescue them.

And the 'Aids scare'? There was none, of course. My own inquiries suggest that routine advice was circulated to firemen, and taken coolly. After all, one would need to have received Lawrence's blood into a tear in one's own skin and the *Mail* does not suggest that he was wounded.

My information is that he was not, but died of smoke inhalation. Still, reporters were able to get a policeman (who knew nothing about it) on record as being 'very surprised'. So there you have your 'story'.

Is anyone interested in the real story? Or such of it as I have been able to piece together from bewildered and (now) fearful friends? Does anyone care that Lawrence was not just an expert and utterly dedicated nurse, but a man of baffling range and depth? That he was an artist, producing beautiful line-drawings? That he sang, composed music, and played the twelve-string guitar? That he was a linguist, a botanist, a gardener, a photographer? That he wrote poetry?

... To whose touch my body leaps,
To whose caress my flesh is laid to bone:
Who in my dreaming safe beside me sleeps
When truth says I am cold and sleep alone ...

Does it matter that he loved his family (he was one of six children) and they him? That he was a superb gymnast, and physically brave? That at different times he had rescued two women from attack? That one stranger attacked by epilepsy on a station concourse awoke to find Lawrence caring for him?

Is it of interest that (as his friend Duncan put it) 'Lawrence had a heart as big as a bucket'? That he was fund-raising for a crippled footballer in his home town? That he did the shopping for the old people in the institution up the road? That he helped a lame old man home from the pub every night? 'It was as if someone had switched on the lights when Lawrence walked into a room,' said his friend Angela.

But she remembers his talking, just once, about being HIV-positive, and his voice faltering. 'I put an arm around him. "It's a bloody stupid way to die," he said.'

It was not Lawrence's fate. The last of his friends to see him was an Italian I have tracked down. Together they had descended the escalator. 'No, Lawrence! There's smoke!' he warned. But Lawrence disappeared, heading straight into the worst of it. 'We heard about him going back to help people,' his pub landlord told me, 'and we said: "That would be Lawrence!"'

Did he in that moment reflect that he had a life of uncertain duration to lose? Angela thinks not. Lawrence would have acted purely on instinct. 'He was brave by nature.'

Here I leave the story. 'No, we cannot see you.' His father summoned words painfully: 'Lawrence was a good son. Now we have laid him to rest. It is better that nothing more is written.' Earlier he had begged journalists to stop hounding his wife and children.

The Nursing Director at the Royal Free Hospital was equally firm: 'Lawrence was a wonderful nurse. The press was terrible. More talk could bring that back.'

And the Italian? He would leave no name or whereabouts, but slipped in to see me in a pub where they raised £500 in Lawrence's name for charity. 'The more the newspapers kicked him, the more the money came pouring in.'

And I have spent two months now, making apologetic inquiries – seldom answered – 'No, we don't want press stories about queers.' And for whom? For some petty criminal? Some wife-beater or molester of schoolgirls? No. For a hero not just at King's Cross, but all his life. A man of such courage and kindness and intelligence that he seemed to dwarf the mean streets and broken people who were the backdrop to his world.

For it to end in that newspaper epitaph . . . the indignity, the injustice rises like a lump in my throat, choking reason.

Lord Mason of Barnsley told their Lordships last month that we must stop the placing of homosexuals 'on a pedestal'. Some pedestal, hey Lawrence? Here then, Lawrence, is a small pedestal, from me.

3.4.88